CRICKET ON THE CONTINENT

CRICKET
ON THE CONTINENT

Tim Brooks

pitch

First published by Pitch Publishing, 2016

Pitch Publishing
A2 Yeoman Gate
Yeoman Way
Worthing
Sussex
BN13 3QZ

www.pitchpublishing.co.uk
info@pitchpublishing.co.uk

A CIP catalogue record is available for this book from the British Library.

ISBN 978-1-78531-203-8

Typesetting and origination by Pitch Publishing

Printed by Bell & Bain, Glasgow, Scotland

Contents

THE PRESENT

Acknowledgements

RESEARCHING and writing a book on a region that has remained very much on the periphery of the cricketing world and its consciousness has been a challenge and I am very much indebted to those who have played and administered the game within continental Europe for their knowledge, insights and support. The thoughts, reflections and proposals set out in this book are my own but have been informed by those whose passion and dedication to cricket in the region is a constant source of inspiration.

I would like to thank Ole Roland, Amjad Khan, Freddie Klokker, Michael Pedersen, Morten Hedegaard, Jeremy Bray, Peter Power, Ed van Nierop, Richard Cox, Tim de Leede, JJ Esmeijer, Tom de Grooth, Paul van Meekeren, Esther de Lange, Peter Drinnen, Simone Gambino, Andrew Northcote, Kelum Perera, Mark Moodley, Rory Gribbell, Tom Liddiard, Brian Mantle, Andre Leslie, Brian Fell, Ken Farmiloe, Joseph Nikitas, Spiros Bogdos, Ralph Dellor, Andrew Armitage, Maija Scamens, Nikolay Kolev, Kamelia Atanasova, Vladimir Ninkovic, Dan Casey, Tim Heath, Nick Pink, Mary Godbeer, Mahendra Mapagunaratne, Darren Talbot, Michael Blumberg and Angus Bell.

I would also like to thank Andrew Nixon, Peter Della Penna, Tim Wigmore and Bertus de Jong for their excellent coverage of cricket in the region and the governance of the global game that helped inform the writing of this book.

Lastly, well almost lastly, a special thanks to Rod Lyall whose vast knowledge of the game and perceptive insight into the challenges cricket faces in the region have been invaluable.

And finally I'd like to thank my remarkable wife who has had to suffer my cricket-related musings that have all too often interrupted the building suspense of a Poirot denouement. If I were to offer any advice to my readers it would be that a romantic meal is no place to review the strike rates of Danish seamers.

Introduction

CRICKET on the continent has hit the headlines twice in the last decade. The first was when the Netherlands defeated England at Lord's in the opening game of the World T20 in 2009. It was a victory celebrated across the world, even by some in England, as a triumph for the underdog and an inspiring example of a team from beyond the game's traditional heartlands shining on the global stage. For the Dutch cricket team it was a moment to savour and an opportunity to capitalise on. As a minority sport in the Netherlands with a player base of only several thousand they had struggled for relevance and recognition at home. But suddenly they were the darlings of world cricket, the photo of Ryan ten Doeschate and Edgar Schiferli having scored the winning runs becoming one of the sporting images of the year, resonating across the cricketing world. The team became celebrities at home too, shaking hands with the great and the good seeking to bask in reflected glory and appearing on television chat shows where they tried to explain cricket to an affable but bemused host and an intrigued but uneducated audience.

The victory in 2009 was a David and Goliath story and at the heart of its journalistic appeal was the amateur overcoming the odds to humble the professional. But this was no fluke. Yes the Dutch team didn't enjoy the funding, facilities and profile of their neighbours over the North Sea but neither were they the rag-tag group of odd-job men the press relished portraying them as. The Dutch team that beat England in 2009 was very different from their forebears who famously defeated Australia on home soil in 1964. A product of the ICC's High Performance Programme, they had a professional outlook and professional preparation. Their success raised some fascinating questions. Could a continental country ever become a leading cricket nation? Did the region have the potential to be a cricketing heartland in the future or was this just an isolated success in a region where the dominance of football was absolute? How realistic was it for cricket to develop from a recreational game on the margins of sporting consciousness? These were questions I wanted to explore.

The second time cricket hit the headlines was in the early summer of 2016 when news of Germany's inspiring work in giving bats, balls and hope to refugees entering the country exploded across the internet and made news bulletins. Once again the ingredients needed to turn a local, specialist story into one of international interest were present. There were the deeply moving human stories of people who had risked their lives and walked thousands of miles to flee persecution and war suddenly to find hope again through sport. There were inspiring pictures of whirling bats and beaming smiles. And there was cricket's role in profound social and political themes that have defined the modern age: the battle between compassion and tolerance against fear and self-interest.

The stories raised awareness amongst the general public and the cricketing world of the character and composition of cricket in continental Europe. It is a region where cricket has changed from a game identified with Englishness and played by Anglophiles who admire its associations with manners, fair play, elegance and sophistication to one identified with South Asia and predominantly played by economic migrants from that part of the world. There are five times more cricketers in the region now than in the mid-eighties, but the number of native cricketers has declined. Less than one in every ten cricketers on the continent is from the majority, indigenous ethnic group.

This has undoubtedly had a transformative effect on the amount of cricket played and the geographic spread of the game within the region. While still very much a minority sport, with all the challenges and constraints that brings, it is nevertheless more widespread than ever before and the passion and enthusiasm for the game in its nexus of outposts is extraordinary and inspiring, presenting much hope for the future. Politicians are taking an interest too, appreciating cricket's role in social integration in their increasingly multicultural countries.

But while this shift in the continent's cricketing fabric brings opportunities it has created a gamut of challenges, sensitivities and criticisms along with a polarisation of opinions that are never far from the surface in continental cricket. There are many who would dearly love to see teams of blond-haired, blue-eyed Germans playing games on silken lawns adjacent to a Bierkeller and representing their country on the international stage. They want cricket to be a German sport, a French sport, a Spanish sport. With its local eccentricities of course, that is all part of the charm, but authentic. In reality native players make up a tiny percentage of cricketers on the continent, national teams are largely comprised of players of South Asian ethnicity and the administration and playing culture reflects the cultural background of participants. In an ideal world the cricketing population and the composition of the national team would reflect general demographic trends but is this realistic in a region where cricket has not even secured a toehold in the cricketing consciousness? This is one of the questions that frame the future of the game on the continent but that have never been addressed. Does it matter that the primary role of cricket administrations in Europe may be to facilitate the playing of cricket amongst particular ethnic groups? In doing so will they further strengthen an already common perception in the region that cricket is a foreign rather than universal sport? Those of a cynical, though they would argue pragmatic, view would also pose this head scratcher: should development funding be targeted only at those countries that have a genuine chance of being a force in world cricket and where cricket either has or has the potential to have broad appeal and participation amongst the majority, native ethnic group?

In this book I will address those questions within the context of both common issues across the continent and particular cultural and cricketing factors in each country. I'll also set out my thoughts and proposals for how to develop cricket on the continent in the future, capitalising on opportunities and overcoming challenges and constraints. The development role of the ICC will of course be critical, although there have been dispiriting signs that they will withdraw active support for the majority of countries in the region. A transformative catalyst to increase the profile and recognition for the sport, and secure vital government funding and sponsorship for cricket, would be inclusion in the Olympics. This has traditionally been blocked by the Victorian governance and short-termism of the ICC, allied to the self-interest and greed of certain cricketing superpowers, but there are now signs that attitudes are changing and there is even the tantalising prospect of cricket in the Olympics if Rome win the bid for 2024. There have been some inspiring examples of development across the continent and these can form the basis of structured plans to grow the game and broaden its appeal.

However, while the big issues are important and can't be ignored I also want to paint a picture of the everyday reality of cricket on the continent. Every summer weekend the passion of cricketers across the region sees them travel up to seven hours to play a game, often on a rough pitch with no changing facilities. The leagues they play in are only made possible by the selfless commitment of a host of volunteers preparing grounds, officiating games and keeping the cricket community together. For have no illusions, cricket across much of Europe faces a constant struggle to survive. Being on the margins of the margins of the sporting scene means access to grounds and facilities is far from assured. In some countries an entire league is dependent on access to a single ground. If the lease expires, or it is developed for housing, cricket in the country is groundless and rootless. And grand plans to qualify for a World Cup, play Test cricket or get 10,000 participants are not as urgent as finding the money to keep bulldozers at bay. It is a different game to that played in England or Australia, where grounds are plentiful and investment assured. It is life on a cricketing frontier and like in all settler communities life is a compelling mix of threat and opportunity. It is this challenge that makes continental cricketers who they are: survivors, innovators, problem solvers. They may play cricket where cricket is largely unknown, but this makes them among the most driven and passionate champions of the game anywhere in the world.

The Past

Brief History of Cricket on the Continent

THIS first section of the book provides an overview of the development of cricket on the continent in the 19th and 20th centuries. Previous accounts have tended to be limited in scope to historical sketches of locations, teams, fixtures and players. While these have provided a rich source of information, memorable anecdotes and no little humour they have not attempted to define or analyse different models of development and explain how these applied in specific cultural and political settings within Europe. They have set out what cricket took place and provided a dramatic narrative of opportunity and challenge within which a compelling cast of missionaries and cricket tragics have been introduced. But they haven't asked those most important questions: how and why?

The development of cricket, more than that of any other major sport, has been studied through the lens of imperialism. And with good reason, after all the founding fathers of the international game were powerful and passionate imperialists who saw cricket as a means of pursuing their ideals and retaining imperial power and influence. When they constituted cricket as a modern, organised sport they did so on an imperial basis. There was no global remit or ambition. It followed therefore that cultural, sociological and political studies of the game focused on cricket and imperialism, its growth, impact and socio-political ramifications. The redoubtable shelves of the Lord's Library are crammed with such lofty tomes. But all this leaves studies of cricket in continental Europe conspicuous by their absence, the forgotten part of cricket's global jigsaw. And this despite the region having the greatest concentration of ICC membership in the world.

While continental Europe has for the large part been written out of an imperial-centric study of the game its close and complex relationship with England is nevertheless the starting point for understanding how cricket was introduced and developed in this geographically close but culturally remote corner of the cricketing world.

The Origin Story

LORD HAWKE, that most aristocratic and sartorially elegant luminary of the Victorian game, once remarked that 'wherever Englishmen go, they take cricket with them'. This simple statement is the basis for the most widely accepted development model for the sport. There is, as you'd expect, a very strong correlation between Britain's imperial control and influence and records of cricket being played. This wasn't merely a case of Englishmen continuing to play the sport they loved wherever they were posted, but part of a planned, systematic imperial strategy.

As Jon Gemmell noted in his study of the history of Irish cricket: 'Encouraged initially as a means to replicate the home environment in the colonies, cricket provided a vessel through which the ruling authorities could instil values firstly into settler communities and through them to the indigenous population.'

It is worth picking this idea apart, for it contains several key themes. At a fundamental level it is natural that people will want to play sports that they enjoy wherever they live, both for enjoyment and wellbeing, but also as an expression of their cultural identity. Therefore it follows that cricket would spread around the world as players who learn the game in a traditional centre of the sport migrate to other areas. This link between migration and development has been a consistent theme throughout the history of European cricket.

Another key aspect hinted at in the quote is class and social standing. It was the colonisers, naturally drawn from the ruling and educated classes, who sought to use cricket as a means of social cohesion and a re-affirmation of an ordered, civilised society. As cricket spread across the world the opportunity to play, in its founding phases at least, was linked with class and social standing. As with its geographical reach this was another form of exclusivity.

Applying this development model in a European setting requires a more nuanced approach. Understanding how cricket's strong links to class, social standing and certain virtues and values applied in Europe, a non-imperial setting that itself comprises of a complex and multi-layered cultural patchwork, is as challenging as it is fascinating.

Despite some persuasive linguistic studies that argue for French or even Scandinavian origins of the word 'cricket' there is no conclusive evidence that cricket existed in Europe before it was developed in England. It is likely that there were variants of similar games involving sticks and balls played across the continent from the early Middle Ages, and this may have influenced the extent to which cricket was welcomed and played by local people. But cricket in its modern form was undeniably an import from Britain or its colonies.

Within a continental European context there are several different forms of British influence ranging from direct control to the movement of people, ideas and ideals. Using this development model as the structure for an assessment of cricket's history on the continent helps to identify common themes and, critically, the extent to which development was inspired and implemented locally. Put another way, while the seed may always be imperial the fruit it bears is European.

I have used the year 1996 as the cut-off for this summary of the past as this was the year when the ICC first considered putting an objective and structure in place to support global development. Before that point any development was bottom up and decentralised. It was also the year a continental European team first featured in a World Cup.

The Colonial Model

Gibraltar

Although the targets for Britain's imperial expansion lay in distant continents where resources were plentiful and resistance limited, in order to exercise its global hegemony and grow prosperous from trade it needed centres of influence and control nearer to home, particularly in strategic arteries of commerce like the Mediterranean. It was for this reason that in 1713 they acquired Gibraltar, an area of less than three square miles at the southern tip of the Iberian peninsula. However, it was ideally situated to give England influence in both the Mediterranean and North Africa.

As with all colonial acquisitions the introduction of cricket was integral to the settlement strategy. Cricket was already firmly embedded within British military culture as a means of instilling unity, comradeship and the virtues of honour, discipline and fair play. It also played an important role in developing the identity and pride of different regiments.

Keeping the men constructively occupied when off duty was a way of keeping discipline and of course many would have been keen cricketers when they signed up for service and would have a personal commitment to continue playing, wherever they were posted. It was military sides that first played the game. In spite of the obvious challenge of playing cricket on a precipitous rock there are records of games from the late 18th century. Initially cricket was played exclusively by servicemen in fixtures organised within the military structure. But one of the roles of cricket within the imperial context was to forge links between the military and civilian administrators, helping ease the tensions that would naturally arise between different working cultures and outlooks.

By 1800 cricket was obviously considered important and established enough to justify the investment in building a ground, just north of the rock itself, in one of the few areas of flat ground large enough. By 1822 there are records of civilians playing. This indicates that interest in cricket, or perhaps in some cases merely intrigue, had seen participation rise though it is not clear to what extent this was a stated objective of the military command. Nevertheless in the context of direct British control, a predominantly British population and British sporting culture it is natural that access to grounds, equipment and facilities notwithstanding cricket developed in a similar way and at a similar rate to any community in Britain itself. In fact it could be argued that a combination of battling homesickness and wishing to emphasise their Englishness in a foreign setting made Gibraltarian cricketers even more passionate to develop the quintessentially English sport.

In 1858 a club for civilians, the Calpe Cricket Club was formed, becoming the Gibraltar Cricket Club in 1883. This ran in parallel with the service and by the 1930s the sport was flourishing, attracting the occasional touring team to play 'the rock', a team drawn from the civilian and garrison clubs. Between the wars the number and quality of local players increased significantly. In the Second World War the ground was commandeered as a vegetable patch causing a long break in play. But when peace resumed a new ground, the Victoria Stadium, was built and became the focal point for the cricket community. The Gibraltar Cricket Association was formed in 1960 but when Britain reduced the size of its military presence there was a greater emphasis on local coordination, especially in schools.

Gibraltar became an associate member of the ICC in 1969, bringing with it a sizeable grant to complement funding for the sport provided by the government. At that time all associate nations received the same level of grant irrespective of size or population. Tiny Gibraltar had the smallest population of any associate nation enabling funding to stretch a long way, not only providing facilities and administration for a strong league structure but enabling an international programme.

Despite limited playing strength, not surprising given the tiny player pool, as an associate nation Gibraltar were eligible to play in the ICC Trophy, the premier international tournament for non-Test countries introduced in 1979. It took part in every trophy from 1982 but never progressed past the first round. The team consisted of a core of expat stalwarts like the Buzaglo brothers and Gary De'Ath, with some Gibraltar-born players like Christian Rocca. They were beneficiaries of the traditional system of an automatic right of qualification by virtue of their membership category. When this was changed early in the new millennium they failed to qualify for the 2005 ICC Trophy and their opportunities within a meritocratic international framework have largely been limited to regional tournaments.

In 1996 they featured in the inaugural European Championships but proved uncompetitive, losing to Denmark by 288 runs in a 50-over fixture.

But the importance of Gibraltar in a European context shouldn't be judged on their own success, whether on or off the field, but rather their role in helping establish cricket in southern Europe. Gibraltar could have served as a base from which cricket could spread north into the Iberian peninsula. However, it is clear that this was not an ambition of either the military or the administration, a result no doubt of political tension with neighbouring Spain over continued British control of the rock. Cricket was a way of celebrating difference from continental neighbours, emphasising British cultural distinction.

Since the 1960s southern Spain has become a popular destination for English expats searching for sun. This has led to the formation of a growing player base and many clubs in the regions that neighbour Gibraltar. While there have been a number of fixtures organised between these sides Gibraltar missed the opportunity to fund and implement a programme to develop cricket in Spain, not helped of course by animosity between respective governments. Some believe that one of the reasons for this was a fear that losing to Spanish sides would potentially threaten funding levels. But whatever the reasons this lack of collaboration is a missed opportunity.

Malta

In 1800 Malta became a British protectorate following a Maltese uprising against the French and the intervention of the British fleet in Sicily. A garrison was established under the administration of a civil commissioner. In 1813 the island was formally incorporated as a crown protectorate and the commissioner replaced by a governor.

As in Gibraltar the garrison would have played cricket, with one of the functions of the game to create a bond of unity between the troops and civil administration. Surprisingly the first reference to a match being played on the island isn't until 1887 when two regiments faced each other at the Floriana Parade Ground, lying just outside the beautiful city of Valletta.

One of the factors that led to wider take-up of the game on the island was the prominent location of the ground and easy public access, drawing local crowds to witness the spectacle. In the first decade of the 20th century this interest led to the formation of several local clubs, including the Colonials, Floriana, Dockyard Union, Silema and Kalkara. In addition to club activity cricket was also taught and played at St Edward's School.

Prior to this one of the most famous cricketers of all had played in Malta when en route to Australia. WG Grace was among Lord Sheffield's Ashes squad who defeated a locally based team comprising the best players from the fleet and garrison. With several grounds and a number of local teams cricket became established as a popular pastime, drawing together different parts of the community, British as well as local. But by the 1950s worsening economic conditions had put pressure on the local cricket community, forcing many to emigrate and others to work very long hours leaving no time to play. It was not embedded sufficiently within the local culture to withstand such pressures and by the 1960s the only cricket on the island was, once again, British. With this contraction to the British it lost its inclusive appeal, becoming a game of the commissioned classes in the military.

Britain withdrew from Malta in 1979 leaving only a handful of expats, some of Asian origin, arranging occasional games against touring teams like the Free Foresters. The game was close to dying out altogether until given a boost by returning emigrants coming home after economic conditions became more favourable. They organised local leagues and formed the Malta Cricket Association in 1989, playing in European tournaments in the 1990s.

Despite an organisational structure being established by the local population the small player base made it vulnerable to player losses, through either retirement or migration. However, the popularity of Malta as a touring destination for English clubs provides plenty of fixtures and impetus for the local players.

Corfu

Corfu, the best known of the Ionian islands, the northernmost island group in Greece, had for centuries changed hands between rival empires before Britain claimed control in 1815 at the conclusion of the Napoleonic wars. It became a British protectorate and was governed by a Lord High Commissioner. Cricket was introduced in the garrison and a ground was established in the Esplanade in the centre of Corfu Town, in front of the governor's residence. The first reference of a game being played on this ground, undoubtedly one of the most historic and picturesque in Europe, was in 1823, recorded in the military memoirs of Major H.R. Lewin.

Corfu became an important naval base for Britain and the garrison arranged games with the crews of passing ships. In this sense the development of cricket followed the classic colonial model seen in Gibraltar, except that in Corfu the local population took to it quickly and enthusiastically. A mere 13 years after that first recorded game two sides had been formed by local Corfiots. It is not known what led to the formation of local teams, though intrigue of a novel game being played in such a prominent location in the town must have been a factor. Rather than being drawn from rival communities the two teams were based on social standing and class, with the nobility forming the *Megaloi* (big) team and artisans and middle class forming the *Microi* (small) team. This suggests that Corfiots saw the role of cricket in conferring respectability and civilisation, perhaps mirroring the structure the English garrison used to construct their teams.

By the 1830s, when curved bats and underarm bowling were still used, cricket in Corfu was played by a mixture of local sides, garrison teams, visiting ships and local residents. This relative complexity developing over a short period of time indicates that cricket was socially important. By 1864 when Britain transferred Corfu back to Greece cricket was well established on the island, with innovations, such as roundarm bowling, gradually introduced by visiting teams. However, there is no evidence that either the British or Corfiots sought to establish cricket further afield in Greece.

Unlike in Gibraltar where British presence has been continuous Corfu offers an example of cricket being introduced in a European colonial setting but then left for locals to organise. British withdrawal did see playing numbers reduce and the Megaloi club, having split into two teams, the Gongakis Company and the Kamvisis club, were forced to merge to form the Gymnastikos in 1893. It also had to widen its membership to attract more players, compromising the social exclusivity of its founding. This was a precarious period for cricket on the island and the Esplanade ground deteriorated, becoming strewn with stones. It is likely that without games against visiting British naval ships the game would have died out. There was enough local interest though for an annual festival to be organised.

After the First World War there was a revival. In 1923, a century after the first match was recorded, a new club was formed called the *Ergatikos* (artisans) giving opportunities to the same social strata as the original *Microi*. A name change in 1930 to the Byron club indicates the enduring link between cricket and British values. The club was run by Corfiots, but rather than seek to Hellenise cricket they deliberately forged a British identity, and in Byron associated themselves with a highly romantic and heroic idealism of virtue and adventure. The Ionian islands was part of Greece, but in incorporating cricket into their social and sporting culture Corfu was emphasising their distinct history. Between the wars matches against the British Mediterranean fleet were the only external fixtures played.

The Second World War had a profound effect on Europe and as with every other aspect of life cricket was impacted. Being associated so closely with English virtues and imperial power cricket was always going to be highly politicised as the continent was divided between Britain and her allies and the Nazi-led Axis powers. Unsurprisingly Hitler and his Allies were hostile towards any cultural allegiances with Britain they found in territories they occupied, and cricket was perhaps the most symbolic and emotive of these. It represented the arrogance of Britain's imperial mission and purported social and cultural superiority. They destroyed all cricket equipment on the island and few players remained. Once again the existence of cricket on the island was threatened.

But once again Britain came to the rescue following the end of hostilities. But this time the development model changed from direct colonial control to military influence. Rather than following a typical structural pathway the resurrection of cricket in Corfu was reliant on the passion and commitment of individuals. If the military mission sent to the island in 1946 had been led by different men, the history of cricket in Greece would have been different. As it was Corfiot cricketers had the luck of welcoming Major George Laing and Major Guy Thorneycroft, both keen army cricketers with a missionary zeal for the sport they loved. They provided equipment, started coaching sessions and encouraged the Gymnastikos and Byron clubs to renew their rivalry. Under their stewardship matches against naval sides recommenced.

Once again politics intervened when the British Mediterranean fleet was withdrawn following tensions with Greece over Cyprus. But another crisis brought yet another saviour, this time in the form of British Vice-Consul in Corfu, Major John Forte. Seeing cricket in a state of collapse he set up an appeal in the *Daily Telegraph* to save cricket on the island, and the £400 raised went towards equipment and the promotion of Corfu as a touring venue for English clubs. By the mid-1960s the island had a busy programme of fixtures against touring sides, providing an impetus for development. In 1962 the island played host to an International XI that included stars such as Wes Hall and Basil D'Oliveira that attracted much attention in the press and helped increase its profile as a touring destination. The links established were formalised in 1970 when an Anglo-Corfiot Association was created, co-ordinating tours, translating the rules of the game into Greek and providing leading domestic players with coaching opportunities in England. This would later become the Corfu Cricket Technical Committee, an organisation recognised and funded by the Greek Ministry of Sport.

By the early 1990s the Corfiots were playing as Greece in European tournaments. In 1995 Greece became an affiliate member of the ICC and the following year the Hellenic Cricket Federation was founded. The federation made limited attempts to reach out to cricket communities elsewhere in Greece, although several Pakistani residents of Athens were incorporated into the national team.

British influence has been critical to the development and survival of cricket in Corfu, through direct control, military presence and diplomatic zeal. But it is also clear that Corfiots adopted the game in part to emulate the social structure and virtues associated with it, as well as emphasise its unique culture and history to mark its difference and distinction within the Greek political sphere.

Croatia

Following victory over the French in the Adriatic during the Napoleonic wars Britain briefly took control of the Dalmatian coast. The governor, William Hoste, introduced cricket to the island of Vis. However, British occupation did not last long enough to establish the game and it died out when they left.

Cyprus

Life Corfu, Cyprus was another island of strategic importance to Britain. Benjamin Disraeli, the enigmatic prime minister novelist of the late 19th century, placed Cyprus under British administration and it was formally annexed in 1914. Cricket was played by the garrison with fixtures against both visiting ships and occasional touring sides from England.

However, unlike in Corfu it was not taken up by the local population. Without such local roots it died out after the British withdrew in the late 1950s, only revived after a wave of economic migration around the new millennium. The British had however provided the grounds to enable cricket on the island to be played.

Military Presence

While British colonial possessions in Europe were limited to Gibraltar and, briefly, Corfu, their military presence has been far more widespread, particularly in periods of war. This has brought players, grounds, facilities and organisation into a region where cricket had either never been played or was limited to small communities with little resources or structure.

Corfu has already provided an example of how British military presence both during and in the aftermath of European conflicts to a large extent determined the development of cricket. But the legacy of British military presence in the major powers of mainland Europe is more complex. The first cricket in Belgium was played by English officers during the Napoleonic wars, including a famous fixture played on the eve of the battle of Waterloo. There are other fleeting references too, proudly acknowledged by cricket federations across the region.

British military teams in the Netherlands provided a much-needed boost to domestic cricket when the country was liberated from Nazi occupation in 1946, helping to schedule matches and strengthen leagues. The British Army of the Rhine brought players and attracted touring teams to the Berlin cricket scene after the First World War and the partition of Germany after the Second World War saw Britain establish a considerable military presence that remained in one form or another for many decades, and was central to the organisation of cricket in the country. Without the grounds they built the revival of cricket in Germany in the modern era would have been much slower.

Diplomatic Presence

The history of global cricket is littered with examples of how British ambassadors have introduced the game and provided facilities and equipment to help it grow. The first Afghanistan national cricket team, that embarked on a fairy-tale journey from refugee camps to the World Cup, had their kit and equipment provided by the British ambassador. In fact the consistent pattern of support across all corners of the globe suggests that establishment and promotion of cricket is an unwritten part of diplomatic training at the Foreign and Commonwealth Office. As in the colonial context, cricket provides a conduit for the values that Britain wishes to promote in the international community.

In many European countries the first references to cricket being played are games organised by British embassies and in some cases these games sparked interest that saw small cricketing communities develop. In Latvia cricket was played by embassy staff in 1998 prior to a club being formed by Indian expats. Another example is British civil servants playing cricket in Luxembourg following the formation of the European Community in 1973.

Indirect Influence – Migration of People and Ideas

Britain only had political control in small, isolated centres at the extremities of continental Europe and therefore its direct institutional influence on the development of cricket in the region was limited.

However, the proximity of the continent made it a natural destination for English emigrants seeking employment or a different way of life.

Some of these emigrants would have been cricketers and while many would have left cricket behind when they left their homeland some were passionate enough to introduce it to their chosen destination. If they were teachers they had the opportunity to play a more profound role in developing the sport, introducing cricket to institutions both as a form of physical exercise but also as a means of promoting British virtues. In some instances the commitment of English teachers on the continent provided a similar missionary zeal to colonial administrators like General Forte. And their passion inspired a generation to ensure cricket spread beyond expat communities and was developed by the local population.

In most cases such emigration led to cricket being played but without the sport spreading into and capturing the imagination of local communities.

Cricket in Portugal

Due to the fondness of the British for a post-prandial tipple, wine merchants settled in the cities of Oporto and Lisbon to keep the decanters of English drawing rooms flowing with port. Clearly these communities counted amongst them a fair number of cricket enthusiasts for in 1855 the Oporto Cricket Club was founded. Five years later a club was formed in Lisbon and from 1861 the two rivals played an annual fixture. A number of press reports survive from these early matches and they offer a fascinating insight into the reaction of locals, or at least journalists representing local attitudes, to the game. Within an understandably befuddled explanation of the rules it is clear that cricket was considered peculiarly English and unlikely to appeal to locals.

Of course the cricket that these journalists were witnessing was the traditional, structured English form, staged as much as an event to re-assert social norms and values as for fun. This social context would appeal to those wishing to appear sophisticated and civilised, but perhaps less to those seeking immediate, visceral entertainment. The social context of the game was a critical factor in how it developed in the region, not just in expat communities but also among locals who adopted it.

The description of the social setting within which the match took place provides a few tantalising clues to how cricket was played by these frontier communities and what function it served. The journalist's report emphasises that a long and sumptuous meal in a specially erected marquee was integral to the game. The match was clearly an important part of the social calendar and an opportunity to network, make introductions and talk business. And because cricket was the context it was culturally exclusive. It provided a natural bond between Englishmen, a way of asserting distinction, difference and perhaps, in the eyes of some, superiority.

The minutes of club committee meetings give credence to the theory that cricket was used by the English abroad as a way of demonstrating greater sophistication and civilisation than the locals they lived amongst. When the question was raised whether Portuguese should be encouraged to play the majority view was that the game was 'too complicated' for them. So while in British controlled corners of Europe introduction of cricket was seen as a civilising influence, there was no such political or moral incentive for small communities of traders. In fact the exclusivity of cricket may well have strengthened its appeal.

In Oporto the club played both cricket and lawn tennis and arranged fixtures with visiting British navy ships. These only provided occasional fixtures but adding football and athletics to their roster meant that the existence of the clubs was not pinned directly on the volume and variety of cricket available. But with the dual appeal of long hot days and free-flowing wine Portugal became a popular staging post for touring teams from England set for more established cricketing cultures. Records attest to famous cricket personalities including Pelham Warner and Percy Fender having turned out for visiting sides. This gave the clubs a steady flow of matches, not to mention social cache.

One of the problems the club faced was grounds, a common constraint across the continent. The decision not to reach out to local communities safeguarded their exclusivity, but it also threatened their existence. For they were only tenants and without either an understanding of the game or a strong case for the benefits cricket brought to their city the municipal authority of Lisbon took the decision to evict the English and use the space for a bullring. In the end the Lisbon team had to buy a piece of land for their own ground.

The clubs survived after the Second World War and touring teams included regular visits from Gibraltar, cricket providing a conduit for forging links between different, isolated English communities on the Iberian peninsula. But ultimately the exclusivity of the clubs was to prove their undoing. Remaining small and culturally isolated they became too heavily reliant on the presence and commitment of a small number of individuals. Once these retired or returned home there was no sustainable base from which to develop a new generation of players. The turf pitch in Lisbon, thought to be the southernmost on the continent for many years, would have been the envy of many players across the continent playing on crude matting on rough areas of ground not considered worthy of any other use. But despite these advantages, a long heritage and ideal weather conditions, cricket in Portugal all but died out, only to be revived by cricketing immigrants from much further afield.

Cricket in Italy

Italy was a popular destination for the Victorian and Edwardian upper classes as they embarked on grand tours of the continent searching for adventure, culture and inspiration away from the stifling orthodoxy and restraint of British manners. It is inevitable therefore that cricket followed in their tread, attested by a game portrayed in the background of a 1772 painting. As in Malta and Corfu it was the Napoleonic wars that first brought organised cricket to Italy, with Nelson staging a game there in 1793, a fixture still proudly cited by the Italian Cricket Federation to show the country's historic links to the game.

Napoleon occupied the Kingdom of Naples and installed a garrison, headed by his brother in law, Joachim Murat. The new ruler asked his aide de camp to find constructive activity for his officials and being part-British, and a keen cricketer, Colonel Maceroni introduced cricket. It was organised in the Capodimonte Gardens, in Rome, and reputedly proved popular with officials from many different cultural backgrounds. However, it was a more orthodox English connection that was responsible for the first cricketing base in the country. The English college in Via Monserrato built a cricket pitch in the grounds of an old monastery it acquired on the shore of Lake Albano, to provide an opportunity for students to play in the summer.

At the turn of the 20th century sport was transforming from a recreational pastime to a more structured, codified and modern form. Drawing inspiration from the Olympic movement administrators sought to promote values, virtues, health and athleticism through organised sport. At this time cricket was the longest established of the major sports and English presence in major Italian cities saw cricket incorporated into new sporting clubs, many of which have now become internationally renowned.

It is hard to imagine that AC Milan, a club so synonomous with Italian style and passion, was actually founded by two Englishmen from Nottingham. At that time the Midlands town had strong links to lace-making firms in northern Italy which drew a small community of English industrialists to Milan. Two such men, Alfred Edwards and Herbert Kilpin, unwittingly created one of the highest profile and successful sporting clubs in the world. Lamenting the absence of the traditional summer game of their homeland they met with friends one evening in a tavern in the city and over a beer or two sketched out a charter for the Milan cricket and football club. It was two weeks before the dawn of a new century, a century that would see these sports become the most played and popular in the world with a defining impact on the development of modern culture. It is pertinent that cricket came first in the title, despite the fact that Kilpin was a talented amateur footballer and an influential pioneer. The famous sporting organ the *Gazzetta dello Sport* reported on the foundation, stating its aims as to 'spread the game of football and to play cricket as widely as possible'.

Edwards, known as 'papa' to historians of the club, became very wealthy indeed from interests in the Pirelli company. He was the first president of the club and bankrolled it, while Kilpin was the captain and star player. While there was an immediate impact on the football field, with AC Milan winning their first national title in 1900 and surpassing Genoa as the leading team in the country by 1906, the extent of their cricketing experience is a matter for speculation.

Two years before that fateful night in Milan Juventus had been formed in Turin by students of the Massimo D'Azelilo lyceum as a sporting club. Cricket is thought to be among those it planned to play, but by 1899 football was the sole focus and the name was changed to the Football Club Juventus. It can only be assumed that there was insufficient interest in cricket within the club for it to continue.

But the honour of the earliest multi-sport club in Italy goes to Genoa, still officially named the Genoa Cricket and Football Club. In 1893 the club was formed by British expats as the Genoa Cricket and Athletic Club. Initially its membership was restricted to British members. This mirrors the wish for exclusivity seen in the committees of the clubs established in Lisbon and Porto. That the club was a patriotic expression is seen from the choice of white shirts to match those of the England team. The club had grounds in the Combasso district, to the north-west of the city. One of the founding fathers of the club was Sir Charles Alfred Peyton, a diplomat who had been transferred from Mogador, Morocco, to the vice-consul in the city in the spring of 1893 and had joined others in the British community in founding the club.

For the first two years of its existence the club played cricket matches, mainly against the crews of visiting ships arriving in the harbour.

Peyton's posting to Calais in 1897 may well have been critical for cricket's future in the city. A year before James Richardson Spensley, a doctor, had arrived in Genoa charged with tending to English sailors on the coal ships. He took responsibility for leading football in the club, becoming its first manager. Acknowledging the burgeoning interest in football amongst the local population and under pressure from the city authorities the club opened its membership to Italians. The locals clearly wanted to play football rather than cricket. In 1898 Spensley established the Italian league and led his team to victory. Although it is uncertain whether cricket was still being played by the club after 1897 it is interesting to note that when a name change was voted for in 1899, cricket remained while athletics was dropped. This may have been in deference to the club's founding purpose, but indicates a willingness for cricket to remain part of the club's activities.

Meanwhile back at AC Milan cricket was being marginalised as the seeds of football fever that would capture Italy's soul were sown. The English founding fathers walked away from the club in 1908, perhaps frustrated that it had not embraced cricket as originally intended. In a few years at the dawn of the 20th century three of the richest and most influential sporting institutions in Italy had played cricket. If only it had survived for a few more years and captured the imagination of Italians the clubs would have provided the organisational capacity and financial clout to establish cricket in the country. This missed opportunity is particularly the case in Genoa, formed before football was widely known outside England and before a national infrastructure for the sport was established. For the first five years of its existence cricket had the upper hand, the bigger profile. But in these crucial years the club didn't allow Italians to join, protecting the exclusivity of their English sport. Cricket in Italy would never have such opportunity again.

With Italians adopting football as their national passion cricket was limited to pockets of English and Commonwealth communities. If any local interest was inspired the fascist government under Benito Mussolini supressed any cultural or sporting links considered unItalian as they sought to remould Italy with the strength and grandeur of ancient Rome.

Naturally Rome proved the strongest draw and there are records of cricket being played between the wars in the grounds of the Villa Doria Pamphilj. The expats had found a sympathetic benefactor, but they lost their ground when it was dug over during the Second World War. As in Portugal the failure to involve locals and earn their support meant cricket was vulnerable to such whims of land-use. After the war the British and Commonwealth community in Rome was sufficient to generate interest in forming a cricket league. A British official was overheard voicing his frustration at the lack of a ground during an embassy function to celebrate the Queen's birthday in 1962. He was fortunate that the couple earwigging were Princess Doria Pamphilj and her husband, the British admiral Frank Pogson. They invited him to their estate to see if there was a suitable space for a ground.

Once a site had been identified a tournament was devised featuring teams from the British Embassy, Australian Sports and Social Club, the Commonwealth War Graves Commission, two colleges and the Food and Agricultural Organisation of the United Nations. The body to coordinate cricket in the city, the Rome Cricket Association, was founded and to generate interest and mirror the rivalries from competing teams the series was dubbed the Rome Ashes.

The initial focus of the association was to make improvements to the ground. Such was the level of interest that the association incorporated other sports and the name was changed to the Rome Sports Association. Efforts were made to attract touring sides to the city for fixtures. This yielded a spectacular result as the Australian touring team, featuring Bill Lawry and Bob Simpson, stopped off to play a match en route to England. But once again these cricketing expats lost access to their ground when the Villa Pamphilj was turned into a public park in 1972.

The revival of cricket in Italy in modern times can largely be attributed to two factors, waves of economic migration from Commonwealth countries and the passion and dedication of Simone Gambino. The former provided the opportunity but the latter has been the driving force.

Gambino grew up in Rome but spent his boyhood summers in England with his maternal grandfather, an American who was an art dealer in London. His grandfather introduced him to cricket and he soon became a regular visitor to Lord's, forming a deep and lasting affection for the game. When he returned to Italy to study history in Rome he was an obsessive follower of the Ashes and played recreational cricket. He was one of the founding fathers of the Italian Cricket Association formed in 1980 by enthusiasts and players. There were no stated objectives or targets but rather a commitment to providing a structure within which cricket could be encouraged while ensuring that it was played in the best possible conditions.

The Doria Pamhilj club had been resurrected a few years before and included four players who had previously competed for the Rome Ashes. The club later changed its name to Capannelle, one of the most famous clubs on continental Europe.

Following the legal process for regulating sport in Italy the federation actively sought to form new clubs. By the spring of 1981 five clubs had been formed in Rome and a league established. These included two teams from English schools in the city. One side was comprised solely of Italians and by the mid-80s these local players had formed two new clubs, Lazio and Roma. In contrast interest in the English-dominated expat teams faded with the college teams slowly dropping out of the tournaments. By 1983 clubs had formed in other regions and a national championship was established, with the winner of a semi-final contested in Lombardy meeting the winner of the Rome competition.

Gambino attributes further growth of Italian cricket to summer tours of England scheduled from 1984, where around half the players were Italian, which attracted considerable media interest. Over time this interest translated into teams being formed in other cities and a subsequent increase in participation, and competition, in the Italian league.

In parallel to domestic development Italy also sought official recognition in the international cricket community. Although an associate membership category had been introduced in the 1960s many emerging cricket nations could not meet the membership criteria and so were left out of the fold. Bertie Joel, a legendary figure in London cricket and creator of the popular home counties cup that bears his name, regularly toured Rome in the early 1980s and sought to use his influence and connections to further Italy's cause. Pressure on the ICC led to the creation of the affiliate membership category in 1984. Beyond Italy being officially welcomed into cricket's global family this brought few practical benefits, in the short term at least. There was no development blueprint or targeted support provided by the ICC and participation in the ICC's showcase event for non-Test teams, the ICC Trophy, was limited to associate members. But Italy's fight was to pave the way for many other European nations in the years to come to access funding, support and a tournament structure.

Simone Gambino became president in 1986 and introduced reforms to the league. It became a requirement of clubs' participation in the National Championships to field seven Italians in their teams, later increased to nine. The strategy was clear, to ensure that the game in Italy was not limited to expats. The board wanted Italian cricket to develop, not just facilitate cricket in Italy. This policy was challenging to implement as the majority of interest in joining clubs was from the rapidly growing expat communities. Clearly by proscribing what players must be picked, the clubs were not always able to field their strongest teams.

The same approach was adopted for selection of the national team. Gambino insisted that the entire XI was Italian, despite ICC guidelines that enabled players to be selected for international games based on residency or holding a passport. It was a show of faith in the development of Italian cricket but such a policy was always going to impact performance in the short term. This was demonstrated in 1989 when Italy lost a one-day game to Denmark by a frankly absurd margin of 409 runs. The philosophy behind the policy was laudable and initially it served to encourage participation by Italian players because they had the strong incentive of representing their country. This may have been a factor in them committing to cricket rather than other, more popular, sports. But countering this was the risk that such crushing defeats would dent morale and enthusiasm.

In 1992 the selection policy was relaxed to a requirement that a player had to have an Italian passport to represent the national team. This policy was to significantly improve their performance on the field in years to come. In 1995 Italy secured elevation to associate status. This provided a significant funding boost thanks to the membership grant. It also gave them access to the ICC Trophy and therefore an opportunity to qualify for the World Cup. In 1995 and 1996 they toured Argentina, South Africa and Namibia. This served as preparation for the European Championships in 1996.

By this time the focal point of Italian cricket had shifted from Rome to Bologna. The university city, known as *Bologna the Fat* due to its love of food, had not adopted football quite as passionately and all-consumingly as cities like Milan. This gave cricket a better chance of generating local interest and participation. The Bologna club was founded in 1983 and six years later in the nearby Apennine hills the picturesque Pionoro ground was built. It was Bologna that had the greatest number and concentration of grounds, making it the de facto capital of Italian cricket and the natural home for national and international tournaments.

Cricket in France

There is a theory, enthusiastically advocated by some, that far from being a quintessential English invention cricket had in fact originated in France. A letter written to Louis XI in 1478 makes reference to a game of 'cricquet' being played in the northern French village of Liettres. Given that an exhaustive search has unearthed no other reference to or description of the game in France prior to the 18th century it is likely that the game in question was an early form of croquet. Nevertheless, it has given tiny Liettres a certain degree of fame and the local tourist board have sought to capitalise on the story by promoting it as a place of pilgrimage for cricket fans.

But theories aside, the first attested reference to cricket being played in France is in a letter written by Horace Walpole dated 1766, around two hundred years after evidence of the game being played in Guildford, Surrey. Eleven years later a match at Saint Omer was recorded. The revolution followed and gentle pastimes gave way to political upheaval and bloodshed. There are no references in French sources to the game at this time, which indicates that it must only have been played occasionally and exclusively by English residents or travellers.

The opportunities provided by proximity were largely negated by the traditional enmity between the two nations. Following the revolution Napoleon seized control and the two great powers went to war again. In this context any sympathy or cultural affinity with England and Englishness would have been actively discouraged. This sentiment must have been hardened by the famous fixture on the eve of Waterloo that ensured that cricket became indelibly linked with England in the French national consciousness. And England was the enemy. It is difficult to assess how lasting and significant a factor this was in determining the extent and pace of the sport's development in France, but it may well help explain why very few native Frenchmen have taken up the game in comparison, for instance, to the Dutch. Cricket's association with class and social order would have jarred too with those who had overthrown their king, humiliated their aristocracy and proclaimed the virtues of 'égalité and fraternité'. While the social base of cricket in England was broadening, it is likely that those with the wealth and leisure to play the game in France were drawn from a class many French had come to despise.

Given this historical and ideological backdrop it is not surprising that references to cricket in the remainder of the 19th century are limited. English communities continued to arrange matches and there are games recorded in Calais, Boulogne, Dieppe and St Omer in the 1820s and 1830s. As in Italy many of the players were drawn from the lacemaking profession. But economic shifts saw them return to Nottingham and surrounding areas in the 1840s, and without them cricket died out in these towns. However, in the final decade of the century sport in its modern, organised form was born and pioneering administrators were spreading the gospel through the foundation of clubs. Mirroring the formation of clubs in Genoa and Milan a group of English businessmen established the Standard Athletic Club in 1892. In Paris the English community was sufficiently large for a 12-team league to have been formed by 1900. Importantly this included an all-French side, Sporting Athletique Garrenois, indicating a degree of cultural assimilation for the game.

In 1900 the city not only boasted a 12-team league but also hosted cricket as an Olympic sport, with a British team defeating a French team consisting entirely of Englishmen in the final. This rather jolly footnote in Olympic history is often used to emphasise the amateur ideal of the Olympic movement at that time, contrasting with its slow but inevitable shift towards professionalisation in the modern era. This high profile event didn't appear to leave a legacy to cricket in France or capture the public imagination. Cricket was played by the English who lived there. From 1906 annual fixtures were arranged with English players living in Belgium and Brussels hosted a cricket tournament in 1920 as part of the world's fair, in which a French team took part. But ten years after the Olympics and almost two decades after the founding of the Standard Athletic Club there were still no Frenchmen in the XI. In fact only one Frenchman was known to have turned out for the club by 1968 and he had been educated in England. It can only be assumed that the club simply did not attempt to broaden its appeal and player base, or if it did its efforts were disappointed.

A game was reputed to have been played atop the Eiffel Tower with an orange as a ball, but such quirky anecdotes only serve to deflect attention from the lack of development of the sport in England's nearest continental neighbour. In 1922 the cricket community was drawn together under the aegis of the Federation Francais de Cricket that organised and supervised a league structure. Nazi occupation in the war both restricted opportunities and saw many players either return to England or join the military. This led to many clubs folding. Standard Athletic lost their ground to allotments, though they reclaimed it in 1947. After the war an influx of potential new players was presented through the founding of offices for NATO and military organisations. SHAPE was based at Roquencourt and the Allied Forces Central Europe at Fontainebleau. These new teams compensated in part for the loss of most of the pre-war teams in Paris, but when these were withdrawn cricket in France was in danger of disappearing. By the late 1960s cricket activity was limited to a few fixtures for Standard Athletic against English touring teams along with the occasional tour to Germany, Holland and Switzerland.

Cricket was saved in France not by another wave of English settlement but by cricketing immigrants from South Asia in the 1980s. Having come to the country to earn a living they naturally wanted to play the game they had grown up with and by 1987 there was sufficient interest to reform a cricket federation. Over this period and into the 1990s new clubs sprang up, such as Saumur and Chateaux Thoiry. The annual fixture against Belgium was revived in 1991 and a new league structure created. But that revival is part of the story of cricket's new Europe.

Cricket in Belgium

To an even greater extent than in France cricket was only ever the preserve of English residents in Belgium. Other than the famous game at Waterloo and a cricket scene depicted in Spa in 1840 the first notable date in Belgian cricket was 1865, with the foundation of the Brussels Cricket Club. Papers from the foundation meeting remain and show that membership was restricted to British residents. A watercolour of the Brussels Cricket Ground painted in 1870 hangs in the Lord's pavilion. As with examples in Portugal and Italy this was an English sporting club that just happened to be located abroad. Cricket was exclusive and the community that played it insular. In 1893 a club was formed in Antwerp.

Despite a determination, a deliberately stronger choice of word than reluctance, not to reach out to the local community links were established with neighbouring Holland, where the game was played by the Dutch. Annual fixtures were staged from 1905–1937 and direct links established between clubs. This suggests that cricket was not considered a game only the English could play, but rather that playing cricket was considered sufficient judgement of character for links to be established. Or it may have been far simpler, and the clubs merely fancied a cricketing tour to see more of the continent.

Though it must have been difficult, given the exclusivity of cricket in Belgium, one local at least did play the game. His name, or to be more specific, title, demonstrates both what kind of people cricket appealed to and who would be accepted into such a closely guarded brotherhood. The Count of Oultrement, no doubt picking up from the English the sophistication and social standing playing cricket conferred, became a champion of the game. There are parallels here perhaps with the legendary figures of Ranjitsinhji and the Nawab of Pataudi, notables of empires who went on to play Test matches for England. They may have been born into a different culture but their social standing, and the innate sophistication this imbued, was sufficient to be embraced in cricketing circles.

The venerable count aside cricket in Belgium remained an English pursuit and therefore the path of its development diverged markedly from that of its northern neighbour. As many clubs across the world have found, a limited pool of players leaves the club ever vulnerable to departures and generation gaps. Following the Second World War, where the Nazis are thought to have destroyed records of cricket in Brussels, the clubs reformed and through a combination of attracting visiting teams from England and playing teams from British military stationed in Grobbeldonk and Olen put together a spasmodic assortment of fixtures to provide sufficient impetus for the clubs to continue. The transitory membership saw some clubs form and then disband but the Brussels and Antwerp clubs were given stability by an invitation from the Dutch cricket board to join their league.

An account from the 1960s of the Antwerp cricket club provides an insight into how the club was run and the challenges it faced. Struggling to attract players it made do with a squad of 15 for the entire Dutch league season of 1966 and had to advertise for players. Those interested were asked to declare their interest to the British vice-consul of the city. The British links continued as the home ground moved from the Rasante Club to the British School in Tervuren. Ted

Heath, the UK Prime Minister, was made its first honorary patron. In 1975 there was a further move, to a site in Blanden. In 1977 the club was bestowed the honour of a becoming a royal society. In Belgium as in Holland cricket was clearly respected by royalty, even if not widely adopted by the country at large.

As well as attracting players, a problem of course largely of their own making, the club also struggled to find and retain a ground. Their original ground was forfeited by the police after a local resident had complained of a ball flying into her toilet window, evidence enough to declare cricket too dangerous for the neighbourhood. Since that time the club have moved to anywhere vaguely suitable.

The formation of the European Union provided the influx of players required as governments, businesses and organisations set up offices in Brussels. This, allied with economic migration from South Asia, saw interest in cricket increase. When Ken Farmiloe, a long-standing chairman of Belgian cricket, moved to the country from England in 1988 he found immigrant communities playing the game 'to a surprisingly high standard'. Some coordination was clearly required and he was influential in the formation of the Belgian Cricket Federation in 1990.

Cricket in Switzerland

The development of cricket in Switzerland followed a similar pattern to that seen in France and Belgium, with English communities playing in several major cities with a boost in interest and participation following Geneva becoming the seat of the League of Nations.

However, away from the major cities a different development model was applied in a small rural village on the banks of the river Inn. Here cricket was introduced through an institution rather than by migration. When Gordon Spencer moved to Zuoz college, an exclusive boarding school, as its games master in 1923 he introduced cricket, supported by the English groundsman, Mr Parslaw. He would remain at the school for 40 years and under his stewardship cricket became a major sport with fixtures organised against English residents in the nearby valley. In 1927 the school employed a specialist cricket coach brought in from Cambridge University. With this commitment and resource cricket was in secure hands within the school itself but it was the old boys that created a greater legacy within Switzerland as a whole. Having been inspired in their schooldays many boys naturally sought opportunities to play beyond their alma mater and some went on to play cricket in Berne and as far afield as Holland.

The Geneva Cricket Club was founded in 1951 by four men drawn from large industrial enterprises and global organisations based in the city. Although Geneva was blessed with many sporting grounds the club failed to secure an area exclusively for cricket and therefore played on matting wickets on football fields. The club found opposition from teams formed by organisations such as the Nuclear Research Agency, International School and British civil servants. But their main rivals were the Standard Athletic Club from Paris. Being the base for the UN Geneva had a very cosmopolitan population by the standards of the day and this was reflected in the ethnic mix of the team.

Cricket in Germany

The history of 20th-century Europe has served to emphasise the cultural and political differences of Britain and Germany. The silver-haired amongst us growing up in England were raised to view Germany with mistrust and suspicion. The propaganda posters on both sides accentuated cultural differences and contrasting values. It is perhaps surprising therefore that cricket took root in Germany to a greater extent than most other countries on the continent. Of course the divide and polarisation was largely the making of one man and in the 19th century, amongst the upper classes at least, there was considerable cultural affinity. Royal bloodlines were linked, after all. Modern Germany was forged on principles of order, respect and discipline. These principles find a very natural home in cricket, as demonstrated by its high popularity and participation in the military. It is perhaps these subtle similarities that help to explain why the game had more appeal in Germany than in France.

In the 1880s groups of British students were playing both cricket and football in Berlin. Following a trend seen elsewhere this interest consolidated with the formation of the Berlin Cricket Club in 1883. Football was the more popular of the sports amongst the locals but unlike in Italy the local football teams were inspired by cricket and by 1889 four of them had incorporated cricket into their clubs. This meant that football and cricket leagues existed in parallel with many club members playing both sports. Organisation of the two sports was linked and although cricket was the junior partner it nevertheless could draw on the infrastructure, resources and backing of clubs rapidly growing in scale and influence as the popularity of football surged. In 1891 the German Football and Cricket Association was formed to organise the games. The German approach to regulating and structuring these modern forms of sport was to provide them with a classification and status. Cricket was given a high status in this process and cricketers within clubs given significant responsibility within the association.

Meanwhile in Hamburg football had been introduced into the secondary school curriculum by educationalist Dr Rudolf Heegmaan who had also championed cricket's inclusion. It is a measure of how much the game was known and respected that the Minister for Sport gave his blessing to this aim. A record of a fixture against a touring team from Copenhagen shows that the majority of the Berlin team were of British origin, suggesting that few German cricketers had yet mastered the game, but despite this cricket had won influential supporters in education and politics. In similar circumstances this had been conspicuously lacking in France and Italy. By 1896 there was a cricket league in Berlin and evidence of clubs composed solely of German players scheduling cricket matches as part of football tours.

Cricket continued to grow in Berlin in the first decade of the 20th century, albeit at a considerably slower rate than football. A Dutch team visiting in 1906 were surprised by the need to line up 15 minutes before the start of play to be inspected. It seems order and discipline were seen as critical facets of cricket by the association. By 1908 there were six teams in Berlin and slow yet steady growth was being maintained. By the outbreak of war this number had doubled and in 1913 a dedicated Cricket Association (the Deutsche Cricket Bund) had been created that not only encompassed Berlin but teams in Nuremberg, Furth, Frankfurt, Mannheim and Hamburg. While not the level of growth seen in the Netherlands and Denmark cricket was nevertheless increasing its profile, participation and geographic spread. It was not sufficiently widespread or popular to form part of the national sporting consciousness but it was officially recognised, endorsed and supported by German-run organisations.

The advent of the First World War could not have come at a worse time for German cricket, just as it was claiming a foothold within a fast developing sporting and cultural landscape and a year after a dedicated organisation had been established to drive development. Unfortunately the DCB didn't survive the war. However, recovery on the resumption of peace was encouraging, helped by the impetus and players provided by the British Army of the Rhine who remained in Germany to oversee the terms of the Treaty of Versailles. They were influential in attracting teams to play in Germany, including Dutch clubs, touring sides from England and British military teams. This influence carried the risk of re-anglicising cricket after it had been taken under the wing of German backers before the war but in fact by the late 1920s there was a much higher proportion of locals playing than prior to 1914, although the number of clubs in Berlin had reduced to four. This boost in local participation came in spite of the anger and resentment that must have followed defeat in the war and the humiliating terms of the Treaty of Versailles. Germany had to submit to occupation by its victors, crippling financial reparations and tight controls over its financial and military recovery. And yet sportsmen were being drawn to an English game.

In 1930 a team consisting of German nationals drawn from Berlin clubs, as opposed to a team of Englishmen that happened to reside in Germany, went on tour to England. Unfortunately their arrival didn't generate the interest or media coverage they deserved, as their visit coincided with that of a certain Donald Bradman. But they made a sufficient impression to encourage the Gentlemen of Worcester to tour in 1936.

By the early 1930s the Nazi party had come to power and Hitler was, it seems, distinctly unimpressed by cricket's lack of physical contact. In his view stronger, more powerful games were better suited to the Aryan ideal. Cricket was actively discouraged by local Nazi officials, which clearly compromised management of the sport and threatened the very survival of the game. But remarkably in such circumstances cricket continued. This was in part due to the tacit support of the *Reichsportfuhrer*, who as strange as it might seem was something of an Anglophile and had enjoyed watching cricket on a visit to England. While not actively supporting cricket he didn't act to prevent games against Denmark taking place and even several sides touring Berlin.

Felix Mendel

The leading German cricketer of the inter-war period was Felix Mendel. He first appears as an opponent of Leicester Cricket Club's tour of Berlin in 1911. A jeweller by profession, he was to prove an influential champion of the game in what were to become increasingly challenging circumstances. He is reputed to have hit the biggest six ever seen in Germany but his strongest suit was devilishly nagging medium pace. In 1930 he was the star player in a German team that toured England, led by his brother Guido. Had the tour not coincided with the presence of a man who was famously to finish his career with a Test average of 99.94 the German visitors would have excited considerable interest in the media. Amongst his team-mates on the tour was the goalkeeper of the German hockey team and Pastor Harold Polchau, who would later become a leading opponent of the Nazi regime. Mendel took 24 wickets at an average of six on the tour.

Though Hitler was not yet in power the tour was nevertheless not without diplomatic tension. The worthies at the Oval barred him from the pavilion, only later to apologise and offer a conciliatory meeting with the great Jack Hobbs. His ambition and drive to develop the game in Germany is shown by his request to the MCC that they organise a tournament for developing cricketing nations on the continent. The *Daily Mail* reported on the proposal but it seems there was never a response, or at least not a positive one.

Following the 1930 tour Mendel worked tirelessly to entrench the game in Berlin and arrange fixtures against visiting teams to galvanise the cricket community. His influence must have been considerable for despite the Nazi party's active opposition to the game teams continued to tour right up until 1939. He exerted this influence from outside the party having never become a member. It is likely he used his business connections to smooth over any problems and get the tacit permission he required to ensure tours were if not welcomed then at least tolerated by the authorities.

During the war the Nazi party banned any contact with the forced labourers who were brought to the country from occupied territories. But Mendel defied this and skilfully and secretly arranged casual games with Dutch and Danish. There is a great story that after the war the officers stationed at Checkpoint Charlie, the border between east and west when the city was divided, were amazed to be approached by a German civilian asking if they fancied a game of cricket. With his home city in ruins around him and his country on its knees, Mr Mendel remained focused on cricket. Such commitment to the game surely pulls at the heartstrings of all who have the game in their soul. He was influential in rebuilding the Berlin league and even after he moved to Frankfurt in middle age he returned each year to Berlin to play cricket into his seventh decade.

As Dan Waddell, who became fascinated by Mendel when researching his book on the 1937 tour to Berlin by the Gentlemen of Worcester, concluded:

'He made sure cricket survived in Germany despite the death of his friends, the annihilation of his city by war, and hostility from the most despicable regime the modern world has seen.'

In the late 40s the cost of the war to cricket across the continent was clear. In Germany, where Bomber Harris and his Lancasters had systematically laid to waste many of its cities, cricketers had died and grounds been destroyed. Many in the cricket community had left the country, while others had matured past a playing age. Ironically given the destruction of the city they had overseen, it was once again the presence of the British Army that provided an impetus for recovery. An insight into the challenges German cricket faced at this time is provided by an account by Mr E Abbotts, an official in the British military government, who noted that 'the almost complete lack of grounds and even the provision of equipment presented almost insuperable difficulties'.

In the desperate circumstances they found themselves in the remnants of the German clubs looked to the British military for support. They provided equipment and helped the four pre-war clubs, Berlin, Germania, Preussen and Victoria reform. Karl Reitz, a team-mate of Mendel, reformed the Berlin league. Reitz had learnt the game in a prisoner of war camp in the Great War and became a successful all-rounder in the league in the thirties. But it was his commitment rather than his ability that left the greatest legacy to German cricket. He recognised that the local player base was diminishing with the remaining players entering the venerable veteran stage, and set about campaigning for cricket to be introduced to schools in order to inspire a new generation of players. He identified growing obsession with football as a major threat, especially as the winter season was extended to 11 months! This encroachment of football remains one of the biggest challenges to cricket on the continent today.

A constant theme in the history of continental cricket is the critical role of individuals in protecting cricket from oblivion in a region where the game is not well known or understood. This is attested in a reflection in 1967 by Mr Drummond, coordinator of cricket for the British Army of the Rhine:

'As I see it there is very little hope for cricket continuing in Berlin as far as the German side of it is concerned, should anything untoward happen to Reitz. The main core still rally to him but they are so few, and, unfortunately, are so divided without him that some would be persuaded to withdraw their support.'

But although a cricket structure had been reformed the level of German participation was minimal, with the vast majority of players drawn from the British military. Although stalwarts like Mendel and Reitz remained involved cricket was no longer attracting German players as it had before the First World War. In the first decade of peace the British military played over a hundred games against German clubs, encouraging the attraction of younger players. But very few were found to replace those with terminally creaking knees. In fact by 1966 there was no longer enough local Germans to field a team in what was now a British league, so they had to recruit Indian students to field an XI.

The influx of men from all branches of the British military saw clubs founded in Cologne and Rheindahlen. But as their foundation was reliant on British players so was their continued survival.

Undoubtedly German notions of nationhood and cultural identity had developed over the course of the 20th century, for much of which they had been in conflict, both militarily and ideologically, with England. Perhaps this cultural divergence and a re-alignment of Germany's class consciousness reduced the innate appeal of cricket. Though in practice the surging popularity of football, the lack of a powerful and resourced governing body to spread the game in local and educational institutions and limited access to grounds were also key factors.

By the late 1950s the cricket community was heavily reliant on British military bases, for players, administrative zeal to arrange matches and for the grounds to host them. This offered clubs opportunity for fixtures and grounds to play them on, but was masking a decline of cricket in local communities. The construction of the Berlin wall in 1961 saw clubs marooned and six clubs reduced to two. Soon there was only one club left in the city. German cricket had been reduced to an English game played by the British military in British military camps. Cricket was played at a school in Husum, South Schleswig, but this was isolated.

However, the 1960s saw the first wave of immigration to Germany from the subcontinent as students from India and Pakistan enrolled at German universities and brought cricket with them. Their enthusiasm attracted fellow scholars to the game and over time new clubs and local leagues emerged incorporating the British military teams and clubs founded by British servicemen. This conglomeration of players and institutions created a demand for games and events. An example was the forming of a six-a-side tournament in 1964 that attracted 16 teams. In 1988 interest had recovered sufficiently to reform the DCB. The following year a tour to Denmark was organised and in 1992 a German national team entered in the European Cricket Federation's Nations Cup in England. While there they earned a creditable draw against the MCC at Lord's.

In Germany a batsman is a *Schlagman* and an umpire a *Schiedsrichter.*

Cricket in Denmark

In the middle of the 19th century Denmark was embarking on an industrial revolution and a key component of this was building a railway network. Seeking guidance and expertise from industrial pioneers the Danish government naturally looked to British engineers to oversee this programme. These engineers brought cricket with them and introduced it to towns they were billeted in. The railwaymen who built the Funen railway started a cricket club in Odense in 1865, the year the railway was opened. The game was also introduced in this way in Jutland and Zealand.

This temporary influx of British and their introduction of cricket may have proved a mere footnote in the history of the game, with the railwaymen returning and cricket soon forgotten, perhaps only recorded in the briefest of references by a local who witnessed them play. But from this brief incursion cricket took root to a scale and in a way not seen anywhere else on the continent except the Netherlands. There are several reasons why this proved the case.

At the same time as cricket was introduced by the railwaymen a small group of aristocrats from Copenhagen returned home from an English education with a passion for the game. They belonged to the Copenhagen Ball Games Club and naturally sought to introduce cricket to its roster of sports. Had this been the limit of their ambition cricket may have remained an elite sport, played by a select few in a single sporting club. But once again it was to be the drive and commitment of an individual that would ensure the game developed. One of these men, Mr Hoskjaer, wrote an article about his experiences of playing cricket in England and a brief explanation of the game to a publication called the *Illustrated Times*, that was published in June 1866. He had copies of the article printed and sent to the Ministry of Culture requesting that they be distributed to grammar schools, secondary schools and teacher training colleges.

Hoskjaer did not leave to posterity his reasons for such decisive action but it is clear that he returned to Denmark not only enthused by the game he had learnt but convinced of its physical and educational value. It was a time when modern states were forming and high ideals of cultural vitality, physical purity and spiritual wellbeing were not just popular but passionately espoused. These ideals would certainly have been imbued by his schoolmasters and he wouldn't have been alone in his generation in striving for a better, purer and more principled future. But what is most remarkable is not one man's vision but that without hesitation the ministry wholeheartedly endorsed his article and distributed it as requested. As all batsmen know timing in cricket is critical, and this may have proved so in this case. In the 1860s cricket was the most established of the sports that would go on to have such a profound impact on 20th-century culture. Its rules were codified, it was regulated by a powerful, influential and greatly respected organisation in the MCC and it had widespread media coverage in the British empire. In this sense it pioneered the model for a modern sport while other games remained parochial, amateur and embedded in folk traditions. Football and rugby would not have such formalised structures for another four decades. So for governments seeking a means to encourage health, athleticism, moral fortitude and the virtues of teamwork and fair play cricket must have proved an attractive proposition. In any case the ministry was certainly sold. We must assume too that Hoskjaer's judgement was highly respected and that he made a compelling case.

Prior to cricket being introduced the Copenhagen Ball Games Club had played a traditional game called *langbold*. This was a bat and ball game similar to rounders but in which players accumulated runs in a similar way to cricket. The fact that it hasn't survived suggests it wasn't particularly exciting or well suited to competition. But it would have required similar skills, such as hand-eye coordination, and it would have been easier to introduce cricket to those already skilled at *langbold*. Quickly identifying this similarity the club produced and arranged publication for a manual of the two sports, with cricket getting by far the greater emphasis. It didn't have a named author but we can assume Hoskjaer was heavily involved. In this sense although it was an English game it wasn't entirely foreign.

The text of this manual reveal what Hoskjaer and his fellow Danish cricketing pioneers considered the game's virtues to be. Its emphasis on individual skills within a team format, its contribution to mental and physical development and its appeal to all classes were emphasised. The manual covered in particular detail the benefits to health, revealing the fear predominant at the time in the dangers of slothfulness, laziness and a sedentary lifestyle. Cricket was also said to develop self-control and strength of spirit.

The manual compares cricket favourably with horse racing and rowing, which it decries for encouraging bets and lax morality. The tactical and strategic facets of the game were also championed. To the modern ear the phrasing is almost laughable in its hyperbole:

'One dares to suppose that just as cricket is beneficial in developing physical powers and suppleness so it is in developing the mental capacities, and that not least through this game requiring the making of quick decisions and an energetic execution of these, so does this strengthen that energy of decision which is the Englishman's chief advantage over other Nationalities.'

This last point is worthy of further consideration. The author not only passionately advocates the virtues of cricket but also implies that England has moral superiority over other nations. You'd expect Britain's officers of empire to subscribe to such a view but to spring from the pen of someone of a nationality outside the empire, especially from a nation recently embroiled in a conflict with Britain (they had been in opposing sides in the Napoleonic wars) is surprising. Anyone who advocates England as an exemplar model for society would naturally be drawn to a game most closely associated with its ideals. This link between the Corinthian ideal, cricket and England is another constant theme in continental cricket.

At the back of the manual a price list is printed for cricket equipment available from an ironmonger in Copenhagen. This suggests there was at least some demand before Hoskjaer and his companions returned from England.

Although the manual identifies, almost celebrates, the Englishness of cricket it also refers to an old Nordic sport of *knatt*. This was a simple game, without cricket's labyrinthine rules, played with a hard ball and a bat. The implication is that hard ball sports have much greater inherent value than soft ball equivalents. But again although cricket was an imported game, in *langbold* and *knatt* there were local games with similarities.

But these were not the first references to cricket or similar forms of game that appear in Danish print. As far back as 1801, in a book translated from German, a description of cricket is included in a collection of gymnastic games. And in 1866 in the same year as the manual was published, cricket, under the name *portbold*, was described in a book by J Lauritzen called *Entertaining and Refining Physical Exercises for the Young*.

The year 1866 was certainly a crucial year for the development of Danish cricket for it also yields the first references to matches played in the country. Newspapers reported two games played on 7 October, one by Hoskjaer's Copenhagen Ball Games Club against the Ball Players of Soro Academy in Zealand, and another between clubs from Aalborg and Randers.

One of the players in that first match, Sophus Hauberg, who was later to become a prominent industrialist, was a boy at the time but 66 years later wrote an account of the game. This reveals that cricket was introduced into the Soro Academy in the spring of 1866 to replace *langbold*, probably due to the fact the PE teacher had been persuaded of its merits by a Copenhagen player. He admits that he and his classmates found *langbold* boring, which appears to vindicate Hoskjaer's belief, supported by the ministry, that cricket would be a source of greater educational inspiration. The boys were given the rules and two members from the Copenhagen Ball Games Club showed them how to play.

Cricket proved popular at the Soro Academy and was also introduced by an English teacher to a rival public school in Herlufsholm. But cricket in the capital was declining and after one of its guiding lights, Mr Hilarious-Kalkau, was posted away from the city the existence of the game was in grave jeopardy. But two former Soro pupils who had moved to Copenhagen after leaving school and finding opportunities to play cricket limited joined a newly formed football club (Kjobenhavns Bold Klub – KB) and tried to persuade them to start a cricket team.

This was unsuccessful so while retaining membership of KB they joined another small club and managed to dominate it and force a name change to the Copenhagen Cricket Club. This club only ever played one game before the membership transferred en masse back to KB.

As part of a recruitment drive the committee of KB wrote to local schools providing a description of the game and inviting them to the club. This initiative saw 80 juniors recruited, with senior players taking responsibility for coaching. The club sought regular fixtures and details of their games provide evidence of clubs in the Jutland towns of Horsens and Aalborg, Odense and the island of Bornholm. By the mid-1880s there are also records of teams at Svendborg and the islands of Lolland and Falster. Young players from these provincial teams, along with a constant flow of Soro students, came to Copenhagen to further their studies and thereby the cricketing community grew and the standard improved.

As in Germany and Italy the organisation of cricket and football was closely linked and in 1889 both sports came under the jurisdiction of the Danish Ball Games Union (DBU). Crucially its first chairman was the leading cricket coordinator in the KB club. The union included clubs where both sports were played, but also cricket-only clubs from Aalborg, Kolding, Hjorring and Saeby. As well as being an enjoyable sport cricket also formed an important social function, with a match at Horsens in 1890 followed by a banquet and ball for the players. This indicates that the English social context for cricket that had been so prominent in the 1866 manual was still very much part of the ethos of the game in Denmark.

Copenhagen and Jutland had separate unions but met each other with combined XIs. In 1890 a Danish side toured Berlin and having previously been played on common land, the KB club acquired their own permanent ground.

By the turn of the 20th century overarm bowling had been introduced. This proved dangerous on the simple, uneven grounds and led to clubs importing matting wickets from England.

Charles Buchwald

Charles Buchwald was the first star of Danish cricket. He made his debut for the Aalborg club in 1896 at the age of 16 and by the time he retired aged 49 in 1929 he had made just shy of 10,000 runs with 28 centuries. None of his contemporaries came close to matching those statistics or approaching his class. He was the first batsman to take a disciplined, professional approach to batsmanship, ensuring attacking shots flowed from a sound defensive technique. While other players may have had greater power and higher scoring rates they would often give their wicket away, when Buchwald would compose a long and match-winning innings. The character of the man is demonstrated by the fact that his highest score, 205 not out, was made in the second innings of a match in which he had missed the first opportunity to bat due to suffering with Spanish influenza. His technical ability is also illustrated by the fact that he made three half-centuries against English opponents in 1926 in what was his first experience of grass wickets. He could also bowl, though he preferred to save his energy for batting, once taking 12 for 32 in a league match.

Buchwald was a talented all-round sportsman and played international football, featuring in the Olympic final of 1908. In his career he reached the pinnacle in the civil service becoming Permanent Under-Secretary of State at the Ministry of Public Works. Given such prominence it is hardly surprising he was honoured by the state, becoming a Knight of the Order of Dannebrog.

* * * * *

Following the first British touring team in 1900, the Royal High School, Edinburgh, clubs visited regularly and this helped to improve standards. This culminated in a tour by the MCC in 1922. In 1929 in an effort to increase standards further an English coach, H.P. Chaplin, was engaged. Chaplin, who had played county cricket for Sussex, made an immediate impact and league cricket was strengthened considerably. In the same year an important development occurred with the creation of the Copenhagen Cricket Ring. The Ring was founded to encourage and arrange tours from English clubs, promote junior cricket and to publish a periodical of Danish cricket. Once again the importance of links with England and educating people about the game was evident. The publication included reports from across the country sent in by local correspondents. The ring was also successful in attracting star-studded teams to Denmark, fixtures that resulted in the first all-Denmark sides being selected.

As well as encouraging English teams the new organisation also sought to organise regular games against Holland, the strongest cricketing nation in continental Europe. A proposal was made for a triangular tournament featuring Denmark, Holland and the MCC to be played in 1933, but this never materialised. Nevertheless the game was beginning to flourish in Denmark with better coaching producing better players and a greater variety of skills. There was even a talented leg-spinner, Eskild Larsen.

As elsewhere in Europe the onset of war came just as cricket was establishing itself as a sport across the country. Nazi occupation saw travel restrictions and curfews, making arranging cricket matches problematic. But cricket continued in spite of these difficulties and playing this very English game may have been seen as a form of resistance to occupation. But naval blockades meant cricket equipment couldn't be imported from England, and clearly the ironmonger in Copenhagen was no longer providing a local outlet.

Without bats how could there be cricket? But one man was determined to enable the game to carry on in what must rank as one of the most inspiring stories of defiance in cricketing history. Frederick Ferslev ran a business importing goods from England. A keen if modestly gifted cricketer, he heard that clubs were running out of bats and determined to make them himself. But he struggled to find appropriate wood from timber merchants. His first attempt used poplar, and despite these proving too heavy and soft they were nevertheless called into service in the 1943 season. He learnt the technique from an article in an old edition of *The Cricketer*. Learning that bats are made of willow he searched the country, even placing adverts in newspapers. When he at last sourced some, he discovered they had been used for herring boxes only two weeks before. He eventually found a stock on the island of Amager. But finding a press was an even greater challenge as all workshops in the country had been commandeered by the Nazis. Somehow he managed to design a press and get a company to make it without detection. By Christmas 1943 his Danish willow bats were made and distributed out to the clubs. He later diversified into balls as well.

* * * * *

After the war cricket activity revived, helped by new opposition provided by British military bases, but it became clear that the sport was being marginalised within the DBU. Calls for the engagement of an English coach to improve batting techniques were ignored. The DBU saw itself as a football federation that just happened to have an irritating responsibility for cricket. This led to the proposal for cricket to break away and form its own organisation. Many clubs were resistant to this change at first but in 1953 the Danish Cricket association was founded. Kurt Nielson, who had instigated the break away, was elected chairman. The Danish Cricket Ring was absorbed and funding was secured from the Danish Sports Association. The Association put in place annual matches against Scotland and Holland, regular tours to England and regular visits from England touring sides. A new national league structure was implemented replacing the old regional unions. However, efforts to get cricket accepted on to the school curriculum were unsuccessful. At the time of the foundation of the DCF there were 31 clubs in the country. The federation put an emphasis on youth, introducing age group sides. They also returned to the practice of employing English instructors over the summer, to work on techniques both with the federation and individual clubs.

Morild – a Family Legacy

Undoubtedly the most famous family in Danish cricket is the Morilds, who produced some of its finest and longest-serving players. Hailing from the north Jutland town of Hjorring, the first in the dynasty was Thomas, a left-arm seamer, who made his debut around the turn of the 20th century at the age of 13. At the age of 60 he was still one of the leading bowlers in the country and had been long invested with legendary status. To mark his birthday the Hjorring club organised a Morild XI against the rest. In the side were Thomas's son Svend and his 11-year-old grandson Carsten along with four of his nephews. It was young Carsten who was to become a great, amongst the most talented players ever produced on the continent. He dominated Danish cricket in the post-war years. Others in the family to have long and distinguished careers were Axel, Svend, Karl, Kristian and Peer. Six Morilds played for the national team and on two occasions four played in the same side. In 1955, against Holland, Svend and Carsten, father and son, played in the same XI.

* * * * *

In 1966 Denmark became an associate nation of the ICC. This provided additional funding in the form of a membership grant and representation in decisions relating to the game. But at this stage the ICC did not have either a development programme or a tournament structure for non-Test sides. So the focus remained on domestic cricket and the annual two-day contest against Holland, which they won for the first time in 1973. Regular bilateral series were also scheduled against Ireland and in the late 1970s the national team toured fellow associates, East Africa and Canada. Denmark made the semi-finals of the inaugural ICC Trophy in 1979, confirming them as one of the leading non-Test teams in the world. The quality of league cricket was improving and a new generation of talented Danish players was emerging through the system.

Ole Mortensen

As a young boy in Denmark Ole Mortensen tried his hand at most of the major sports and like most of his friends joined a football team. But one day, after football training, he witnessed a cricket match being played and paused to watch. Fortunately this momentary interest was spotted by the chairman of Svanholm CC who explained the principles of the game to the boy and invited him to practice. That was in 1966 and over the next two decades Mortensen was to become the best and most famous cricketer Denmark has produced and the most prolific cricketing professional produced outside a Test nation.

Having become one of the leading bowlers in league cricket by the mid-1970s Mortensen made his international debut in 1977 when just 19 years of age. Basing his action on Dennis Lillee he was discovered at a cricket clinic run by Derbyshire and invited over to the county for a trial in 1982. He won a contract, becoming only the second continental cricketer, after Dutchman PJ Bakker, to do so. In his debut season he took 66 wickets, making him the leading Derbyshire bowler by some margin. In a bizarre and audacious marketing ploy Carlsberg offered to double Mortensen's wages if he move to Northampton, their UK base. But he stayed for a 12-year stint and became a county legend, taking 434 first-class wickets at an average of under 24. In his testimonial year Derbyshire fans showed their love and respect by wearing Viking helmets.

He soon gained a cult status on the circuit with a nickname of 'Eric Bloodaxe' and a propensity to issue Danish slurs and shout 'satan' when frustrated. Another nickname was 'Stan', after the famous English footballer who shared his surname. His county commitments left him little time for an international career, although he did take 63 wickets in 26 ICC Trophy games at an average of 10! He was the best of a generation of talented fast bowlers, some of whom, like Sorensen and Vestergaard, joined him, albeit briefly, in county cricket. The impact he could have made on a broader international stage is perhaps hinted at in his performance against Australia in 1989, when he took three wickets for 15 runs off ten overs. But Denmark never quite made it to the global stage on which he may have shone.

When his county career was over he returned to Denmark where he combined cricket with business interests. Playing for Glostrup he was Denmark coach for five years from 2005 and later had spells coaching Germany and Norway.

The momentum gained in the 1970s stalled in the 1980s partly due to financial constraints (the team was unable to fund participation in the 1982 ICC Trophy). Despite a relatively wide proliferation of clubs cricket had never achieved a breakthrough into the country's sporting mainstream. It still had a relatively low profile, a limited number of players and lacked the institutional recognition or financial backing of rival sports. Though club communities were strong interest in wider Danish society was negligible.

Netherlands

The introduction and development of cricket in the Netherlands was defined by the sport's appeal to the educated elite and that class's management of the game. It cannot be assumed for instance that its pioneers set out to make it as popular and widespread a game as possible in the country. In the Dutch context it is not as simple as charting how cricket fared against other sports such as hockey and football for profile and participation. For it is clear that from its genesis in the mid-19th century cricket's development in Holland was governed by a desire to retain its exclusivity. Cricket was a sport for the virtuous and sophisticated and jealously guarded from those who may not subscribe to its ideals or withhold its gentlemanly standards.

As early as the late 18th century English travellers reported seeing games of cricket being played in the Netherlands. With its close proximity to England and the strong mercantile trade between the countries it is not surprising that cricket was part of the cultural exchange that naturally accompanies the flow of people and ideas. The first written reference of cricket being played was in 1845 at the Noorthey boarding school in the village of Voorschoten, between The Hague and Leiden. The school was founded in 1820 by educationalist Peter de Raadt whose philosophy, shaped by a tour of influential schools across the continent, was that children needed physical and mental exercise and inspiration. The esteem in which the school was held and its standing amongst the elite is shown by the fact King William III entrusted Noorthey with the education of his son. Cricket was an ideal fit for the school's philosophy, combining athletic activity with mental stimulation and instilling the virtues of fair play and team spirit.

It is not clear whether an English teacher working at the school or English students actually introduced the game but whoever the nationality of the pioneer it clearly caught on as Noorthey was to participate in the first national leagues established nearly 40 years after willow was first wielded by its students. In the 1850s South African students were playing cricket at the University of Utrecht.

Although Noorthey was an independent school a similar philosophy was endorsed in the highest category of public education, known as gymnasium schools. Roughly equivalent to English grammar schools, these were designed to prepare the most intellectually gifted for university and positions of power and authority in society. At this time children at these schools were generally from privileged backgrounds. As their name suggests these schools drew inspiration from the physical and intellectual ideals of Ancient Greece. With its gentle rhythms and enchanting mix of physical attributes and intellectual acumen cricket was the perfect choice of sport. With such schools often attracting teachers from England and its empire, it is not surprising that in some cricket was introduced and enthusiastically adopted.

In the 1870s and 1880s the enthusiasm for cricket in many elite schools translated into the formation of clubs by students eager to play beyond term times. Given the current concentration of cricket in the urban areas of the west of the country it is perhaps surprising that the first cricket club in the country was founded in the eastern town of Deventer, in 1875. An English student and some classmates were clearly inspired by their classical education as they called the club *Utile Dulci*, meaning 'work and pleasure' and taken from a verse of the poet Horace. That teenagers would adopt a Latin motto for a bat and ball sport illustrates both the educated, sophisticated class to which they belonged and the fact that cricket represented something far more virtuous than a fun game to be played with friends.

In 1878 The Hague Cricket Club was founded and two years later an English teacher at the gymnasium in Haarlem formed a sporting club appositely named 'Progress', for teenagers under his charge. The name appears cloyingly idealistic to our more cynical modern ears. But Mr Wilson, the founder, and his peers saw themselves as spiritual guides to a generation who would forge the modern world. There is a clear parallel with the authors of the Danish pamphlet extolling the virtues of the game to the Ministry of Education. The devotees to progress would meet to play cricket on a sandy strip nestled behind the sand dunes that protected them from North Sea breezes. That is until some found a more suitable surface in a forest glade. Some of these players formed the Rood en Wit club, and proudly sported red and black jerseys. Progress indeed. Despite the impetus provided by an Englishman, the rest of the founding committee were Dutch. Haarlem became a cricketing centre with other clubs soon springing up, some, such as 'Unity', adopting a similar theme. Three clubs were formed in Amsterdam in the 1880s, Amstel, Volharding and RAP. These would merge to form VRA in 1914. Many of these clubs remain leading lights in the Dutch league today, and tradition and conservatism still very much part of their cricketing culture.

In 1881 Uxbridge Cricket Club became the first to tour Holland. They were met by a Dutch representative side consisting of players from The Hague, Haarlem, Deventer and Noorthey. At this time there was no standardisation of rules and regulations, with each club having adopted their own conventions. These local idiosyncrasies reveal a great deal about what attracted these pioneering players to the game and why they played it. For instance the Deventer club adopted a gentlemanly approach in the Corinthian spirit of fair play. Scoring behind the wicket was considered unfair and given the derogatory label 'Spanish hitting', referring no doubt to the Duke of Alba who had been the despised governor during the years of Spanish Habsburg control.

The tour by Uxbridge Cricket Club drew considerable local interest. But it also caused a certain degree of embarrassment that the local players did not know the rules or apply them consistently. This was the equivalent on a national level of deflecting a ball behind square. It literally wasn't cricket. Coming from such educated, cultured backgrounds to be perceived as gauche and unrefined would have been unthinkable. This shame provoked the clubs into establishing a national organisation to coordinate cricket and, crucially, to ensure it was played properly. Properly in this context meant mirroring the standards of English clubs, which in turn meant emulating the standards and ethos of the MCC.

When the Nederlandsche Cricket Bond was founded in 1883 it was only the second national cricket association in the world, after the MCC. To put this into context Dutch cricket was coordinated at a national level nine years before the Australian Cricket Board was established and over 20 years before any international coordination of the sport. But while Australia had defeated England at home the year before, leading to the burning of ashes to signify the death of English cricket, the standard of play and facilities in Holland was very poor. But despite such profound limitations needing to be addressed the NCB focused its early efforts on hosting cricketing festivals. This reflected the wish of its upper class members for cricket to have a social function. Early tournaments lasted several days and featured banquets, processions, brass bands and medals. The clubs meanwhile instigated membership qualifications to protect their exclusivity. Prospective members had to be nominated by existing players and vetted and approved at board meetings. Clubs with their origins in gymnasiums limited their membership to players from the alma mater.

In 1899 the NCB employed an English coach to improve standards, particularly batting, which was best described as cavalier. Arthur Bentley had toured Holland with his club from Newton Abbot, Devon, in 1886 so was well aware of the scale of the task in hand. He introduced overarm bowling to the country and dramatically improved batting and fielding standards. Despite a local league being established clubs continued to look to England for both opposition and an exemplar of standards and behaviour. They also played matches against a team of English expats in Clingendaal. A representative side sent by the NCB to England in 1891 wasn't termed a Dutch XI but rather the Gentlemen of Holland. Is it reading too much into this to suggest that they saw greater kinship with the gentlemen of England than from other classes in their own country? In a second tour of England in 1894 a fixture was scheduled against the MCC at Lord's, with a certain Ranjitsinhji stroking a century to consign the Dutch to an innings defeat.

Although employment of an English coach had increased standards, levels of participation started to decline in the 1890s. Two-day fixtures represented a significant commitment of time and many of those that worked simply couldn't spare the time. Others joined the diplomatic service and were posted abroad. This player drain was exacerbated by the anti-English sentiment stirred by the Boer war, where Dutch-descended Afrikaners fought bitterly against the British. But despite this pressure Dutch clubs still sought to protect their exclusivity and they forced Rood en Wit to abandon efforts to develop a youth section through fear that it would attract the wrong social class. By the end of the century participation levels had dropped to isolated groups whose wealth shielded them from the pressures of work.

Cricket had been introduced and established in Holland before any of the other modern sports that would become such an intrinsic part of popular culture in the 20th century. However, this window of exclusivity had been limited and by the 1890s the popularity of football and tennis was growing rapidly. Due to the exclusive membership of its clubs it had not taken advantage of this head start to broaden its base and establish itself as a major sport in the country. Competition from other sports, especially those requiring less facilities and equipment, also saw the game stop being played in many of the gymnasium schools. As these were the main source of recruitment for the clubs participation levels began to dip.

The domestic game was facing considerable challenges in the lead-up to the First World War. But the NCB was focused on attracting teams from England and addressing the gulf in standards between domestic cricket and that found across the channel. The MCC visited in 1902 and despite animosity caused by the imperial struggle between the British and the Boers, affability on the pitch remained, as did the appetite on both sides to schedule fixtures. In 1905 annual games were commenced against British expats in Belgium and the Netherlands took part in a tournament marking the Brussels exhibition, once again taking the opportunity to play and fraternise with the MCC. At this time there were also cricket tours made to Berlin.

By the time of the First World War Holland had established clubs in a number of cities and towns, ran a national league, developed links and established tours with England, Belgium and Germany, boasted a number of talented players such as Ricker, Feith, Hisgen and Posthuma, improved playing standards through employment of a professional coach and had a national governing body. But the NCB had looked outwards, particularly in fostering links with England, rather than to consolidating and growing cricket in the country itself. This is perhaps explained by the ethos of exclusivity that pervaded the governing body and the clubs. In this context it is easy to imagine that organising a tour to England to play at Lord's would have generated more excitement for players than spreading cricket in schools and in so doing potentially diluting the very exclusivity they so cherished.

Carst Posthuma

Carst Posthuma was the most talented cricketer to be produced on the continent before the wars and proof that even small cricketing communities could produce players of world class standard. It is fortunate indeed, given cricket's relatively modest spread in the country, that Posthuma was born in Haarlem, one of the strongest cricketing centres in the Netherlands. Had he been born several hundred miles to the north or south he may never have come across the game and his talent graced other sports instead. Still referred to with reverence as the Grand Old Man of Dutch Cricket, Posthuma was born in 1868 and as a young man joined local club Rood en Wit. He established himself as the leading player in domestic cricket by the 1890s, principally as a high-class left arm seamer – but also as a hard hitting batsman, making the first century ever scored in Holland in 1894.

In 1900 he became the first Dutch bowler to take 100 wickets in a season and in all he took 2,338 wickets in the Dutch league at an average of under 9! He clearly had the talent to play at a much higher level and in 1902 against the touring MCC took 19 wickets in two matches. These performances saw him invited over to play for London County, a first-class side captained by no other than W.G. Grace. The faith in their foreign recruit proved justified when Posthuma took ten wickets in his debut match, against Leicestershire. In all he took 23 wickets in five matches at an average of 15. Given that he was 35 years of age at the time, these figures suggest he would have been a very successful bowler at first-class level and perhaps even have played Test cricket had he been born over the Channel. Even seven years later and in his forties Posthuma took 11 wickets against MCC in the International Exhibition match in Brussels.

Perhaps inspired by W.G.'s career longevity, though some would argue in Grace's case it was more a stubborn refusal to leave the crease and the limelight, Posthuma continued to play for the Dutch national team until he was 60. In an international career begun in 1892 and ending in 1928 he played 72 games. Given they didn't have any formal fixtures and were not part of the ICC these were largely against touring teams or on tour in England, with a few fixtures against Denmark. His international debut came against Hull. But it wasn't just on the pitch where Posthuma had an impact. He left a more lasting legacy to Dutch cricket through his campaigns to improve pitches and facilities.

* * * * *

Holland had remained neutral in the First World War but the army needed men to guard its frontiers, and this saw clubs lose many players from what was already a dwindling base. But following the British defeat at Zeebrugge, many troops finding their retreat cut off took refuge in Holland. The officers were based in Scheveningen and other ranks in barracks near Groningen. Several Dutch clubs took the opportunity to arrange fixtures and in 1916 Posthuma organised a cricket week in Haarlem, with Dutch sides facing English ones. This not only provided opposition but also helped improve standards as the local sides sought to emulate the techniques and behaviour of their opponents. By the end of the war the officers at Schveningen had formed two clubs, both named 'prisoners of war', and entered the Dutch league. These included several players of sufficient pedigree to later play county cricket. This influx also saw Dutch clubs bolster their ranks. While this undoubtedly strengthened the quality of the league, it may also have limited opportunities for aspiring young players.

Once peace was declared the 'prisoners of war' returned to England and the quality of the league once more declined. The NCB once again busied itself with arranging tours and international fixtures. Games were played against the British Army of the Rhine and invitations made to English touring clubs, such as the Free Foresters. Although they didn't leave a direct legacy to the Dutch cricketing structure the regular presence of touring teams did give local players a standard to aspire to and a source of inspiration and advice. Many who toured Holland regularly during the wars attested to a significant increase in standard.

The concept of touring clubs clearly appealed to Dutch cricketers for in 1921 the 'De Flamingo's' club was formed. This had links to but was not formally part of the NCB and soon became the body responsible for arranging international tours and selecting players for them. But as membership of the club was by invitation only in effect you could only represent Holland if you were the sort of person they wanted to tour with. It was yet another layer of exclusivity introduced into Dutch cricket. However, the Flamingos soon broadened their focus to helping develop cricket within the country too, sending sides to regions of the country where cricket was less established to encourage development and organise youth tournaments. The Flamingos still play this role today and recently won a development award for an indoor tournament they ran.

In the mid-1920s cricket had revived to the extent where the NCB sought to expand the domestic league structure. Traditionally the top division had only consisted of the six strongest clubs and as these were all from the cricketing centres in the west of the country the geographic reach of the league was limited. To encourage development of the game elsewhere in the country new clubs were promoted, seeking to build on the impetus provided by the De Flamingo's domestic programme. This reform was encouraging and signalled a desire to be more inclusive. However, in truth the concentration of talent in the traditional clubs of Haarlem, The Hague and Amsterdam, whose players had benefitted from selection for representative games and foreign tours, meant they proved far too strong for the newer clubs with less experienced players. This inevitably resulted in very one-sided games and consequently a decline in interest. The noble experiment was ended in 1932 with a return to a smaller first division. To this day the configuration of leagues is one of the biggest talking points in the Dutch cricket community.

The dominant domestic team in the 1920s was The Hague Cricket Club. Already one of the strongest clubs in the league they recruited Fred Warburton, a professional coach from Lancashire. He developed a generation of players who would dominate Dutch cricket. In fact such was their dominance that the club's second XI was promoted to the first division and became the only viable challenger to the first XI for the national championship. With such playing strength in their ranks it is not surprising that the vast majority of the national XI was drawn from the club. The VRA club in Amsterdam followed the example and contracted an English coach, who also developed talented players for the national team.

The resources and ambitions of specific clubs has been a major factor in the development of Dutch cricket. There is no doubt that the top clubs in the country were powerful and influential. Connections in England, cultivated through De Flamingo's, gave them prestige and influence. This was demonstrated by the fact that HCC were able to attract an MCC side featuring Pelham Warner in 1928 to celebrate its 50th anniversary. It is telling that the MCC were the chosen opposition, rather than a local rival. Dutch cricket had always looked to England for example and kinship.

By 1928 it is estimated that there were 1,200 cricketers in the Netherlands, four times as many as when the NCB was founded in the 1880s. By 1932 there were 54 teams, more than double the number in 1918. This was partly the result of the regional development programme of De Flamingo's that had seen new clubs form and old clubs revive. But it is also evidence that cricket had found its niche in the cultural sporting landscape of the country. It was still a sport of the elite, and this naturally limited mass participation, but its ethos of fair play and honour attracted those wanting to associate themselves with a sophisticated pursuit that furthered the Corinthian ideal.

The 1930s was to be a period of growth and has sometimes been referred to as a golden age of Dutch cricket. In 1930 the first women's team was founded in Haarlem. By 1934 there were several more and the Nederlandse Dames Cricket Bond was founded and a league introduced. In 1937 the Australian women's team played a game in Holland during their tour to England. This was 17 years before the first tour by the Australian men's team. In 1931 the NCB founded a weekly magazine called *Cricket* that was distributed to its member clubs. This provided official information and match reports and helped galvanise cricket across the country. In 1933 the MCC were once again invited to Holland, this time to celebrate the 50th anniversary of the NCB. The hosts won chasing down 133 in three-quarters of an hour. Two years later the South African Test team, featuring Dudley Nourse, toured Holland. The standard of play had increased significantly from before the war and Dutch representative XIs won as many games as they lost, and were dominant against other continental teams.

The heroes of the Golden Age included de Beus, the first Dutch leggie, the attacking batsman van Manen, the accomplished run-scorer Glerum and the fast-medium bowler Terwiel, who took a record 144 wickets in the 1938 season. The best players in Holland were good enough to have played at a high standard in England.

The story of how Dutch cricket survived Nazi occupation in the Second World War is an inspiring tale of defiance and a make do and mend philosophy. When Rotterdam was bombed in May 1940 the country's only sports dealer selling cricket equipment was razed to the ground. Faced with shortages cricketers came up with innovative ways of extending the life a ball. One such method was rubbing balls in boot polish which strengthened them to the extent that they would last ten matches. It was a modification much beloved of swing bowlers. Others painted hockey balls red, though this led to rather too many broken bats and fingers to be sustainable. As well as a lack of equipment, cricketers also had problems getting to matches with use of private cars banned and rail travel restricted. Several clubs fashioned tricycle carts to transport the team's kit to the grounds from the nearest station while others cycled more than 30 miles to play.

The risks for cricketers were considerable, particularly as the sport was considered un-Aryan by Hitler and actively discouraged. They made an obvious target for officers tasked with recruiting men for forced labour. Many of the best grounds in the country were requisitioned while poles were planted in others to ensure they couldn't be used as impromptu landing grounds for Allied planes. Sight screens and pavilions had surrendered their wood for fuel. Incredibly, given such constraints and pressures, the NCB were able to organise 300 matches in 1944. With such exertion and persistence required to play and with severe rationing of food cricketers would be exhausted after a match, but their spirit revived by a glass of Jenever. A significant factor in this collective will to ensure play wasn't stopped was that cricket, surely the most English of sports, was a demonstration of defiance against Nazi occupation and cultural suppression. It was also in its own way a show of solidarity with the Allied powers who would liberate them. This may have been an important psychological factor in the broadening of the game's appeal to different sectors of Dutch society in the post-war period.

It was natural that cricket would be part of the jubilation and relief of liberation with impromptu games organised against British troops. In these circumstances the stuffiness and formality of cricket gave way to a purer, simpler form played wherever possible with whatever equipment available. The army units, playing in their khaki uniforms and gym shoes, provided sandwiches, cigarettes and sometimes even petrol for the mower. It is estimated that around 300 matches were played against the liberators. Furthermore Pelham Warner, who had regularly toured Holland before the war, set up a Save Dutch Cricket fund, which provided 200 bats and 100 balls for the NCB. The boot polish could once again be used for boots. With such a generous donation the NCB were able to restart the national league in 1946 with 58 teams taking part.

The links to England, the forging of which had always been central to NCB strategy, had been strengthened by the war with cricket a symbol of the cultural difference, perhaps in some eyes even superiority, over the brutality of fascist Germany. It was in this spirit that club teams from English towns and villages sought to twin with those in Holland, arranging regular games and developing bonds and friendships between players. Although development of young players had been curtailed in the years of occupation the national team performed well in the immediate post-war seasons with De Flamingo's defeating the MCC by five wickets at Lord's. In 1947 J.J. van der Luur became the first Dutchman to score a century on the hallowed turf. Such accomplishments mattered, and were recorded as key milestones.

The 1950s saw Dutch cricket take a further step forward both in standard and levels of participation. What was particularly encouraging was the introduction of government support. Early in the decade a government subsidy enabled the NCB to organise coaching courses run by the MCC Youth Cricket Council. Further funding was provided by cricket's share of the proceeds from the legalisation of the football pools. Thanks to a talented new generation including Wally van Weelde, Piet Sanders and Peter van Arkel, the Dutch XI was competitive against even the strongest touring sides. In general there was a greater emphasis on youth development and Dutch clubs began to send junior teams on tours to England to play school sides. This investment ensured that talented young players could come into the team when pre-war cricketers hung up their boots.

By the mid-1950s the long commitment to attracting touring teams to Holland saw the league season punctuated by a wide range of visitors from club sides to Test teams hopping over the Channel during their tours of England. Holland was established as a cricketing centre and its representative team deemed worthy opposition, even for sides of Test calibre. In 1955 regular fixtures were instigated against the best continental opposition, Denmark, though in truth Holland were much the stronger side. In 1958 on its 75th anniversary the NCB was given royal endorsement and the name was changed to the Koninklijke Nederlandse Cricket Bond. By this time there were 97 clubs in the country, a 60% increase over the previous decade. There were by then 12 visiting tours a year and a further four of five at youth level, largely from public schools.

Victory over Australia 1964

The Ashes-winning skipper, Bob Simpson, was sitting in the clubhouse at the de Dieppput ground, The Hague, as his opening batsmen put on their pads. It was a chance to unwind after a long tour to England and see something of the continent before flying home. After all, the serious cricket had been played and bragging rights over the Poms secured. However, the stakes were much higher in the home dressing room. It was only the third visit of a Test match team to the country since the war and so a rare chance to prove themselves against a leading cricket nation. A chance, too, to get recognition and respect in a sport in which despite having the second oldest national cricket board in the world, they had been denied a stake and kept on the periphery.

Whether the steadily building crowd sensed history in the making or were just intrigued to see what the fuss was about it is difficult to say but several thousand were watching on as Bill Lawry and Wally Grout strode to the wicket. It was at this point that one or two seeds of doubt may have entered their minds in what previously must surely have seemed a mere end-of-tour jolly against amateur opposition. Rather than closely mown grass they made their guard on a matting strip. They had to swop their spikes for plimsolls. The pitch proved something of a brute with the Dutch bowling attack of Trijzelaar, Pierhage and Vriens making the most of viscious bounce to get the Aussies hopping and dancing. Lawry fell for five and Grout's stumps were uprooted to leave them two wickets down for just 36. Attempting a hook off Trijzelaar, Jack Potter, who had waited patiently all tour for his first cap, only to be given a consolation run out against the Dutch, missed and was retired hurt with a fractured skull. Despite O'Neill's 87 the Australians could only muster 198. Not as many as they would have hoped, and they had lost a player and broken four bats in the process, but surely enough.

The Dutch sensed an upset though and with knowledge of conditions made an assured start, with the opening pair of Pieter Marseille and Pim van der Vegt falling one short of a century stand. But Marseille and captain van Arkel kept up the pressure, making 77 and 45 respectively, and bringing the Dutch close to the target. Now fearing an embarrassing reverse that could taint an otherwise successful tour the Australians finally upped their game and the hosts slumped to a precarious 181-7. In the gloaming they required 24 runs off the last three overs. In the end it came down to two men. Australian off-spinner Bob Cowper who had choked the Dutch middle order and got his team back into the game and young batsman Ruud Onstein who needed to hit a seemingly improbable nine runs for victory. Requiring seven off four Onstein launched Cowper out of the ground to bring the scores level and then hooked the next behind square for four. The Dutch celebrated wildly, and with good reason. It was their first victory over a full member and the most famous in their history.

For a sport that only had 50 clubs in comparison to the 4,400 football boasted it was a justly proud moment. To be able to produce players of sufficient quality to defeat an Ashes-winning team was testimony to what could be achieved within a relatively small community. They were even missing one of their key players, all-rounder Nico Spits, who was representing his country at hockey against Great Britain the same day. The Australian press were furious at what they took to be a complacent and contemptible performance. Furthermore some questioned why they had even scheduled a fixture against an unworthy opponent. There was no mention of how well the Dutch had played or even how encouraging the result was for development of cricket in the region. The following year the Netherlands were to join the ICC, though the victors were certainly not to keep the spoils.

For the members of the Dutch team legendary status awaited, within the cricketing community at any rate, and match-winner Ruud Onstein was to become a key figure in seeking to build press coverage and increase the sport's profile, always to be seen, crisply attired, at international matches.

* * * * *

In addition to the headline-grabbing victory over Australia the national side was talented enough to get regular draws against strong English teams including Oxford University and Combined Services. The Hague Cricket Club had continued to dominate domestic leagues, with 42 national championships to its name. As well as an increase in the number of clubs cricket had also spread within the country with Alkmaar and Den Helder in the north of the country founding clubs. By this time Holland had become an associate member of the ICC and the KNCB chairman, H Grijseels, became the Dutch representative at the conference.

Although membership of the ICC brought little practical benefit to associate nations prior to the foundation and funding of a development programme in the 1990s it nevertheless provided an opportunity for international matches against peers. Holland had been playing international representative games for years but as they were not an imperial nation they had been excluded from membership of the ICC and therefore denied any official endorsement or status accorded to their matches. They had been allowed into the fold following the ICC's reconstitution as the International Cricket Conference in the 1960s.

In this context fellow associate members became natural opponents. Teams such as Canada, Sri Lanka and Bermuda were the barometer for how strong Holland were in the global pecking order and, critically, how strong their case was for playing Test cricket at some stage in the future. Tours by Bermuda and Sri Lanka were planned in 1968 but were cancelled.

When the NCB was founded in 1883 there were 18 clubs and approximately 300 cricketers in the country. By 1968 this had increased to more than 50 clubs and over 5,000 active cricketers.

These clubs produced 135 teams who played in a four-tier domestic league structure, complemented by youth and veteran teams.

The game was still strongest in its traditional centres in the west of the country. Fourteen of the 16 teams in the top tier were from the region known as the Ranstad. As well as strong representation from the traditional centres of Haarlem, The Hague and Amsterdam, there were sides from Rotterdam and Schiedam. But helped by the regional tours organised by De Flamingo's the game had slowly spread to other parts of the country. The two remaining teams in the top tier were Bilthoven, located near Utrecht in the centre of the country, and Nijmegen, lying close to the eastern border with Germany. In the lower tiers there were clubs from other eastern towns such as Enschede, Arnhem, Deventer and Apeldoorn. Cricket had not spread to any great extent in either the south or the north, though there was a club in Groningen.

But despite an increase in teams and a much broader playing base cricket was still run by gentlemen for gentlemen, with privilege and Corinthian principle guiding the board's decisions. Despite a tiered league structure being in place promotion and relegation were decided off the field rather than on it. It was the KNCB board rather than league rankings that determined the fate of teams. The preferences and prejudices of half a dozen denizens decided who could join the elite and who would be protected from the infamy of demotion to the ranks. It was only after sustained pressure during the late 1960s that promotion and relegation were made automatic in the 1969 season.

By the late 1960s the KNCB had implemented several sub-committees with responsibility for different aspects of the game. As well as management of the league, selection of the national team, maintenance of the journal cricket and records there were sub-committees focused on youth development and publicity. There were just under a hundred umpires and the board ran courses to encourage transition from playing to officiating. Each year there were two youth camps organised for boys under 17 and these would generally attract around 80 youngsters. In addition to this some ad hoc camps were held to introduce children under 8 to the game. The league structure was divided into four tiers, with two leagues in the top division, six in the second, three in the third and six in the fourth. Complementing this were two dedicated divisions for veterans and a one-day knockout tournament.

Below the league structure regional associations affiliated to the KNCB organised lower grade cricket, generally with a focus on youth. The strongest clubs had five or more senior sides in various tiers as well as youth and veteran XIs. The vast majority of players in the league structure were ethnic Dutch in the late 1960s, though a small percentage originated from Suriname and the Antilles. There were also around 40 players from either England or the Commonwealth.

By 1968 the De Flamingo's club had played over 700 matches. They had arranged more tours to England than they had within Holland.

Although initiatives of the KNCB and De Flamingo's had helped grow the domestic game the structure of clubs was also important. Generally in Holland clubs play a number of different sports. This has undoubtedly helped provide financial stability and access to facilities for cricket. As in Denmark and Italy the older clubs generally played both cricket and football. But clubs that were established after the Second World War tended to focus on hockey with cricket as a summer sport. The VRA club in Amsterdam is a prime example. This connection with hockey has been a significant advantage to the spread of cricket in Holland. Players attracted to clubs to play hockey in the winter would naturally be encouraged to play cricket in the summer. This proved a very effective recruitment tool and gave cricket a much greater reach than its limited profile warranted. While limited access to grounds and facilities has made cricket very vulnerable elsewhere on the continent, in Holland the link with hockey has provided relative stability. Fluctuations in playing numbers, popularity or funding while being a concern for the boards were not critical to survival. This helps explain why in Holland cricket has not endured such a hand to mouth existence as in neighbouring countries.

The advent of a limited-overs knockout tournament, that had proved popular in England, provided an opportunity for those with work and other commitments to play the game. It was also intended to provide a more entertaining and engaging spectacle to broaden the game's appeal. In the time poor modern age this was to be a significant development for the global game, but perhaps even more so in nations where cricket was a minority sport. This greater accessibility and a relaxation of the exclusivity of old was a significant factor in an increase in playing numbers through the 1970s and 1980s to a peak of around 6,500.

The next important reform domestically was the introduction of player/coaches in 1978/79. This enabled the richer clubs to pay salaries to lure quality players, often with first-class experience, to the Dutch league. Many of these, having qualified through residency, became stars of the national team. While many had a very positive impact on developing the next generation of talent, others just took the money and a spot in the team that otherwise may have been given to an emerging player. There is a long list of international stars that have played for a spell in the Netherlands.

The switch in emphasis to limited overs was also a major influence in international cricket, especially for the associates who were not given Test status or any other form of endorsed multi-day cricket. The traditional 'Tests' against Denmark were reduced to one-day games and the fixtures organised with Scotland and Ireland were similarly curtailed. This meant that a programme of fixtures against different opponents could be organised in the limited time players were able to get released by their employers.

Twelve years after a limited-overs tournament was first introduced in county cricket the ICC finally introduced a global one, the World Cup. In addition to six Test nations the strongest associate nation, Sri Lanka, was included along with a composite team from East Africa. They were there to make the format workable, rather than through any altruism on behalf of the ICC. However, it set an important precedent that ICC events would be opened, albeit to a limited extent, to its associate nations. The success of the World Cup saw the ICC introduce the ICC Trophy in 1979, a tournament for its associate members that served as a qualification opportunity for the World Cup itself. The Netherlands, with a long cricketing heritage and established domestic league, were well placed to take advantage.

The ICC Trophy was open to all associate nations and was the first ICC-run event that enabled an assessment of the relative strength of non-Test nations. There was a considerable gulf in class between countries close to Test status like Sri Lanka and weaker associates like Malaysia and Israel. The two European teams that participated in the inaugural tournament in 1979 were Denmark and the Netherlands. The Dutch team was comprised of leading Dutch players who had represented their country in the ad hoc fixtures against visiting teams and De Flamingo's tours. The entire XI were Dutchmen. Though they could adjust better than many of their opponents to the English climate they had to contend with turf pitches, having played their domestic games exclusively on artificial wickets.

The Dutch were placed in a difficult group with Sri Lanka, winner of the tournament and soon to be promoted to Test status, and ended the tournament with only one victory, against Israel. They came close in a rain-affected match against Wales and their match against the USA was washed out. Humiliatingly for the Dutch their continental neighbours Denmark, albeit with a more favourable draw, progressed to the semi-finals.

The 1980s was a successful decade for Dutch cricket, both domestically and internationally. From their first round elimination in 1979 the Dutch were finalists in the ICC Trophy in 1986 and 1990, on both occasions losing to future Test nation Zimbabwe. Though they had not yet qualified for a World Cup they had cemented their reputation as a leading associate nation, eclipsing any other in Europe by some margin. This was of course in the period before Scotland and Ireland became ICC members in their own right. They also took some notable scalps on home soil, defeating the West Indies in 1990 and South Africa in 1994. Like the Australians before them the trip to Holland wasn't quite the restful break in their tours of England they were hoping for.

This success was based largely on a talented generation of Dutch cricketers emerging through the domestic set-up. The strength of the Dutch club structure and increased emphasis on youth was undoubtedly a factor. While many players were still drawn from the upper middle class milieu that had always dominated the KNCB the player base was broadening. While still very much a minority sport it was becoming slowly more inclusive with limited-overs formats more conducive to those wishing to balance sport with employment, family and other interests. Many of the players that started their international careers in the 1980s emphasise the importance of access to cricket through the BBC to developing a lifelong passion and commitment to the game. England wasn't only merely across the water but its summer game was available in every living room. To some extent this compensated for cricket's lack of penetration into the national psyche. It had a very limited profile in the country, but anyone flicking through the TV channels had access to it.

* * * * *

One of the elder statesmen of the team in the 1980s was keeper-batsman Rene Schoonheim. Born during Nazi occupation in 1944, he had played alongside elder statesman Wally van Weelde when facing Denmark in 1964. In 1966 his national team commitments were limited to games against Oxford University and the Combined Services. But two decades later his itinerary had changed dramatically, with the ICC Trophy, three fixtures against India and two against New Zealand. He would go on to play league cricket until 2002 and had the pride of seeing his son follow in his footsteps and be capped for the Netherlands too. His was a career that spanned different eras of Dutch cricket. They had become if not quite a force then certainly a fixture of international cricket, regularly playing in tournaments and embarking on a programme of international tours.

* * * * *

An indication of the quality of the Dutch league by the early 1980s is that it was producing players capable of making cricket their career. This wasn't simply a question of talent, with many of the finest cricketers in the country very content adopting the role of gifted amateur. But for some the proximity of England and the lure of a professional career for an English county was attractive. Being noticed was difficult as Holland was not generally on the radar of county scouts, unless perhaps a player's ability stood out during a tour. But there was an opportunity through second XI games to give players a trial. The first to go down this route was the off-spinning all-rounder Frank Lubbers who made several appearances for Derbyshire second XI in 1978, a year before playing in the ICC Trophy for his country. Though he never enjoyed a career in county cricket he would go on to represent his country at a World Cup and later join the KNCB board. The following year the supremely gifted Ron Elferink played a match for Worcestershire. He didn't get a chance to bat, which was a shame because his ICC Trophy average of 48 serves notice of his ability.

PJ Bakker

Paul-Jan Bakker was born in Vlaardingen in 1957. A medium-fast bowler with a probing line and length he played his club cricket for Quick Haag, making his Holland debut relatively late at the age of 26 against the MCC. In the summer of 1985 he came to England to play for Southern League side Old Tauntonians. The following year he made history by becoming the first Dutchman to play county cricket when he played for Hampshire against Gloucestershire in Bournemouth in late May, taking the wicket of future England bowler Syd Lawrence. The following month he drove to the Midlands to represent his country in the ICC Trophy. He made an immediate impact, taking five wickets for 18 runs against Papua New Guinea in the first game.

He played two championship games for Hampshire in 1987 but finally cemented a place in the side by the end of the following season. 1989 was his golden year, finishing the season as Hampshire's highest wicket taker with 77 wickets at an average of 22. He played for the county until 1992, taking 193 wickets in all at an average of 28. He was an integral part of a bowling unit that included Malcolm Marshall, Tim Tremlett and Cardigan Connor. One of his proudest moments though came off the pitch, when he was a guest at David Gower's wedding.

Despite his county commitments he continued to represent his country as often as possible. Against the Australians at The

Hague in 1989 he took an impressive trio of scalps in Mark Taylor, Dean Jones and Tom Moody.

After ending his county career he returned to Holland and Quick Haag. Though he had lost some pace his experience at the top level was valuable and he remained in the national team, fulfilling his dream of representing his country at a World Cup in 1996. He was very much the veteran of the squad at 38 and only took three wickets, though one was England opener Alec Stewart.

Overall he played 51 matches for the Netherlands over a span of 13 years, taking 161 wickets at an eye-catching average of 13.

In 1995 the ECB invited the Dutch to participate in the NatWest Trophy, a 60-over knockout competition. Their recent qualification for the World Cup and the South African scalp the previous year may well have been influential in being welcomed into the fold, though it is likely that filling a gap to provide an even number of teams may have been the more practical reasoning behind the decision. For the KNCB, who had since their creation been determined to forge strong links with England, this represented quite a coup. It provided further exposure and high quality opposition for their leading players as they sought to be competitive on their World Cup debut the following year. Though it only provided one guaranteed game a season this link with the ECB was part of a subtle shift in Dutch cricket that increasingly saw the development and programme of the national team diverge from the clubs and domestic leagues. The Dutch lost that first game against Northamptonshire though in posting 270 they demonstrated they were good enough to compete against county opposition.

In 1996 grass wickets were laid in Deventer and Amstelveen. This not only enabled players to improve their techniques and skills through experience of playing on grass wickets but also meant that the Netherlands could host top level fixtures and tournaments for which turf wickets were a requirement. This was to prove crucial in the years to come.

That same year saw the first European Championships held. As expected the Netherlands proved the strongest of the continental sides though they lost to Ireland in the final.

Themes

English Influence

THE introduction and development of cricket was an important part of Britain's imperial mission. It provided entertainment and cohesion for its military and administrators and symbolised the ideals of order, sophistication and sportsmanship that it was seeking to impress on its new dominions. But in continental Europe this structured model of development was limited to colonial enclaves at the extremities at Gibraltar and Corfu. Here the insulation of the communities meant that cricket was closely guarded as a means of demonstrating difference, perhaps even in the views of those that played it, superiority. Cricket did not spread through the continent from its toeholds in Greece and the Iberian peninsula.

The presence of the British military at certain times certainly gave a boost to cricket communities across the continent, providing opposition and in some cases equipment and grounds. This was particularly important following the Second World War when cricket on the continent was extremely vulnerable. British migration also played its role with railway workers in Denmark, wine merchants in Portugal and weavers in Italy. English teachers introduced cricket into public schools, in some cases enthusing students who would become pioneers of the game in their nations.

But for the game to take root it needed local champions. In Paris a relatively large English expat community founded leagues but didn't leave a lasting legacy. In contrast in The Hague and Copenhagen, cities with much lower levels of English migration, cricket became established and participation levels grew. In the Netherlands and Denmark cricket was adopted by the same class of people that helped embed it in English culture. They respected the game's combination of athletic and cerebral challenge and the role this could play in the physical and spiritual development of young people. The Danish example shows that these pioneering cricketers found willing champions in government and educational institutions. But it wasn't just the inherent virtues of the game that appealed, but its representation of Englishness and the sophistication that link bestowed. As the most powerful empire and developed nation of the period Britain had defined the standards of modern civilisation. It is natural therefore that many on the continent, particularly those from educated, privileged backgrounds, would have looked to Britain for an exemplar of civilised living. Cricket as an embodiment of all those virtues and so modern in comparison with the simple pastimes that predominated in agrarian societies, was the perfect way to reflect that sophistication they aspired to.

The early champions of cricket on the continent were to a greater or lesser degree Anglophiles. In Denmark the influence of an English public school education was a major factor but even where there wasn't a direct link the pioneers measured themselves against English standards, sought English opposition and established as many cultural links as they could. In the Netherlands the KNCB devoted much of their energies to attracting English touring teams and planning tours across the Channel. Improvements in standards often came about through the shame of not matching the standards of their English guests. The wish not to appear gauche, raw and unsophisticated was an ambition that guided the actions and strategy of the national boards.

The grainy photographs of early touring sides from the Netherlands around the turn of the 20th century show how the players mimicked the style of dress and codes of behaviour they saw in their English opposition. The MCC was held in total reverence as the arbiter not only of the rules but the etiquette and standards of the game. It is not an exaggeration to suggest that the primary motivation of the early administrators of the game in Holland was to play in England or against English opposition. Even when domestic leagues were established and cricket became self-sustaining locally, ties with England were retained, nurtured and strengthened. When the Dutch cricketing elite formed the De Flamingo's club, their primary focus was on crossing the Channel.

Given the cultural differences between England and the continent you might have expected cricket to have developed differently. But in practice the national boards took great efforts to crack down on any deviance from the way it was played in England. Both the Netherlands and Denmark employed English coaches to ensure conformity to established techniques and when the MCC introduced any reforms, such as allowing overarm bowling, the boards strove to follow suit. The same applied in conventions and behaviour. The only localisation was the invention of cricketing terms in the local language. Such was the desire to match and uphold English standards of sportsmanship that it was taken to even greater extremes than in the shires themselves as in the case of it being frowned upon to play shots behind the wicket.

Cricket's embodiment of English ideals and sophistication was certainly a compelling draw for early cricketers in the Netherlands and Denmark. It was a significant factor in generating the enthusiasm and commitment to the game that saw leagues and organisations founded and therefore a platform for the game to become established. But the game's association with England, emphasised by those who played and ran the game, would have had less appeal beyond moneyed, educated classes. In this sense the Englishness of the game became part of its exclusivity. Even if those from a broader social spectrum became aware of the game their judgement of cricket would have been formed through the prism of its social setting. While the game itself may have instinctively appealed the way it was played would probably not. The shaping of the game to conform to English ideals and social conventions was a means of protecting its exclusivity. In this social and class context cricket was always going to be constrained in its appeal and reach. It was difficult for an English game to become rooted in the national consciousness. For many it would have been perceived as a foreign game played by people very different to themselves. Foreign and different can be appealing, but generally people are drawn to what is known and accepted. Breaking down these perceptions has been one of the defining challenges of the modern era. To really succeed cricket needed to have a universal appeal, like football, but in truth it never has.

Corinthianism

Cricket has long been associated with the spirit of fair play and the Corinthian ideal. It has been a distinguishing feature that has drawn many people to the game and given it a reputation as a civilised, gentlemanly pastime. Even beyond traditional cricketing centres this aspect of the game is well known, even for people for whom the objective and the rules remain a mystery. In my journeys through Europe I've heard the phrase 'it just isn't cricket' cited with relish in many different accents.

Even in the 21st century sledging, mankads and not walking when you've nicked it are minor scandals that fill many column inches. But there is a greater acceptance now as younger generations base judgements on adherence to the rules rather than to a gentlemen's code of honour. But in the late 19th century such codes were considered inviolable to any self-respecting gentleman cricketer, and this was particularly the case on the continent. While they may not have been capable of matching the quality of English teams they could certainly be their equals for sportsmanship.

That these ideals were central to clubs is shown in their names. In Holland Sparta and Hercules betray the classical ideals of their founders. Others chose English names like Quick. It is clear that having fun was not the primary objective of these clubs, but rather instilling ideals and virtues to young people. It was as much educational as recreational. These Corinthian values reflected those of their founders and proved attractive to others of their class, equally enthused by such values through the education provided by a privileged background. In this way the clubs could reinforce the exclusivity they wanted by emphasising this aspect of the game. How well you played was less important than the spirit in which you played. Many a paltry batting average has been forgiven due to good breeding and peerless behaviour.

Exclusivity

Such has been the focus on development since the birth of a new millennium that it is natural for many to define the history of cricket on the continent as the struggle to overcome barriers and constraints to it becoming a mainstream sport. But this view presupposes that the pioneers of the game in the region shared this ambition. In each country where it took root cricket's development was indebted to a handful of individuals whose passion for and dedication to the game saw fixtures organised, clubs formed and structures of governance and administration put in place. But they did not lay these foundations to convert their countrymen and make cricket a national sport. In fact often the decisions they made served to protect the exclusivity of the game and ensure that cricket did not become a mass participation sport. It was a sport for gentlemen and had to be protected from those classes of society who may not uphold its values. This view pervaded both the clubs that were formed and the organisations created to run the game, which naturally mirrored the views of their founders. In this way exclusivity was woven into the fabric of continental cricket and steered its destiny. Many clubs put restrictions on membership and it was only deemed appropriate as an activity for the scions of the privileged at the best kind of schools.

To understand why cricket developed in this way you need to consider what drew early cricketers on the continent to the game. It is clear from first-hand accounts that it was not the elemental thrill of bat striking ball that was the primary attraction but rather the social context in which the game was played and the collective affirmation of mutual ideals held by the cultural elite that it provided. This can be seen in the way that cricket was played. Matches were stage managed as society events held over several days with bands, banquets and bonhomie. In this sense they were more a celebration of what the game stood for than a demonstration of cricketing talent. Cricketers in Europe adopted a social context for cricket just as if not more willingly than those in England and the empire. In the same way that English wine merchants in Portugal didn't think cricket a suitable game for the locals so the elites that adopted the game in northern Europe thought it too sophisticated for their fellow countrymen.

This social context was critical to how cricket was perceived and how it spread. Social envy amongst the educated classes, for whom the sport's deep connection with sophistication, Corinthian ideals and Englishness would most appeal, saw cricket spread from its founding centres to towns and cities with a similar social-cultural composition. This was particularly the case when students graduated from the few select schools that had adopted the sport and formed clubs in their home towns or wherever they went for employment. But though in Denmark and particularly the Netherlands this process resulted in the geographic spread of the game it remained restricted to the educated elites. There was no attempt to broaden its social base, at least not until deep into the 20th century. This exclusivity was preciously guarded and this was a factor in ensuring that cricket established a social-cultural niche, albeit very dependent on the commitment of a small number of players and administrators for its survival. Its appeal may have been limited to a very particular social class, but for this minority no other sport offered what cricket did and this galvanised the communities.

As cricket was very much a gentlemen's game it was organised and played in a way that reflected the social background and sensibilities of its players. This meant that even in clubs where membership was not explicitly restricted the organisation and social setting of games would not have been accessible to those of other classes. If a passer-by happened to witness a game in their neighbourhood and stopped to watch they would have seen men very different to themselves, dressed in smart clothing playing a game whose rules must have been baffling. Even if intrigued by the spectacle many must have concluded that this was not a game for them. In this way the manner in which it was played would have reinforced its social elitism. Another factor that further strengthened this connection between cricket and class was that it required a lot of free time. Even if working men were not put off by the social and sartorial (striped blazers may not have appealed to everyone's notion of hard-working masculinity) elements of the game, they simply would not have been able to commit several days to play. Cricket was a game for the leisured classes, one of the luxuries that time afforded them.

As cricket is very much a minority sport on the continent there is a paucity of evidence on its social impact. With the exception of a handful of references by travellers who witnessed cricket on their journeys the only records of cricket being played are from the archives of clubs and governing bodies. These fixtures were by their nature formal. It is possible that cricket was played in less formal, unstructured settings but has been lost to historical record. But getting access to specialist equipment would have been difficult and expensive and with clubs proudly protecting their membership it seems very unlikely that people from social classes not courted by the clubs would have adopted the game. In this context the exclusivity of cricket would have limited its potential growth to a very small percentage of the population. In turn this meant that it never achieved the social reach necessary to become part of sporting consciousness in Europe.

But social contexts change over time and in both the Netherlands and Denmark cricket became more inclusive in the second half of the 20th century. This was partly through necessity. The leisured classes had far more options for how to spend their time than previous generations, as many took up tennis, golf and other pastimes. The ideals of Corinthianism were not quite as in vogue either and cricket's link to Englishness perhaps not as strong a pull as in Victorian times. This meant that clubs had to broaden their appeal in order to replenish their numbers and ensure that leagues were still viable. There is no doubt that the introduction of one-day cricket in the 1960s was a significant contributing factor to breaking down the old class divisions that had characterised cricket before the war. Working men could play games at the weekends and balance cricket with career and family commitments.

In the Netherlands participation levels grew steadily after the war until a high in the 1980s largely thanks to clubs reaching out to a broader spectrum of society. But awareness of cricket in the country was very limited, with little or no media coverage and only a select few schools teaching the game. The board established committees to address these challenges but made little headway. It was more inclusive but still very much a minority sport. The critical factor in Holland having higher participation levels than other continental countries was its multi-sport clubs.

This ensured that those attracted to clubs by popular sports like hockey and football would also be exposed to cricket and be encouraged to take it up as a summer sport. This club structure acted as a much more powerful recruitment drive than cricket could have achieved through its own profile or resources. Access to cricket on television was also a significant factor.

Birth of Modern Sport

Football became so dominant in 20th-century Europe that all other sports faced a challenge to match its appeal and level of cultural saturation. This dominance has seen football claim the lion's share of funding, sponsorship and media coverage which all contributed to it becoming a cultural phenomenon. Even at the peak of cricket participation in Holland the sport had less than 1% of the nation's footballers. In this context all other sports have had to play second fiddle and seek to co-exist as a junior partner. But it did not always enjoy this hegemony.

Although forms of both football and cricket were being played in England from the Middle Ages cricket was the first to develop from a pastime to a modern sport by codifying its laws in 1744. It was more than a century later in 1848 when rules were first codified for football. Similarly cricket was the first to have coordinated organisation when the Marylebone Cricket Club was formed in 1787 and became the rule-maker and arbiter of the game. The Football Association was not formed until 1863. This pattern is repeated on the continent, albeit with a much shorter time delay. The first cricket club in a country beyond direct British influence was in Holland in 1857. This was 22 years before a football club was first formed. The Netherlands Cricket Board was established in 1883, six years before its footballing counterpart.

For the last quarter of the 19th century the two games coexisted on the continent, but with cricket having the earlier foundations and in many cases a greater number of clubs. It wasn't until the first decade of the 20th century that football really took off. Cricket therefore had a short window of opportunity to become an established sport. This window coincided with a period when governments and educational institutions saw the value of sport to social cohesion and physical and spiritual development. The Corinthian ideals that cricket propagated were popular in the high Victorian age, especially amongst the political and ruling classes. So why did cricket fail to capitalise on this unique opportunity?

In Denmark the pioneering cricketer Captain Hoskjaer wrote to the Ministry of Culture in 1866 extolling the virtues of the game and advocating its adoption in schools and colleges. This was 13 years before football was established in the country. Many of the merits of the game he set out could equally be argued for any team sport but cricket had stolen a march on its challengers. His wishes were granted by government ministers who were drawn from a similar class and who could see the value to society as clearly as he could. Danish sporting press archives show that cricket got far more coverage than football in the late 19th century, largely because it was longer established and better organised.

But in spite of this head start it was nevertheless soon eclipsed by football, that went on to become the national sport. Denmark was after all the first national football association outside the United Kingdom.

Cricket was also introduced before football in Italy where several now famous clubs were founded by Englishmen keen to play cricket. But in the crucial years in the 1880s and early 1890s before football had taken root, when cricket had an opportunity to appeal to a broad social demographic eager to play sport, access was guarded to protect its exclusivity. In some cases clubs restricted membership to English expats. Italians who may have become fine cricketers and champions of the game in their country were denied the opportunity and turned to football instead. It may well be that even if membership had been inclusive cricket wouldn't have captured the national imagination but the restrictive policies of early clubs certainly served to instil the idea that cricket was a foreign and exclusive sport.

The extent to which exclusivity nullified any opportunity for cricket to become established in these critical formative decades is also seen in the Netherlands where clubs restricted membership not by nationality but by social class. Although cricket leagues existed before football ones awareness and access was limited. Football was far from immune from class distinctions, having originated as a game played in English public schools, but it had a more universal appeal and was easier to play in an informal setting. It was more adaptable and could be played anywhere by anyone.

But it was institutional endorsement that could have proved a breakthrough for the sport. If it had been introduced to mainstream schools generations would have been introduced to the game and it would have gained a more universal appeal. The perception of cricket as an exclusive, English sport for the social elite would over time have been altered.

The critical role of cricket in schools to the development of the sport in several countries illustrates what may have been possible, had it not been limited to select private schools.

Conditions for establishing sport in the last quarter of the 19th century were propitious and it is hard to ignore the conclusion that had cricket's pioneers across the continent taken a more inclusive approach that cricket would have become established in more countries. Whether it would have grown and prospered once football had taken such a stranglehold of the sporting consciousness in the early 20th century is another question. But there is no doubt that cricket had a unique opportunity to become part of the social fabric in this formative stage of its development in Europe. That many of the continental cricketers of this period wanted to be distinguished from the social fabric helps explain why cricket remained a game played by the few.

Why Did Cricket Not Flourish on the Continent?

Since the millennium there have been many initiatives to revive grass roots and schools cricket in England to arrest a decline in participation levels and a narrowing of its social appeal. This shows that even a game deeply rooted in English culture faces challenges to remain relevant and fun in a world where pleasures and diversions are many and varied. Even with highly developed infrastructure, ready access and broad social awareness it can be difficult for many clubs to put an XI on the field come the weekend. This brings into sharp focus the sheer level of challenge facing the game on the continent where grounds are scarce and awareness of cricket limited to small and often isolated communities.

In a historical context cricket was such an integral part of the imperial mission that throughout the empire cricket was introduced, organised and encouraged. Its development was an administrative exercise carried out with the industry and purpose of a certain class renowned for their administrative zeal. Not everyone in the empire would have liked cricket but they would certainly have been aware of it and had consistent opportunities and encouragement to play. The circumstances were very different in Europe. Cricket would not find you, in fact over much of the continent it would be a miracle if you stumbled across it. Even if you did you may not be welcomed and encouraged by those playing. As access and awareness was so limited it is difficult to judge the extent to which cricket was suited to the national characteristics and cultural settings of specific countries. Put another way, is there something about the English that makes them like cricket more than, say, an Italian? Does it appeal more to northern European character than a Latin temperament?

Accounts of cricket played on the continent in the 19th and early 20th centuries show that the social setting was much more significant than the mechanics of the game itself. Had the game been invented in the modern world with a much greater flexibility of format, playing style and duration it would be easier to assess any variability in a natural inclination to play. But in the formalised setting of multi-day cricket it is more likely that any reaction would be based on a feeling of social inclusion or exclusion rather than a propensity or otherwise to strike a six or shatter the stumps.

In England and the empire the social setting for cricket gradually became less significant over the decades as class stratifications relaxed and perceptions shifted. But this process was only made possible through consistency of opportunity. Gradually the game of the social elite became the game of the people too. They stripped away the social airs and played the game for fun. In a sense they liberated cricket from its social context. But on the continent cricket has never had the level of government and institutional support to provide the level and continuity of access necessary to reach this tipping point. It undoubtedly became more socially inclusive after the Second World War but awareness has never reached a sufficient level to make it populist.

Denmark and the Netherlands are the only countries where cricket was established and not reliant on expat communities. There are several reasons why this may have been that are worth exploring in more detail. The first is proximity. But while this was certainly a factor in the development of cricket in those countries by this logic France and Belgium would also have adopted the game to a certain level. Even with a relatively large league in Paris the game never broke far beyond its expat communities. The next is cultural links. Such has been the historical animosity and mutual suspicion between the English and French it is perhaps not surprising that the French have not taken to a quintessentially English sport. There is no such historical baggage with the Netherlands and Denmark and both share mercantile and maritime heritage with Britain. Restraint, understated refinement, dry humour and modesty are all mutual characteristics. These all fit well with the subtleties and slow but cerebral passage of a cricket game. It is also a sport where the efficiency of a team generally triumphs over the flashes of individual inspiration. This is consistent with a northern European approach to life. The Latin and Gallic temperament is perhaps more suited to the visceral passion and showmanship of football and other sports.

Global and Regional Governance and Development

The history of the governance, organisation and structure of the international game has shaped how cricket has developed in different parts of the world. Perhaps more so than in any other sport the politics that have dictated decisions have left a lasting yet imbalanced legacy across the globe.

England had invented the game and spread it across the globe as it expanded its empire. It was such an integral part of its imperial mission that administering cricket was as natural as administering territory. The Marylebone Cricket Club had been founded in 1787 and by the 1870s was firmly established as an arbiter of the laws and de facto governing body for county cricket and the England representative side. It was therefore the MCC that accepted an invitation from the Victorian Cricket Association to play a fixture in Melbourne in 1877. This would later be awarded the status of the first Test match, though at the time was just a match privately arranged between two organisations. Just over a decade later in 1888/89 another MCC side toured South Africa to play two Test matches.

During this period neither South Africa nor Australia was a unified country and both had a complex relationship with England. Australia was comprised of six separate colonies until unified in 1901 and South Africa remained fragmented between English and Afrikaans communities after independence had been granted in 1852. The leaders of the MCC were also passionate imperialists and their decisions were taken through a political lens. They viewed cricket as a means to consolidate the imperial family and strengthen imperial ideals, further Britain's foreign policy ambitions and protect racial bonds. Their focus was very much imperial rather than international and this was to have profound and prolonged impacts on global cricket.

This was the political context for the formation of the Imperial Cricket Conference in 1909, the precursor to the modern ICC. This came only four years after the conclusion of a bloody and bitter conflict between the British and the Dutch-descended Boer Republics. It was the brainchild of South African diamond tycoon, politician and sometime cricketer Abe Bailey. Two years previously on a visit to England he put a proposal to the MCC that was cleverly worded to appeal to their imperial sensibilities:

'Inter-rivalry within the Empire cannot fail to draw together in closer friendly interest all those many thousands of our kinsmen who regard cricket as our national sport, while secondly it would probably give a direct stimulus to amateurism.'

There are several notable aspects to reflect on in the formation of the first ICC in 1909. First is that beyond the obvious political context it was so limited in ambition. Its sole purpose was to establish a triangular tournament between three teams and ensure a standardisation of rules for those games. It was in essence merely a framework for scheduling matches. There were no commitments to develop the game or even to collaborate on any issues other than staging Tests. The reason for this startling lack of ambition or the adoption of any form of democratic decision-making process was almost certainly because within this very limited imperial club the MCC would naturally have the moral authority to dictate all aspects of the game. This was formalised in the appointment of the MCC president and secretary as the ex-officio chairman and ex-officio secretary respectively. In turn this cemented England's dominance in the governance of its imperial game. Derek Birley blithely described the ICC as 'the MCC's colonial branch'.

The second and most significant aspect of the formation of the Imperial Cricket Conference was how exclusive it was. New Zealand formed its own Cricket Council in 1894 and had hosted MCC sides while cricket was well established and played to a high standard in the

West Indies and India. Beyond the empire the game was flourishing in Philadelphia and there were national cricket boards in both Denmark and the Netherlands. In defining membership by imperial ties and race the newly formed ICC had afforded much of the cricketing world a lower status. Only the three ICC teams could play Test matches. This allocation of status was neither transparent nor based on performance. For instance a West Indies combined side had defeated an English touring team just after the turn of the century. There was no selection process or stated criteria for membership that each team could strive towards. It was simply, as Abe put it, based on kinship and political expediency. It was the start of an obsession with status and inherited rights that have informed every major decision in international cricket ever since.

The impact of this exclusion on the Netherlands and Denmark is difficult to quantify but it was certainly a missed opportunity to raise the profile and standard of the game. Had the I in ICC been International rather than Imperial then both sides would have enjoyed regular, high profile international matches that would have generated widespread interest in the public and press and almost certainly led to more interest and investment. Even if the disparity in standard had been considered too high to ensure a balanced contest and they had not been awarded 'Test' status the very inclusion in such an organisation would have surely led to an increase in standards and performances. At a time when international football was still in its infancy this could have transformed the development of cricket in those countries. There would have been a significant logistical advantage to their inclusion too. Rather than months on a steamer tours would have only required a short hop over the Channel, providing greater opportunity for fixtures and forging links between clubs and schools. But development of cricket outside the empire just simply wasn't a priority for the MCC. It was their game: a game of their empire. The fact that others played it was no more than a curiosity.

The foundation of a global governing body for football in the first decade of the 20th century was very different and the absence of a political motive or vision undoubtedly facilitated a much more inclusive approach to develop. The founding members of FIFA in 1904 were European, as this is where football had taken root at the time, but membership did not mirror any political affiliations or French colonial interests. By the First World War there were FIFA members in Africa, North America and South America. The onus was on facilitating international fixtures and boosting the global profile of the sport, in marked contrast to the ICC that only wanted imperial teams to play and where status and moral authority were always more important concepts that inclusivity and equality.

The fact that the Netherlands and Denmark were left out of the fold doesn't mean that all contacts were severed. Cricketers and administrators in both still sought guidance and respect from English peers and arranged tours across the Channel whenever they could. The very MCC who had denied them any status or stake in the global game were still revered.

The plan was that the tri-series between the three Test nations would be held every four years. But the inaugural competition held in England in 1912 was deemed a failure, with rifts in Australian selection leading to a weakened team and the wettest August of the 20th century forcing dull, damp draws. The *Daily Telegraph* were certainly not impressed:

'Nine Tests provide a surfeit of cricket, and the contests between Australia and South Africa are not a great attraction to the British public.'

It seems the natural kinship was felt less keenly between the public than the administrators. Nevertheless it was memorable for Aussie bowler Jimmy Matthews who became the first and remains the only bowler to take two hat-tricks in the same match.

After this failed experiment the ICC reverted to organising bilateral Test tours. In 1926 the founding members agreed to India, West Indies and New Zealand joining the conference. But they didn't want this to result in a distillation of their authority or influence and so implemented a two-tier voting system, with founding members retaining a veto over any proposal. The other caveat for the new members was that Test status was not automatically afforded. Indeed the New Zealand tour to England in 1927 did not include any Tests. Over the next few decades the ICC did remarkably little beyond arranging bilateral series. Duration of matches and types of surfaces for pitches varied from country to country with standardisation only introduced in the 1950s. In 1952, five years after its partition from India, Pakistan were admitted as members. They were to play a key role in challenging the status quo in the decades to come.

There was no globally coordinated programme of matches at this time. Each member could choose their opponents and the frequency of tours. South Africa, for instance, only played other white teams. The MCC continued to rule the roost, playing host to the conference, setting the rules and retaining their power of veto as a founding member. This cosy, Anglo-centric rhythm would have no doubt continued largely unchallenged were it not for political influence. South Africa had voted to become a republic in 1960 and in the context of widespread opposition to apartheid they withdrew from the Commonwealth. This was a problem for the ICC because one of its only membership criteria was that members had to be from the Commonwealth. In addition there was extreme political sensitivity around South Africa's decision to run society and sport along racial lines. The Conference fudged the issue to buy time but Australia, England and New Zealand showed solidarity by committing to tours. This caused a division within the ICC between the white founding members who used their power of veto to ensure South Africa, albeit with some caveats, remained in the fold and India, Pakistan and West Indies who were firmly of the view that they should be ejected.

This split certainly unsettled the historic balance of the ICC where decisions had traditionally been endorsed on the nod of the founding members. It was not in the MCC's interest to increase the remit or ambition of the council seeing as they already independently held the power over rule-making. However, their veto meant they didn't have to fear any rocking of the established order. But the newer members, emboldened by their moral opposition to apartheid, were becoming more ambitious. In 1962 *Wisden* reported that Pakistan had advocated the establishment of a second tier of members to incorporate those countries where cricket was established. This included Denmark and the Netherlands. This was more influenced by politics than altruism as Pakistan sought allies to challenge the hegemony of the founding members, though in practice this would only amount to building further pressure as the founding members could always use their veto. Nevertheless the proposal was discussed at the conference and took the form of a junior section. It is worth noting that any official fixtures played by these countries would presumably have been intended to be either Tests or first class, as the one-day cricket revolution was still some years away.

In 1965 these proposals finally bore fruit and ICC created associate member category. In doing so the ICC had adopted members beyond the Commonwealth and therefore changed its name to the International Cricket Conference. Denmark and the Netherlands were amongst the initial cohort. But it was clear, initially at least, that England and Australia had only acceded to the proposal to appease Pakistan and the others who had opposed their support of South Africa. Although the Netherlands and Denmark, almost a century on from the foundation of national boards, were now officially cricketing nations there didn't appear to be any benefits. They didn't even get a vote at ICC meetings, so had no influence at all over the running of the game. The founding members finally relented in 1971 although their veto remained jealously guarded. Neither did they get any fixtures. They weren't afforded Test status and there was no league or mechanism introduced to give them official fixtures either against Test nations or fellow new members. It was like being welcomed to the party but then facing snub after snub.

The ICC, despite its name change, remained an organisation that had a very limited remit. It oversaw the standards of cricket in its member countries and facilitated matches between them. Well, at least matches between some of them. From 1965 it added a third tier of members. There were the founding members with a veto, other full members who could play Tests and associate members who were in the fold but had no power, no status and no matches. From its inception the ICC had no stated ambition or plan to develop the game. Presumably because it covered cricket in the empire it reasoned that the officers of empire had developed the game already. But remarkably even with the creation of a membership category that included teams beyond the Commonwealth it still didn't set out any development aims or support. It was not functioning as a governing body of a sport. It was a members' club with an Orwellian view that some members are more equal than others.

For the new associate nations like the Netherlands and Denmark very little changed. They had a glimpse into the corridors of power at conference meetings but had no influence within them. In practical terms their cricket carried on much as it had done for decades with domestic leagues interspersed with games against touring teams. Their associate status may have given them slightly more leverage in attracting Test teams touring England to visit but there were precious few practical benefits.

It was the emergence of one-day cricket that presented both the ICC and the associate members with an opportunity. Having not deigned to offer their new members Test status, which in truth many members may have found difficult to fulfil as their cricketers would have struggled to get time off their jobs to commit to long tours, one-day fixtures would be easier and cheaper to organise. With conservatism and risk avoidance the default operating model for the ICC it naturally took them almost a decade to recognise the importance of the limited-overs game. But when the World Cup was finally staged in 1975 it was a resounding success. And what is more it included two associate members, Sri Lanka and a composite East Africa team. This set an important precedent. Associates were excluded from Tests but could play on the global stage in the quicker stuff.

For the second World Cup in 1979 the ICC took the decision to create a tournament for associates that would serve as a qualifying route to the World Cup itself. Thus was born the ICC Trophy, the first taste of official international cricket that most countries had played. There was no qualification for the tournament itself with all associate members able to participate. Fourteen years after welcoming new members the ICC had finally offered them a carrot in the opportunity to play on the global stage against the best teams in the world. Such was the prize that countries like the Netherlands and Denmark reframed their scheduling to enable tours against other associates to prepare for the ICC Trophy. Sri Lanka and Zimbabwe were the heir-apparents to be awarded Test status but the European associates showed that they were quality teams certainly in the leading group of the chasing pack.

But while the ICC Trophy was a positive step forward it was only held every four years and in between the associates had no more structured cricket than they had before being granted membership. Associate membership did not bring with it first-class or List A status for domestic fixtures and there was no requirement for full members to play games against them. There was a theoretical prospect of elevation to Test status but the criteria required to make this jump was not transparent and therefore could not be the basis for development plans implemented by the associate boards. However, formal status afforded by the global body did at least give boards a stronger hand in securing support and funding from national sporting bodies.

The next major change to the ICC's structure in the 1980s came about through pressure applied by another European country. In order to attain associate status countries had to meet certain criteria set by the ICC. These were around numbers of players and teams as well as structural and governance requirements. These were not achievable for many countries at the early stages of their cricket development. Italy through their passionate chairman Simone Gambino and supported by well-connected champions in England successfully lobbied for inclusion of these emerging cricket nations and the affiliate membership category was introduced in 1984. Again the practical benefits were virtually non-existent, beyond the pride of being part of the global cricket community and greater leverage to secure government support. Affiliates were not permitted to enter the ICC Trophy and therefore had no official tournaments or matches to play and no opportunity to qualify for the World Cup. But it got them on the ladder, albeit only to the giddy heights of the lowest rung.

With the elevation of Sri Lanka to full member status in 1981 the balance of power in the ICC board began to shift away from the founding members. With more associate members joining there were more voices at the table and a potential challenge to their power. Historically the ICC had only made recommendations to its members but in 1989 it took the significant step of making binding resolutions that its members would have to comply with. This reform in theory brought it closer to how other global sports were governed, with decisions made for the good of the sport overall rather than freedom for members to further their own interests. However, the founding members ensured that there were sufficient caveats to protect their historic right to shape the game. Although a motion could be passed with a majority vote an additional clause was added that this had to be supported by two thirds of the full members and that this must include a founding member. This ensured that the traditional powers continued to dictate governance and that they could not be marginalised through a blocking group of associate members and newer full members. In this context any attempt to introduce progressive reforms would inevitably be outmanoeuvred by those seeking to protect their self-interest. However, with Zimbabwe's promotion to full member in the early 1990s the pressure increased.

Ehsan Mani, who would later become ICC president, recently reflected on his initial views when he first encountered the ICC.

'In the late 1980s I was struck by the reluctance to admit new members. This was for a number of reasons: lack of funding to promote the game and concerns over the long-term implications on the voting structure of the ICC, which carried with it the possibility of a change in the balance of power within the governing body.'

Although the number of associate members was growing and the affiliate category had been introduced there was no pathway for these aspiring cricket nations to progress and no funding to support their development. As Mani noted, 'Any development in the associate member countries depended on the enthusiasm and passion of volunteers who loved the game and wanted to play it but did not necessarily have the resources or the expertise to promote, develop and sell the sport to the masses.'

By the early 1990s England's hegemony of cricket governance was coming under increasing pressure from Asia. The vast majority of players, followers and fans of the game were in the subcontinent and there were more full-member nations in Asia than any other continent. If cricket was to flourish as a sport in the modern entertainment age and compete against football for revenue, reach and coverage the impetus would have to come from Asia. Not only was cricket a cultural religion in the region but it was also central to political aspirations to assert nationhood and growing international influence on the eve of a new millennium. Put another way India, Pakistan and Sri Lanka were no longer willing to let their former colonial masters shape the destiny of a game they had taken to their hearts and which defined their national character. This was the context for the schism in the ICC created over the choice of venue for the 1996 World Cup. The sport was braced for change.

The Present

Cricket Today

CRICKET on the continent today has been shaped by two movements that began late in the last millennium: a profound philosophical shift in the global game and a significant demographic change in the region underpinned by economic migration. Together these factors altered the cricketing map of Europe, presenting opportunity and challenge in equal measure.

Given what was to come later it was ironic that opportunity sprang from Indian ambition. In cricket's traditional, colonial frame of reference continental Europe was a virtual irrelevance. It made for a culturally diverting place to tour but it had taken almost a century for any European team to be accepted as a member. However, India were determined to wrestle control of the game from their former colonial masters and in doing so they set in motion a chain of events that would see the ICC broaden its ambitions. Continental Europe was as far from the nexus of power as ever, but it would belatedly at least attain relevance.

In the early nineties the game was still governed by convention and historical privilege. England assumed, naturally, that it would host the last World Cup of the millennium. They had after all always been the default host for global tournaments. This was vehemently opposed by India who wanted to maximise profits and interest by hosting the World Cup on the subcontinent while also asserting their right to shape the future of the game. But England had cunningly and cynically put instruments in place to block any insurrection by newer members, even if those members held the future of the game's fortunes in their hands. India was not in the mood to quiver and made a robust legal challenge that a decision on the venue for the World Cup did not fall under the decision-making filter that would allow a blocking motion by a founding member. The battle lines were drawn.

The minutes of ICC meetings of this period illustrate just how bitter this schism within the organisation was and how hard England and its founding member allies fought to reassert their moral authority over the game. But in the end they had no choice and India was confirmed as host. At this time profits from a World

Cup were retained by the host country with a playing fee given to each participating nation. In the past it had been a useful funding boost for the host but not transformative for the sport. In 1996 India changed all that and showed the sport just how blinkered they had been. They made $20m and paid each full member $500,000, thus returning a handsome profit. With this shift in the power politics of cricket came an appreciation of how much money could be made if the sport capitalised on growing media interest. With England's stranglehold over cricket governance successfully checked this money could be invested into the ICC.

In 1993, 84 years after its creation, the ICC remained a tiny adjunct of the MCC office. It comprised a president, chief executive and three other members of staff and had an operating budget of just $250,000 a year. Given the scale and reach of the global game its remit remained remarkably limited. But this changed quickly as the profits from the 1996 World Cup brought money into the game and with it far greater levels of ambition. A professional secretariat was created and for the first time the ICC decided to focus on the global development of the game. It is remarkable that although the ICC had created new membership categories as far back as the 1960s it had never set out its development objectives or strategy. It was palpably not, as would later be brutally shown in an independent report, acting as a global governing body for the sport. But it now had ambition to set out objectives and it would soon have the funding to deliver them.

When Clyde Walcott stood down as chairman in 1997 there were two rival candidates to replace him, the Australian Malcolm Gray representing the status quo and Jagmohan Dalmiya determined to cement India as the dominant voice in cricket following their successful and money-spinning staging of the World Cup. In the lead-up to the vote Dalmiya courted the favour of associates by promising them greater financial support and an ally in their aspirations. The Netherlands, who with perfect timing had qualified for their first World Cup on Indian soil the year before, and Denmark had much to gain. This courtship helped him secure 25 votes to Gray's 13. However, Gray had the support of the majority of full members and therefore an impasse was reached. At this delicate juncture a compromise was proposed by John Anderson, the head of New Zealand cricket, who advocated the chairman be replaced by a president that rotated amongst the full members supported by an executive board that would run the game. To appease the ambitions of India he proposed that Dalmiya be the first president.

This new governance model was a mixed blessing for associate nations. Although greater ICC resource meant potential support in development their decision-making power was further diminished.

Rather than having a vote each, albeit diluted in significance by the two-thirds rule and the founding member veto, they now had only three votes between them. The shift to Asian dominance of the game was also seen in associate representation, with Malaysia and Bangladesh getting votes, along with Kenya. In this way not only had England's wings been clipped but the Netherlands and Denmark had also been marginalised. As this reform limited associate votes to three there was now no block to cricket's global family growing further, as they wouldn't gain any votes with which to rock the boat. India had gained control of the ICC through associate sponsors and had then all but disenfranchised them.

But while they lacked power they still had much to gain from an organisation with money to burn and eyes open to opportunities. As part of the professionalisation of the ICC several new committees were established with South African Ali Bacher heading one focused on development. This would oversee the implementation of a development plan that would be delivered in each region by development offices. The ICC was extending its reach and the development of the game in Europe was primed to have a guiding hand. Naturally the regional office for Europe was based at Lord's. Amsterdam would have seemed a more natural setting, but perhaps the objectivity assured by the North Sea was politically astute. Although some coordination of cricket at European level had been introduced in the late 1980s this was the first time the ICC had directly focused on developing cricket in the region.

India had proved that cricket could maximise its revenue by taking advantage of the money pouring into sports broadcasting. Cricket's mass audience and considerable global reach made it attractive to both sponsors and advertisers. This transformed cricket into a hugely lucrative 21st-century sports entertainment business and in turn enabled the ICC to flex its muscles and significantly expand its remit. Its traditional role of maintaining standards and scheduling matches was now secondary to further leveraging its marketing appeal. Cricket was becoming corporate and those who could influence its decisions were guaranteed a significant return on investment. This remit now included development, though it was not yet clear what the level of investment would be, how it would be allocated and the extent to which the ICC would directly intervene. But the Full Members were naturally wary of this new-found philanthropy and didn't want to give up their historic windfalls to support growth elsewhere. Funding for development would have to come from a separate pot. It would be new money for a newly discovered conscience. This was provided in the shape of the Champions Trophy, a biennial global one-day tournament first held in 1998 that would fund the development programme.

Although the creation of a development programme in the late 1990s and the structure to financially support it were laudable it was from its inception only a bolt-on initiative. The development programme created by Ali Bacher, the development team and its regional branches had a clear remit to boost participation and performance in existing members and enlarge the cricketing family as the sport sought to obtain a truly global footprint. But the development wing of the ICC could not implement its vision in isolation, for it was answerable to and governed by the ICC board. The ICC remained a membership organisation rather than a democratically run global governing body. This meant that it existed principally to serve its members, which in practice meant its full members as associates had all but been frozen out of any say on governance and strategic decisions. The development programme could implement any reform as long as it didn't impinge on the privileges and financial interests of the full members. As the next decade would show there were very few meaningful reforms that didn't. The board basked in the good news stories its development programme produced. After all it offered them the veneer of being a truly representative governing body for the sport. But it would never countenance the compromise of the interests of its full members.

This tension between the objectives of the development programme and the narrow focus of ICC governance meant that development was interpreted in a particular way. In a very different way, it should be noted, than sports of comparable popularity and global reach. This is clearly seen in its attitude to membership. The best teams in football have much greater popularity and financial muscle than the worst. But FIFA gives all teams the same membership status. Cricket meanwhile retained a hierarchy of membership categories dating back to Victorian ideals of class and moral superiority. As if that wasn't enough it didn't even have a clear process or criteria for how teams could progress from associate membership to full. In this sense cricket did not so much welcome a new member when an affiliate joined but add an acolyte.

Affiliate members were in relative terms a negligible drain on the sports resources but creating a new full member would mean each existing full member taking a smaller share of the sport's burgeoning wealth. Since its inception the development programme has had to frame development in a way that does not threaten the self-interest and inherited rights of full members. This has undoubtedly constrained what they have been able to achieve. Critics of the ICC, of which there are many, have often failed to appreciate the internal dynamics that dictate its decision-making and this has led to some unfair criticism of the development programme itself.

One of the leading associate nations of the 1990s was Kenya. From a relatively modest domestic structure a golden generation had emerged including Steve Tikolo, Maurice Odumbe, Ravindu Shah and Thomas Odoyo. Their performance at the 1996 World Cup was sufficiently strong for the ICC to grant them ODI status, as a stepping stone to becoming a full member. This was a rather fudged compromise but it set an important precedent that an associate member could play official status international fixtures outside a global tournament. Corruption, complacency and mis-management were to ensure that Kenya squandered this opportunity.

Moving into the new millennium the top priority for the ICC was maximising income generation from its global events, which accounted for the lion's share of the ICC budget and therefore kept full member boards in pocket. In order to ensure they attracted the highest bids possible for broadcasting rights they looked to tailor the composition and format of the tournament to meet the needs of broadcasters. In practice this meant ensuring the maximum number of blockbuster games between the world's strongest teams. Or to be more accurate the most number of games between teams that attract the largest audiences. This presented the ICC with something of a moral dilemma. On the one hand they had just launched a development programme to boost cricket across the world and appearing on the global stage could be a transformational opportunity to raise the profile of the sport in these emerging cricketing nations, but on the other hand they were working with companies who had very clear-cut demands to maximise return on investment by attracting the biggest audiences possible in the most lucrative markets. Had the ICC had a different governance model it may well have taken the long-term view that the benefit of developing new markets outside its historic centres outweighed the short-term imperative to secure the highest bid possible. But full members wanted to maximise their dividends then and there. The compromise the ICC struck was to invest in the High Performance Programme (HPP).

The HPP provided a unique opportunity for the best non-Test sides to become leading cricketing nations. Not full members perhaps, but competitive, professionalised teams with a potentially lucrative global profile. But it speaks volume of the limitations of the ICC that such a significant reform was launched with such a narrow ambition. That ambition was to ensure that the teams that qualified for the 2003 World Cup didn't embarrass themselves and undermine the future earning potential of the tournament.

This objective meant that the HPP had a very specific focus, to improve elite performance. Development of domestic cricket and infrastructure was secondary. As long as the World Cup squad had sufficient quality to be competitive the strength of its cricketing culture more broadly was largely irrelevant. It was public facing success that was critical rather than a strengthening of associate cricket nations at grass roots level, though of course the former could certainly support the latter.

The HPP was a commitment to raising the elite performance of the best of cricket's second-tier nations. But it was not a programme to fast track new full members. For while maximising revenue from the World Cup was in the financial interest of the world's leading teams, reducing their financial remuneration and influence by adding to their number most certainly wasn't. The HPP was a laudable initiative but one implemented by a members' organisation rather than by an independently governed body tasked with growing the global game.

For associate nations like the Netherlands and Denmark the timing of this injection of revenue into the game and a belated focus on development was critical. For in selecting countries that would be incorporated into the HPP a line was drawn at a particular point in time. The decision was taken to increase the number of competing nations at the 2003 World Cup to 14 teams. These were comprised of the ten full members, including newly appointed Bangladesh, Kenya, who had been granted an intermediary ODI status, and the top three teams at the 2001 ICC Trophy. It was a very propitious time for associates to have a strong tournament and the Netherlands, Namibia and Canada not only qualified for the World Cup but also for the additional funding and tailored support the High Performance Programme offered. But while it was good timing for some it was a defining moment for those who missed out. Denmark had regularly been among the leading teams in the ICC Trophy in the 1980s and early 1990s. Had the HPP been introduced at that time they would have been included and their development given a significant boost. But by the new millennium they had slipped from being one of the leading nations to part of the chasing pack. In 2001 they finished sixth, a few places under the line that was drawn.

Given that the principal goal of the programme was to make associates more competitive at the World Cup it is logical that it was the teams that qualified that were given access to additional funding and support. But it did not follow that the Netherlands, Namibia and Canada were necessarily the best teams or had the greatest potential for development. They had simply been the three most successful teams in a particular tournament. The fate of teams was determined by how they fared over a handful of games in a tournament held once every four years. The strongest team could have its key players unavailable, be unlucky with injuries or simply have a dip in form just when it mattered most. Alternatively a weaker team could secure a top three place on the back of a golden patch of form, a modest player in the form of his life or an outrageous run of luck. In the absence of the application of a more robust set of criteria judging performance and development over a period of time the ICC were gambling that they were investing in the teams with the greatest potential. But then of course it wasn't a development programme as such, but rather an insurance policy that teams wouldn't embarrass them at the World Cup.

The ICC's stated outcome for the HPP was to 'develop the quality of on-field and off-field structures in order to close the gap between associate members and full member playing standards at both senior and under-19 level.' There was no mention of helping participating countries to fulfil the criteria to become full members themselves. So while it aimed to close the gap it did not go as far as to ensure there was no gap at all. It was also solely focused on playing standards.

In practical terms the HPP consisted of a series of high performance camps, consultancy advice on developing elite talent and access to world class coaching and infrastructure. It offered an additional level of support over and above that provided by the ICC's regional development office. This enabled a select group of players from participating countries to develop in a professional structure. The intensity of their training and the time and attention paid to skills development was intended to prepare them to make the difference for their teams in crunch World Cup encounters. It wasn't so much about natural talent as adopting a professional outlook. Amateur players with amateur preparation may wilt and capitulate on the global stage with a mass audience witnessing the discomforting spectacle. But the professionalised had a chance to compete against the professionals. Over time the programme took advantage of the elite performance facilities that were built as part of the ICC's headquarters at Sports City, Dubai. There the leading associates benefitted from coaches of the calibre of Rod Marsh and Dale Hadlee.

In adopting and advocating a professional approach the HPP changed the way that cricket was viewed in the leading associates. Rather than the national team simply being drawn from the most talented of the domestic player pool, elite performance began to be seen as something separate. The Netherlands were blessed with a golden generation of players in the 1990s and this talent had made them one of the leading associates and ultimately qualified them for the HPP. But once in the programme the desire for professionalisation gradually changed the ethos of Dutch cricket from a celebration of the talented amateur to a commitment to the dedicated professional. Over time this created a division between domestic cricketers focused on enjoying league cricket and an elite national team squad. The pressure to remain in the HPP also promoted a cynical approach to selection, with players with first-class experience qualifying through residency or passports chosen ahead of young native talent. HPP nations adopted the short-termist attitudes of the ICC. To be fair to them they had no choice if they were to retain the additional funding and resources the HPP provided.

Despite the focus on elite development there was no change in the status or amount of cricket played by leading associates for several years after the formation of the HPP. But after the 2003 World Cup a new tournament structure was created beneath Test cricket. The first was the brainchild of visionary coach Bob Woolmer. He passionately believed that the best way for emerging cricket nations to improve their technical ability was to play first-class cricket. This would not only serve as preparation for Test cricket but would also improve players' techniques and concentration levels to enable them to compete with full members in shorter formats. While the ICC had a commercial interest in the HPP mitigating the risk of uncompetitive, unattractive fixtures in the World Cup there was no ulterior motive in launching the Intercontinental Cup in 2004. It demonstrated a commitment to development for development's sake. An injection of money to the game gave them the luxury of supporting development in parallel to serving their full member constituents.

The Intercontinental Cup was first devised as a 12-team tournament played in a regional structure. The ICC showed their commitment to the competition by awarding the fixtures first-class status. This was important symbolically because after years of offering very little to their associate members they finally had a show of faith. It meant a lot to individuals that they had the recognition and pride of being first-class cricketers. Until this time the careers of leading associate players were virtually invisible. Even if they had a 20-year career and played several hundred games for their country they left hardly any trace in the record of the game. The awarding and withholding of status has been a controversial talking point in the modern game, but the launch of the Intercontinental Cup was a sign the ICC were starting to be more inclusive.

Its first-class status gave the cup profile and the rhetoric at the launch was that it would be a proving ground for Test cricket. Bangladesh had endured a chastening first few years as a Test nation since their elevation in 2000, losing many games by an innings. This had led many to criticise the ICC for awarding them Test cricket too early and in the process undermining the credibility of Test status. Some commentators went as far as to say that it made a mockery of statistics, inflating batting averages to an extent that players could no longer be compared statistically across eras. For the

ICC this unease was a significant threat both to the integrity, and therefore marketability, of Test cricket but also to their judgement and decision-making. For every advocate of development there was a vocal and haughty traditionalist forecasting plague and portents if the game became more inclusive. It was into this cauldron that the Intercontinental Cup emerged.

For the participating teams and the HPP it was certainly seen as a pathway to Test cricket. Given the Bangladesh example it seemed very prudent to give teams experience of competitive multi-day cricket to hone their skills before being given Test status. It was natural that many would refer to the tournament as a second division of Test cricket. But this it most certainly wasn't. After all, in virtually all other sporting settings a second division team would have the opportunity to earn promotion to the first. And conversely poor performance in the first division would lead to relegation to the second. But the Intercontinental Cup was to prove an opportunity without an outcome. The winner got a modest cash boost but no promotion or play-off game. A tournament where even the winner collects a consolation prize is always going to be met with furrowed brows.

In 2009 the ICC introduced a second division of the Intercontinental Cup branded as the Intercontinental Shield. This was comprised of four teams, the UAE, Namibia, Bermuda and Uganda and increased the number of associate teams playing first-class cricket to ten. There was no provision for promotion and relegation between the Cup and the Shield, or indeed to the Test championship. However as part of the 2009 reforms $250,000 prize money was made available with $100,000 for the winner of the Intercontinental Cup and $25,000 for the winner of the Intercontinental Shield with further prize money for runners-up in both tournaments and for an outright win.

The Intercontinental Cup was an example of a positive initiative compromised by weaknesses of ICC governance. Its introduction was a triumph for the development team and the High Performance Programme but for the board and the full members it presented risk. The full members had a vested interest to both restrict the number of chairs at the top table of the sport to protect their financial interests and to resist any notion that status be based on performance. For if good performances by an associate were rewarded then logic may follow that poor performance by a full member would have consequences. This wasn't a palatable concept, however fair it might appear to an impartial observer. Even if the ICC themselves wanted to apply an equitable approach it was the full members and not them that had voting power.

There was a simple solution to this seemingly intractable problem. By de-coupling the link between full membership and Test status the financial disincentive for full members would have been removed. This way the winner could have earned Test status. What is more the entire tournament could have been formally made a second division of Test cricket. As Bangladesh had shown the standard of Test cricket was only ever arbitrary. There was no transparent performance criterion. If every player in a Test team fell ill the night before a match and was replaced with an inferior XI the match wouldn't be downgraded in status because the quality had dropped. But the full members were almost as protective over their status as the rights and financial windfall their membership gave them. By limiting Test status and ensuring the top of cricket's global pyramid remained narrow they could continue to claim the lion's share of revenue the game attracted.

While the Intercontinental Cup was to draw much interest from fans, even beyond the competing nations, and achieved encouragingly high following through online commentary and scorecards it didn't attract live broadcasting. Had it been awarded Test status it may well have done and this increased profile and income could have further boosted development of the game. But the ICC did not see the development opportunity status provided, but rather took the more cynical and short-term view that status had to be protected to ensure it provided a gold standard that could be marketed at a premium.

While the competing teams knew that there was not a pot of gold at the end of the rainbow they hoped that consistently strong performances would make a compelling case for further support and perhaps, hope beyond hope, recognition that they had earned a higher status. The Europe group consisted of Ireland, Scotland and the Netherlands. Despite being consistently competitive at the ICC Trophy and being one of the oldest cricketing nations outside of the empire Denmark missed out. The winners of each region contested semi-finals from which the finalists emerged. Scotland was the winner of the inaugural season. In fact European teams were to dominate the competition with Ireland winning in 2005 and 2006. In 2006 the regional format was dropped with each team playing their opponents both home and away. The results of the tournament demonstrated that teams who possessed professional cricketers, for instance Scottish and Irish players playing in English county cricket, generally proved too strong for teams with part-time players.

* * * * *

By 2005 the ICC had 88 members, including 32 associates and 46 affiliates. There had been an extraordinary recruitment drive and the ICC was delighting in its ever growing family. The membership requirements to join as an affiliate were very modest. Any country with four teams, a ground and the most basic of administration could join the club. Continental Europe had been one of the highest growth regions, though in many cases cricket was limited to expat players in big cities. The sheer number of teams meant that a qualification filter had to be applied to the ICC Trophy, which was traditionally open to all associates. Previously any associate was theoretically only ever one step away from the World Cup by reaching the final stages of the tournament. But now most teams faced several stepping stones to get to the ICC Trophy. They had to qualify for the qualifier. While this had limited impact on the leading associates like the Netherlands it completely changed the prospects for weaker but long-standing associates like Gibraltar. They would never reach such giddy heights again.

As in previous tournaments the ICC Trophy served as the final qualifier for the World Cup. The ICC had announced that the 2007 World Cup would be the most inclusive ever with 16 teams participating. This meant Kenya and five other associates could qualify. There was a greater opportunity than ever before to take their place on the global stage. But while this grabbed the headlines an announcement with a more fundamental impact on teams like the Netherlands was made. The six teams that qualified for the World Cup would be given ODI status for a four-year World Cup cycle along with a significant boost to funding. This was an era-defining opportunity for associates and the stakes could not have been higher. If teams were going to progress they simply had to finish in the top five. With performances having such far-reaching consequences there was far more pressure on associates sides than their Test cousins.

Unsurprisingly given the importance of the tournament the games were fiercely competitive. Europe's continental heavyweights met in a fifth place semi-final at the Inch, Dublin on 9 July. The Netherlands smashed 314 and won by 89 runs. They went on to defeat the UAE to qualify for the World Cup and claim ODI status: ecstasy for the Netherlands but agony for Denmark. The Danes were two wins away from competing in their first World Cup. But crucially they were two wins away from changing their trajectory as a cricket nation. Once again for associate nations timing was everything. Teams had to perform at the times when the ICC offered opportunities.

The reason for giving the five qualifiers ODI status was to provide an opportunity for big game experience in the lead-up to the 2007 World Cup. The hope was that this would make them more competitive and avoid any embarrassing mismatches in front of their media partners. But of course it was much more than this. The six ODI teams would be the focus of HPP support and the beneficiaries of additional funding. In effect the ICC was creating a new category of elite associates with higher status and more money than their peers. This represented a significant investment for the ICC and a defining moment in the cricketing history of both those who were lucky and those who missed out. But it needn't have been based on luck.

If performances at the World Cup were not the primary concern the assessment of which teams should be singled out for development funding could have been made by an informed, objective analysis against a range of criteria. This would have given the ICC much greater confidence that they were targeting their funding at the countries with the greatest chance of becoming a leading cricket nation. The strength of domestic structures and necessary prerequisites for sustainable growth could have been assessed. Instead this far-reaching decision was based on form over a single tournament. There are just too many variables in a single tournament to make an informed decision. Injuries, player availability, conditions, form and luck can all dictate a handful of results. This lack of rigour and strategic foresight was to prove costly for the ICC as Bermuda embarrassed themselves and the associate cause at the 2007 World Cup. The ICC had invested in a tiny country with a handful of talented club cricketers, some of whom had a liking for mischief and rule-breaking. If viewed as a corporate decision in the long-term interests of the game it was breathtakingly narrow-minded.

The 2007 World Cup was a defining tournament for the associates. Kenya's progression to the semi-finals in 2003 had shown that associates were more than making up the numbers and could be competitive against the Test nations. This was vindication for the HPP and supported the expansion of the tournament to 16 teams. It was branded as a World Cup, after all, and the ICC had close to 100 members. Without the associates the tournament would have been virtually indistinguishable from the Champions Trophy.

There was naturally a considerable focus on the expanded format and whether the associates were worthy of the increased opportunity afforded them. The HPP and regional development offices saw the tournament as a chance to showcase the increased competitiveness and professionalism of the leading associate sides to gain further support and profile for development. A more inclusive World Cup was a critical part of growing the global game and expanding the reach of its interest, marketability and profitability. But this long-term view was not shared by the commercial arm of the ICC whose focus was to ensure the highest bid possible for the next rights cycle. This conflict between long-term success and short-term profits was to be a point of building tension between ICC departments. With full members holding the controlling interest, long-term strategy was always going to play second fiddle to short-term gain.

The 2007 World Cup will always hold cherished memories for the Irish. Their qualification against the odds to the Super 8 stages was the defining moment in their cricketing history and an underdog story worthy of the Hollywood treatment. They had picked up the mantle from Kenya and were flying the flag for all associate and affiliate members. Their defeat of Pakistan was one of the most dramatic and exciting sporting spectacles of modern times. The victory won Ireland legions of fans across the world and social media was ablaze with interest and opinion. It demonstrated that associate teams were a considerable draw for fans watching the tournament, that their progress was equally as compelling as the traditional match-ups between the world's leading sides. A more inclusive World Cup had added a new dimension to the tournament, more subplots, more drama and more human interest. But Ireland had progressed at Pakistan's expense and losing one of their major markets early in the tournament had been a commercial blow for the broadcasters.

The inclusion of six associate nations was blamed for a bloated, over-long tournament that failed to grip the public imagination. This was not helped by the woeful performances of Bermuda who lost several games by over 200 runs. It was argued by many that a more inclusive approach could not be allowed to detract from an exciting tournament that showcased cricket at its best. In truth the duration of the tournament had more to do with the format rather than the number of participating teams. In trying to engineer as many blockbuster fixtures as possible broadcasters had not been keen on a knockout format but this meant that the mini leagues in each pool took time. The ridiculous decision to ban any musical instruments and set ticket prices too high for locals meant that the tournament didn't enjoy the sense of fun and carnival atmosphere which is usually a hallmark of cricket in the Caribbean. The associates were a scapegoat for what was billed by many as an unsuccessful tournament. This naturally led to a debate on how inclusive future World Cups should be.

The debate about inclusiveness revealed just how top-heavy the sport was. Most mainstream commentators and media focused solely on the impact of associates on the tournament itself rather than consider what role the World Cup should play in development of the global game. As cricket broadcasting and writing was dominated by former Test players it was naturally presented from a certain perspective. Many suggested that the most important consideration was the integrity, popularity and marketability of the tournament. A popular argument was that the World Cup had to be exciting and the play of the highest quality in order to showcase cricket to the world and show that it remained relevant and popular to the next generation. Including weaker teams compromised this aspiration and was therefore a risk to the game. But there was a potentially much more significant risk that this widely held view ignored: the risk of failing to develop the sport, ignoring opportunities to build a truly global audience and create lucrative markets beyond the imperial heartlands of the game. It was an argument that was to rumble on in the years to come.

Following the 2007 World Cup the ICC completed its reform of development structures with the introduction of the World Cricket League (WCL), a 50-over tournament that served as a qualification mechanism for the World Cup. The ICC heralded it as a 'meritocratic pathway', an opportunity for all international teams to progress by merit to the pinnacle of the global game. The WCL overlay a regional tournament structure enabling even the newest affiliate nation to climb from the lowest rung of the ladder to the promised land. The dizzying recruitment drive of the noughties had created a handful of new members every year so that membership soon passed 100. The WCL gave these teams a focus and a development goal. It also provided players with an opportunity to gain experience and develop their techniques in a range of different conditions and climates across the world against teams of similar ability. This experience would in turn help them be competitive at global events, wherever they were staged in the world. The ICC had set out a strategy for a bigger, better global game and with a three figure membership and a truly global tournament structure it was beginning to deliver.

The WCL was widely lauded for its fair and transparent structure. If a team continued to deliver results it continued to progress. On the other hand if a team stagnated and performance levels dropped it would be demoted. Afghanistan started at the lowest rung and secured four successive promotions to become one of the leading non-Test teams and, ultimately, qualified for the World Cup. This remarkable, uplifting and emotional journey was charted in the excellent film, *Out of the Ashes*. Though given political and ideological differences it appears a strange metaphor to use, they were the embodiment of cricket's very own American dream. The ICC was quick to seize on their success to demonstrate that aspirations and dreams could become reality in cricket's meritocratic modern age.

But for every winner there was a loser and the introduction of the WCL exposed the weaknesses of several high-profile, long-standing associates. Argentina began the tournament in division 2 but with a small player base and limited access to expat talent they plummeted down the divisions. Naturally it took several years to bed down before the tournament provided an accurate barometer of the relative strength and weaknesses of international sides. After a time definite trends began to emerge. Over the first eight years teams from the Americas region had on average been demoted by more than two divisions while Asian teams, led of course by Afghanistan's spirited example, were on an upward trajectory.

Teams were placed within the original five team structure based on rankings determined by the 2005 ICC Trophy and regional tournaments. Division 1 consisted of the six High Performance Programme teams that had qualified for the 2007 World Cup. As these teams had ODI status division 1 was an ODI tournament. The teams placed 7 to 10 at the ICC Trophy were placed in division 2 with the 11th to 13th ranked teams in division three alongside the highest ranked teams in regional qualifying tournaments. The entry level 5th division featured 12 teams, double the number in the other divisions. These teams qualified through regional tournaments. Fixtures in division 2 were awarded List A status by the ICC. The top two divisions had to be played on turf wickets. Divisions 3 and below were not awarded status for the fixtures and games could be played on artificial wickets.

For participating teams it was not merely a question of winning promotion and climbing up the global rankings. Performances were also critical in ensuring a fixture schedule for the years ahead. So for instance while Afghanistan guaranteed a regular programme of international fixtures by progressing through each division, thus gaining experience and having crucial time together to develop as a squad, this was in contrast to teams like Norway, Japan or the Bahamas whose five games in division 5 were their only international 50-over games until the next round of regional tournaments. The impact of this has been underestimated. The momentum gained by countries on an upward curve like Afghanistan enabled the creation of a unified national squad that trained and played together regularly, gained experience across the world and instigated a virtuous cycle of development and performance. But conversely teams that failed to get promoted were left with no fixtures and therefore no focus for the national squad. Players would go back to their employers and it would be difficult to retain unity, focus and standards. Coaches would have limited time with the players to develop skills and elite performance and the development programme of the country would lack a natural focus point to inspire players and youth programmes.

Continental Europe had five teams in the original structure. The Netherlands in division 1, Denmark in division 2, Italy in division 3 courtesy of being the highest ranked team in the regional qualifier, and Germany and Norway in division 5. For Italy, Germany and Norway this represented their first participation in ICC-sanctioned international tournaments.

When the 2015 World Cup qualifying structure was introduced in 2009 the WCL was expanded further to eight divisions. This reflected the continued growth of ICC membership and the ICC's wish to ensure as many teams as possible were incorporated into the global qualifying structure for the World Cup. This gave an opportunity for more teams to qualify through regional tournaments and Gibraltar became another representative from continental Europe.

T20: The Great Hope for the Global Game

England introduced a T20 league to its tournament structure in 2003 to attract a younger audience to the game and arrest a decline in crowd numbers and sponsorship revenue. T20 internationals were first played two years later but the ICC were slow to embrace the format, fearful perhaps that franchise-based tournaments could draw away interest and finance from its global events. The first World T20 was not staged until 2007. It was clear from the financial success of domestic tournaments that the format had significant potential to revitalise cricket in its core markets, attract a younger and more diverse audience and lead to a significant boost in revenue and sponsorship interest. It was widely billed as the format that would enable cricket to compete in the modern era of sports entertainment.

The ICC enthusiastically championed T20 as the format that would take cricket to every corner of the world. With a shorter duration and emphasis on fun it would be easier to promote and could therefore play a critical role in boosting player numbers, increasing profile and generating public interest in countries where cricket was a minority sport. Most cricket writers and commentators agreed and predicted a proliferation of T20 leagues from Baltimore to Beijing. At international level the prevailing logic was that it would give non-Test nations a much better opportunity to be competitive against the world's top teams. It was considered a much more natural and sustainable format for these teams than Test matches and it soon became established logic that if associate and affiliate nations wanted to compete on the global stage they should focus on the shortest format.

The first ICC World Twenty20 featured two associate nations, Ireland and Scotland, who qualified by reaching the final of WCL division 1. The ICC mirrored the qualification process for the 50-over World Cup by creating a World Twenty20 qualifier in 2009 from which the top teams qualified for the global event later that year. The participating teams were the six countries in the HPP. The two qualifiers both received a $250,000 funding boost. The next qualifying event, in 2010, was expanded to eight teams but rather than being based on a meritocratic basis the ICC invited two sides to join the six HPP sides. The beneficiaries were the hosts, UAE, and the USA. This was a clear indication that the ICC were once again seeking to capitalise on the vast potential of the US market. There was financial merit in the decision even if it side-stepped the meritocratic tournament pathway it had introduced.

A much fairer and more equitable qualification process was introduced for the 2012 tournament with 81 countries participating in regional qualifiers. This incorporated more teams than qualification for the 50-over World Cup, reaching out to virtually all ICC members. In Europe this gave teams like Bulgaria, Slovenia and Estonia their first taste of ICC-sanctioned global fixtures. The World Twenty20 qualifier itself was expanded to 16 teams, consisting of the six HPP nations and ten regional qualifiers.

A Bigger, Better Global Game 2011–15

By the end of the noughties the ICC's investment in development had transformed the game below Test level. Its membership had swelled to 106 and the vast majority of teams were incorporated into regional tournaments and had a meritocratic pathway to qualify for global tournaments. The strongest associate nations enjoyed a significant boost in funding, received tailored support for elite development through the HPP and played regular international cricket across three formats. The World Cup had been expanded and the World Twenty20 had been created, giving greater opportunities to appear in global flagship events.

To build on this success the ICC launched a strategic plan at its annual conference in Hong Kong in the summer of 2011 entitled 'A Bigger, Better Global Game'. The overarching aim of the strategy was to 'target more players, more fans, more competitive teams'. While this appeared to be a development focused plan it was clear from references to 'targeted support' and delivering 'return on investment' that commercial aims continued to be pre-eminent in ICC strategy. Put another way the ICC's commitment to meritocratic pathways could be trumped by commercial gain, as shown in its special treatment for the USA and reluctance to create new full members or extend Test match or ODI status. The inherent tension within the strategy was balancing a stated aspiration for a more inclusive approach while retaining a primary focus on revenue generation. While most agree that these two objectives are in harmony over the long term they potentially conflict over the limited constitution of an ICC board.

The explicit reference to return on investment presented a challenge to the development programme. The ICC could divert funding to other priority areas such as tackling corruption, supporting the women's game and rejuvenating Test cricket. The audit trail for the impact of development funding was not clear. Although participation levels had increased significantly this was largely due to economic migratory trends that saw cricketers from the subcontinent relocate to other countries across the world and take up cricket there. The level of penetration into local communities was limited. Although Ireland and Afghanistan had shown excellent progress on the field the level of development of other HPP countries, such as Canada and Kenya, had been disappointing. There were undeniably more teams but the jury was out on whether they were better.

One of the most eye-catching commitments made in the strategy was to carry out an independent review of governance. The existing governance model where decisions were made by less than 10% of the membership was increasingly at odds with a more inclusive approach and a global development remit. While the sport had modernised and expanded its governance remained anachronistic and patriarchal, encouraging short-term decision-making favouring the vested interests of the few over the needs of the many. The recommendations of the review and the appetite of the ICC to adopt them would determine whether development would be embedded into the culture of the organisation or whether recent reforms would be compromised.

Woolf Review

The boldest commitment made under the Bigger, Better Global Game strategy was for an independent review of governance. This was to fulfil a stated objective of the ICC's strategy to ensure that it was a recognised leader in the field of sports governance. It had the potential to have a far more profound, long-term impact on the global game than the boost in funding and creation of tournament frameworks under the development programme. Full member nations were not impacted by the development programme; it was something happening below their sphere of interest. But governance of the game was central to maintaining their vested interests. Lord Woolf was stirring a hornets' nest.

The scope of the review was agreed in August 2011 and ratified by the ICC board in October and, perhaps surprisingly, didn't flinch from addressing the big issues. It covered the effectiveness of governance structures within the organisation with an explicit remit to compare these to other sports and comparable international organisations. It also reviewed membership structures, criteria and status along with voting structures and the independence of committee and board members. Finally it reviewed nomination and election processes and procedures to deal with corruption and breaches of ethics. In short, Woolf had a mandate to investigate, question and criticise the very fabric of cricket governance. He was tasked with presenting the ICC with a plan of action to become an exemplar for a modern sports governing body, with specific recommendations under each theme.

Lord Woolf and his team carried out extensive interviews of the ICC board, Chief Executives' Committee and the management team. This included representatives of associate and affiliate members. Former ICC presidents and chairmen were interviewed and may have been more candid than those still employed by the organisation. There was no question that it was a top-down approach as the team reached out to smaller member nations and a range of journalists with no organisational affiliations. These included the chairmen of the Dutch, Belgian and Italian cricket boards along with leading ICC critic Gideon Haigh and Rod Lyall, a passionate advocate of global development and ICC reform and future vice-chairman of the KNCB. In addition to these structured interviews an email account was set up for anyone to provide their thoughts. Submissions were received from 38 countries. There were clearly many with an opinion to share, or indeed an axe to grind.

There is no doubt Woolf was given chapter and verse on the limitations, shortcomings and inequalities within the cricketing world. It remained to be seen whether he agreed with them, what he would propose and what impact this would have.

It was inevitable that an objective organisational review comparing the ICC with modern organisations would highlight significant issues. After all the ICC was an anachronistic body, established to serve vested interests without any meaningful reform in over a century. Indeed the ICC had admitted in its own strategy that its structures and guiding principles were created when the landscape of cricket was very different. They knew modernisation was required, but they can't have anticipated such a thorough, at times brutal, dissection of their modus operandi as Woolf provided.

To his credit Woolf addressed the fundamental issues before reviewing the details. He asked what the ICC was for. He found an organisation that purported to govern the global game but was instituted and structured to protect the vested interests of a minority of its membership. He was clearly shocked by the lack of transparency, representation and accountability in global cricket, along with inequality of opportunity and funding.

He strongly criticised the 'members' club' mentality within the ICC, which saw strategy set, decisions made and resource allocated by a handful of powerful member boards that had very little separation between their ICC roles and national, commercial interests. Although membership of the ICC had risen dramatically to 105 by the time the report was undertaken the definition of membership was far from conventional. For 90% of these members had virtually no say in the governance of the game and saw potential opportunities blocked if they threatened the inherited rights or commercial interests of the Test nations. Divisions of status and opportunity reflected the world in which the ICC was created in the early 20th century, but it jarred with modern concepts of equality and governance.

Woolf pulled no punches in concluding that the existing governance was not appropriate for a modern sporting governing body and that unless significant reform was instigated the sport was in danger of reputational damage. He also hinted that the embedded inequality in the sport could lead to schism, instigated by those who saw their progress blocked by the stubborn determination of the elite doggedly defending their historic privileges. His findings gave hope to those members who had felt disenfranchised while making for a very uncomfortable read for beneficiaries of the status quo. Naturally the actual wording was a little more subtle:

'unless significant changes are imminent, many of the members most adversely affected could lose their enthusiasm for trying to improve the situation.'

The report made some very simple yet profound observations. If there was no separation between an individual's role in shaping strategy for the game and his requirement to protect the interests of a member board then policy would naturally be shaped by the interests of the few rather than the needs of the many. This inherent tension within the organisation was predicated on the age of empire belief that a gentleman would always do the right thing. Woolf advocated reforms to the governance structures to ensure independence and the requisite checks and balances to expose and marginalise self-interest in decision-making. He challenged the ICC to make decisions that shape the game themselves rather than delegate to those with a very blinkered view of success.

To ensure the objectivity of decisions Woolf advocated a new formulation for the board, with four directors representing full members, two representing associates, five independent directors and the president and chief executive. This would ensure the independent voices outnumbered those with vested interests.

A prerequisite for an independent ICC was breaking its financial dependence on the full members. As long as the revenue generators were the de facto governors of the game the sport would develop along traditional lines serving the interests of traditional powerbrokers. Woolf highlighted an urgent need for a new revenue distribution model that both gave the ICC the independence required to invest in priorities for the global game and allocated resource based on need rather than perceived historic rights. He pointed out that the ICC had no audit trail for the 75% of the sports revenues that was directly distributed to full members. It was merely transferring it to a commercial body and hoping it would be well spent. This divvying of the dowry was simply an established privilege, not informed by need or directed to achieve particular objectives for the game.

Although they had benefitted from the implementation of the development programme the associate and affiliate members remained disaffected and disenfranchised. They played the game but had very little say or stake in it. If membership of the ICC gave them wings, those wings were severely clipped. For the most part their fate was dictated by the decisions of those who had a vested interest in remaining a big fish in a small pond. It was therefore the associates and affiliates, and by extension global development of the game who had most to gain. Woolf's reforms could be transformational.

The report advocated the urgency of extending full member status to more countries to demonstrate that the ICC was a not a closed shop for the existing full members. He suggested the immediate promotion of two teams with further elevation once the traditional blockers of a guaranteed seat on the ICC board and a share of revenue generation were removed. In doing so he recommended that the connection between being a full member and playing Test cricket be removed. He also highlighted the need for transparent criteria for elevation to full member status, so that all countries could plan their progress with assurance. In addition he suggested the amalgamation of associate and affiliate membership into a single category. Although elevation of a few of the leading associates would not directly benefit those further down the development ladder, including many in continental Europe, it would provide a stronger voice on the board for a development focus.

Many respondents questioned the very notion of membership categories. Rather than be placed in a largely arbitrary membership category Woolf explored an alternative method where membership was based on merit across a range of criteria. This would facilitate both promotion and relegation. While the criteria for associate membership are clear there was a lack of expectation on full members to support global development. Full membership gave countries status, rights and privileges but was not balanced by obligations: for instance an obligation for a full member to support development of cricket in their region.

Woolf also reflected on how traditional notions of categorisation and status were proving a barrier to associates and affiliates. Clearly they were barred from Test cricket, but the vast majority weren't allowed to play official international games in 50-over and 20-over games either. This compromised their ability to play the leading sides and in so doing improve performance, raise profile and generate revenue. The system was designed to protect the interests of the full members who could exclusively benefit from a premium status and marketability that they alone could profit from. Although the top associates had been given ODI status they weren't incorporated into the Future Tours Programme and so struggled to get the high-profile games they needed to progress. The report criticised the ICC for not taking ownership of the international programme to ensure opportunities were fair and that all could benefit. The priority for bilateral series was profit, not development.

Some respondents requested an increase in the size of the High Performance Programme to incorporate more teams and the development of regional development hubs.

Continuing the theme of inequality of opportunity Woolf focused on the constitution of global events. He questioned why full members qualified automatically and criticised the lack of an inclusive approach to provide associate members a springboard for growth. Once again the ICC did not have the independence to run tournaments that supported an overarching vision for global development. Instead full members favoured smaller, more exclusive tournaments that maximised short-term revenue generation and therefore a larger dividend. Woolf wanted access to tournaments to be equal and merit-based. He shrewdly observed that:

'It may be no coincidence that since the significant increase in revenues from commercial rights relating to the ICC events, no new Full Member has been admitted.'

Funding

In the decade preceding the publication of the Woolf report the ICC's financial position had changed dramatically, both in scale and structure. Prior to 2002 the ICC was funded through nominal subscriptions through members and by selling media rights for its tournaments to the host. It provided the structure for governance of the sport but the organisation's own headcount was limited. However, during the noughties the structure was reformed to increase the membership subscriptions and generate direct income for the ICC by bundling media rights over several years. This model generated $22 million in subscriptions and $550 million in broadcast revenue between 2001 and 2008. This enabled the ICC to increase its staff to 130 which in turn enabled a greater focus on development. Rather than negotiating their own media deals as host of tournaments the full members received an even share of 75% of the surplus profits from global events, once 6% had been top sliced to fund the global development programme. The remaining 25% was allocated to associate and affiliate members based on a performance-related scorecard.

Woolf highlighted several fundamental issues with the funding model. The first was that the membership subscription model reinforced a belief amongst the full members that they had the right to dictate decisions. The second was that the distribution model provided an incentive for full members to block elevation of new full members, as in doing so they would give up approximately $2.5 million over a World Cup cycle. Thirdly the ICC are obliged to distribute surplus funding to members. This means they cannot ring-fence funding to support long-term development of the game, have limited control of how money generated by the game is spent and can't assess return on investment.

To overcome these limitations Woolf recommended that the ICC become financially independent by scrapping the subscription model. It could then take a strategic approach to funding, allocating funds to members on the basis of need rather than automatic entitlement, ensuring adequate funding for delivering strategic objectives and enabling targeted assistance.

The report encouraged the ICC to reposition itself from reacting to full members' wishes to proactively shaping governance for the good of the global game. Only by doing this could they switch from a 'service company' to full member boards to an objective, independent governing body.

A False Dawn and the Rise of the Big Three

THE publication of the Woolf report came after a decade of unprecedented focus on and investment in development. There was a groundswell of hope that with the adoption of Woolf's recommendations cricket could become a truly modern and a truly global game. The HPP and tournament frameworks established by the development programme were bearing fruit and the emergence of T20 had provided a unique opportunity to grow profile and participation of cricket in its emerging markets. With more equitable governance and funding structures and the removal of barriers to opportunity the future looked very bright indeed, for continental Europe and other regions in the world.

But the Woolf report proved to be a false dawn. A mere ten days after publication it become clear that however sensible the recommendations and however urgent and compelling the case for reform the traditional powerbrokers of the game simply had too much to lose. In a very blunt rebuttal by their chairman Srinivasan the BCCI said the recommendations were, simply, 'unacceptable'. Srinivasan was both an ICC director and president of the BCCI, an arrangement Woolf himself considered unacceptable. The rejection by the BCCI, which didn't even bother to provide counter proposals to address the shortcomings Woolf outlined, set in motion a nervous few months before the ICC board met in April to discuss the report. If anything the BCCI strengthened the reforming zeal of those pressing for the reforms to be made while highlighting the strength of the vested interests that Woolf had exposed. Other full members had been more guarded than India, indicating that the recommendations should be given serious consideration in order to improve cricket governance. Beyond the member boards player representative bodies gave wholehearted support to Woolf's vision.

In March the Cricket Executive Committee was more positive, showing support for at least some of Woolf's recommendations. These included hosting a global tournament outside a Test nation, creating a version of the Future Tours Programme for leading associates including games against full member nations and an aspiration to increase the number of participating teams in T20 World Cups.

As many commentators observed, the meeting of the ICC Executive Board in April 2012 was a defining moment. It was a unique opportunity, backed up by an objective report commissioned by the ICC itself, to stand up to the BCCI and governance based on self-interest. The meeting would determine whether representatives would courageously fight for the future of the game, or bow to the pressure of power politics. In practice the board shelved the issue, agreeing it required further discussion. By way of a fillip to Woolf's supporters the board announced it was adopting one of the recommendations in separating the role of president and chairman while also introducing a programme of targeted financial assistance to weaker Test nations and leading associates through the TAPP initiative, of which the Netherlands was to be a beneficiary. But these were very minor concessions and only scratched the surface of the urgent reforms Woolf advocated.

The challenge for those who champion global development was reading between the lines of ICC press releases. In a statement designed to generate positive publicity there was never going to be direct rebuttal of Woolf's recommendations or an explanation of the mood within the ICC to accept or reject it. But in hindsight it is clear that the ICC had been cowed by the BCCI and its allies and sought to allow time to take the sting out of a backlash and hide behind a few piecemeal reforms. The full truth was not to be known for another two years, when the ambitions of the big three became clear.

In January 2014 the cricket world was shocked by the sheer arrogance of proposals put forward by India, England and Australia, the so-called big three. A paper prepared for discussion at the Executive Board in late January 2014 set out an audacious power grab that not only ignored all of Woolf's recommendations but arguably made the ICC more autocratic, undemocratic and exclusive than in any point in its history. It was an astonishingly brash statement that those who finance the game had the right to run the game.

The proposals focused on many of the areas Woolf had considered, including the financial distribution model, administrative structures and tournament frameworks. But in stark contrast to Woolf's desire to make these processes fairer, more transparent and supporting long-term development the big three sought dominance in decision-making and a far greater share of the wealth the sport created.

In order to ensure their decision-making would be unchallenged they proposed the establishment of an executive committee that only they would sit on and to which all existing committees would be subordinate. To support this unassailable position of strength they insisted that all key ICC posts should be filled with nominees of the BCCI, ECB and Cricket Australia. Seeking to maximise their revenue generation potential they wanted the Future Tours Programme to be scrapped in favour of a return to bilateral series. They also created a revenue distribution model that reflected the financial contribution the big three made to the global game.

The position paper referred to the existing revenue distribution model as 'distorted' because it did not take into consideration the varying level of economic contribution to the game. India felt they could call the shots because they generated over 80% of cricket's global economy. In their view it was therefore unfair that they should share the profits equally with members who contributed far less. They advocated a sliding scale whereby India's share of the game's wealth would increase as the overall value increased, redressing an historical imbalance.

In order to get support from associate and affiliate members the position paper dangled the tantalising prospect of Test cricket, through the establishment of a two-tiered system with promotion and relegation. However, India, England and Australia would of course be exempt from relegation.

From its inception power politics have dominated the ICC's governance and decision-making and it was perhaps naïve to assume that the new dawn offered by Woolf would become a reality. Woolf himself clearly set out how vested interests had shaped the sport. He also showed that there was much more wealth in the game than ever before that the vested interests could claim for their own. It was meant to be a sad indictment of and a closing of a chapter of a previous age but proved to be a prophecy of what was to come.

India bullied the vote through in February 2014, with Pakistan and Sri Lanka providing tacit opposition by opting to abstain. Although on the face of it other members had no incentive to support the big three, in practice the business models of their own boards were dependent on the revenue tours by India provided. In short, India had everyone else over a barrel and whatever their moral indignation they had no choice.

Srinivasan had achieved his very narrow-minded view of fairness, that the victor should keep the spoils. For India it was the culmination of a long and bitter battle for power in the sport. In the early 20th century they were dictated to by the founding members and they had to fight for recognition. Now they had the financial clout to progress from recognition to dominance. Giles Clarke later admitted that India had used the threat of withdrawing from ICC events as leverage to force their reforms through.

Naturally Lord Woolf was in demand for his view on the extraordinary turn of events:

'It is giving extraordinary powers to a small triumvirate of three people, and everybody else has got no power to say anything or do anything. To say a sport that has got aspirations to be a world-class sport internationally should not have an independent body at the top seems to me to be very surprising. It seems to be entirely motivated by money. I think it will stand out as a retrograde step.'

The founding philosophy that underpinned the reforms instigated by the big three in 2014 was that money should translate into power. For associate and affiliate members, champions of global development and the ICC's own development programme the hope of the Woolf report had turned to despair and despondency. It signalled an uncertain and vulnerable future for all but the most powerful of cricketing nations. At the time of making submissions to the Woolf report associate members complained about a lack of development focus in the game, but they soon came to the realisation that 2011 was to be the peak of the development programme.

But what did it all mean in practice for the aspiring cricket nations in continental Europe? In some ways they were not the biggest losers. After all it was the weaker Test nations that had lost their voting power, had their revenue slashed and lost the financial security of the Future Tours Programme. The associates and affiliates had limited resource and opportunities to begin with. But the rejection of Woolf's funding model based on need and long-term development would leave them isolated. If countries weren't deemed a market they would be cut adrift, and this meant they would have to meet the challenges they faced on their own with less and less funding support.

In a masterstroke of timing and public relations the ICC deflected attention from the pain and heartache to come by announcing the Test Challenge. They had, they claimed, broken the glass ceiling by allowing leading associate nations to play Test cricket by winning the Intercontinental Cup and a four-match challenge series against the lowest-ranked Test nation. This was enthusiastically welcomed by teams like Ireland who still saw playing Test cricket as the pinnacle of cricketing accomplishment. Ironically this was the fulfilment of one of Woolf's recommendations, to de-couple full member status with playing Tests.

But reading between the lines the announcement of the Test challenge was more revealing of the lack of ambitions for development than any fundamental step forward. It signalled the death knell on any aspirations associates had for promotion to full membership. Ireland had put in a formal application and it had been rebuffed, with this theoretical chance of playing Tests once every four years as a trifling compromise. Even if Ireland, the Netherlands or any other associate comes through the Test challenge there is no guarantee of playing a Test. That would be dependent on scheduling a fixture with countries already buckling under fixture pressure.

But the announcement of the Test challenge was even more telling for those countries that have little chance of qualifying for the Intercontinental Cup. For it showed that the big three-led ICC would limit their global development aspirations to the leading associates. This was seen in press releases where there would be regular mentions of Ireland, Afghanistan and Nepal but no reference at all to teams like Belgium or Spain. There was a fear in the associate and affiliate community that once again a line was being drawn, a line which the vast majority of ICC members would fall below.

Back in 2012 Woolf had set out a vision for global cricket in 2015 once a transitional plan had been implemented to prepare the ground for the long-term reforms he proposed. He envisaged an ICC that had wrestled independence from financial dependence on full members and had the freedom to put in place a long-term strategy that saw beyond short-term profits. But this halcyon vision had turned into a Dickensian reality of survival of the fittest. The concept of meritocracy and the tournament structures implemented by the development programme survived. But these were now only serving the top 40 or so associate and affiliate members.

The ICC was concerned by the poor level of play in the bottom divisions of the tournament. With very limited experience of 50-over internationals many teams were getting all out in less than 40 overs and not displaying the technique or game management the ICC expected to ensure a competitive international fixture. This was compounded by the very heavy reliance many teams had on aging expat cricketers. These factors led the ICC board to question the return on investment of the lower divisions in the WCL. There was a feeling within the ICC that it was merely footing the bill for flying club cricketers across the world to play poor quality cricket. The logic went that it would be better for these teams to focus on developing domestic cricket and increasing standards before being re-incorporated into a global tournament framework. Some members of the ICC board favoured a reduction of the WCL to three divisions but the development programme managed to make the case for a return to the original five.

The decision to limit the 50-over World Cup to ten teams from 2019, in order to get maximum bids from broadcasters looking for every game to be a marketable blockbuster, was a retrograde step and fiercely criticised by commentators and fans alike. As many pointed out cricket must be the only world sport that seeks to reduce rather than grow their World Cup competition. To compensate the ICC announced that it would increase the number of participating teams in the World T20. But in practice they merely tacked on a further qualification stage to the event, making qualification for the main tournament harder than it had ever been before.

Under its Bigger, Better Global Game strategy the ICC gave more opportunities to more teams. In the period before the big three takeover the game had developed rapidly in continental Europe with more ICC members, more players and more competitive opportunities for teams. But in 2014 the 'bigger, better' soundbite was being replaced by the more ominous-sounding 'contribution to cricket's global economy'. This was aligned with the philosophy of the big three but what it meant for associates and affiliates was not at all clear.

Long-held fears of lower-ranked teams were realised when new funding structures were announced by the ICC in the spring of 2014. While Giles Clarke had promised that better commercial deals for the game meant more funding for all it was clear that the definition of 'all' was actually very narrow. Of the funding allocated for 95 associate and affiliate members half would go to the top six. This was consistent with the long-standing focus of the High Performance Programme to close the gap between leading associates and weaker test nations. It was good news for countries like Ireland and Afghanistan as they sought to cement their reputation as leading international sides. Their funding would increase further, supporting the development of professionalism of infrastructure, domestic tournaments and the national squad. But it was confirmation that teams below the top six would see funding and opportunities reduce.

Prior to the cost contribution bias that the BCCI introduced to the ICC's funding model the associates and affiliates are estimated to have received $550m in the 2015–23 funding cycle. But under the reforms made in 2014 this was reduced to $300m, only a marginal increase on the settlement for 2007–15. Almost half of this funding was allocated to the top six associates as the ICC look to target funding at teams that can be consistently competitive on the global stage. Surprisingly, although perhaps not that surprisingly if you recall the logic of funding HPP associates in 2006, the ICC selected these teams solely on the basis of their rankings in particular tournaments. You would have thought that such a significant investment would be based on a thorough appraisal against a range of criteria in order to ensure the best chance of return on investment. But, oddly, while such criteria apply through the scorecard funding mechanism it isn't used in determining what countries are eligible for significant funding boosts. As Tim Wigmore has noted the decision to target funding at the top 16 nations is 'an arbitrary number selected at a wholly arbitrary moment'.

In practical terms this means significant funding cuts for associate and affiliate nations in continental Europe just at the culmination of a period when playing numbers have risen considerably and improved infrastructure is desperately needed.

For mid-ranked associates and affiliates the equation is quite clear. They will receive less funding and less support from the ICC. They will have the opportunity to increase funding incrementally through the scorecard model if they meet certain criteria (of which more later), but this will effectively be capped unless they can make a significant breakthrough to qualify for global competitions. Leading associates like The Netherlands have greater access to funding boosts, for instance through qualifying for global events, but these are not guaranteed and failure in particular tournaments can lead to a slashing of funding.

This trend of a further concentration of development funding towards a limited number of leading associates is set to continue as the ICC stress more explicitly that they expect to see a return on investment. The ICC board translate return on investment in this context to teams becoming more competitive on the global stage. This in turn translates to developing teams that can be a net contributor to cricket's global economy and do not compromise the ability of the ICC to maximise revenue from its global events.

A New Hope?

From the nadir of the big three's position paper, prospects for development looked decidedly rosier by the spring of 2016 when Srinivasan, Clarke and Edwards had stumbled from their thrones. Srinivasan's successor as chairman, Shashank Manohar, is a fellow Indian but immediately set out to distance himself from Srinivasan's manic desire to benefit and enrich the BCCI whatever the consequences for the global game. Manohar considered Srinivasan's approach unfair, even distasteful, and agreed to reduce India's cut of the game's profits, roll back from the 2014 restructure and put a greater emphasis on development. In creating an independent chairman, not having to kowtow to a national board, the ICC had implemented one of Woolf's reforms. It enabled the chairman, in theory at least, to base judgement on the good of the global game rather than maximising profits for his board. This still only scratched the surface of what Woolf had proposed though, and the fundamental governance flaws remained. But the removal of the big three was nevertheless a considerable relief to champions of development. It offered the promise of hope, if not yet hope itself, for the future.

Under Manohar Dave Richardson and the development team have grown in confidence in proposing more equitable, development-focused structures for the future of global cricket. These do not represent the wholesale overhaul many have called for but, if implemented, in 2019 and beyond will deliver incremental reform. The ICC finally seem willing to wrestle with the white elephant and sanction relegation for full members. If Richardson's planned structure ever sees the light of day full members face relegation in both Test and ODI formats. A 13-team ODI league, featuring Ireland, Afghanistan and one other associate, would sit atop the current World Cricket League Championship, with a play-off between the bottom-ranked team in the league and the winner of the WCLC for promotion/relegation.

In parallel a two-league Test structure sitting above the Intercontinental Cup is envisaged, with promotion and relegation. This is a far better proposal than the fundamentally flawed concept of the Test challenge. It means, in theory, that any international team can qualify to play Tests. They'd merely have to qualify for the Intercontinental Cup through the World Cricket League and then progress through that. It is, to the ICC's credit, the meritocratic pathway they have long promised. 2016 saw more welcome news for leading associates when it was proposed that the World T20 return to a two-year frequency. The ICC meeting in Edinburgh also saw a consensus grow for the extension of ODI and T20 status to all international teams. Replacing regional allocation of grants the ICC has identified 20 countries for targeted support. These are countries that show promise as an emerging market, not just those with strong performances on the field. The indication is that teams like Germany, whose participation levels have soared in the last few years, could well have shown enough promise to access this targeted support.

These reforms make 2016 an encouraging year for development following a dark and foreboding period under the big three. However, it now looks likely that a two tier test structure, with promotion and relegation, will be blocked by India. The ICC having failed to implement governance reform are powerless to compel full members to support a progressive reform. There is a lot more for an Irishman to cheer than a Belgian. Ireland and Afghanistan have been rewarded for being the leading associate sides of the last five years with a special, very cosy, sub-category of their own, which gives them greater funding and more competitive opportunities against the world's best teams. The definition of providing more funding to associates appears to translate to giving more funding to these two teams, with a little more to those in the World Cricket League Championship and targeted support for those countries considered promising future markets.

The majority of teams in World Cricket League 3 and below are as invisible as ever. For continental Europe this cloak of invisibility rests on the shoulders of all but the Dutch, and perhaps now the Germans, and even they might find themselves being trumped by the exciting markets like Nepal, however they perform against them on the field.

ICC and Global Development

For the majority of its long history the ICC did not even have a stated objective to develop the global game. National boards were solely responsible for developing cricket domestically and securing international opposition. The influx of money into the game following the 1996 World Cup enabled a development programme to be financed and this saw the creation of a host of new members who were provided with tournament structures, grant funding to support development and a pathway to qualify for global events. But as the ICC's membership grew to a peak of 106 members so the funding was increasingly targeted at teams that could be competitive on the global stage.

The ambitious strategy to build a bigger, better global game undoubtedly led to a significant increase in participation and performance levels in continental Europe. But in the last five years cautious optimism has turned to concern for the future due to a switch in ICC policy. The failure to implement Woolf's reforms and therefore lay the foundations for equitable governance and a long term commitment to development has left the majority of countries in the region marginalised, with reduced support and funding.

To his credit Dave Richardson has consistently challenged full members to accept tournament structures based on merit and in the last few years there are finally some precedents that full members can be relegated across different formats and that they need to qualify for tournaments, rather than get a 'bye' from qualification. If these proposals get voted through there will be a pathway for countries to play Test cricket and participate in World Cups. How they will do this, however, without sufficient funding, remains the elephant in the room.

Regional Support

BEFORE the establishment of regional ICC offices in the 1990s the only regional support available for countries in Europe was through the ECB and MCC. Neither organisation had any formal commitment to supporting the development of cricket on the continent and naturally they focused resource and effort on their core remits. The ECB have only given lip service to what might appear a natural, paternalistic role to help develop cricket in their region and the ICC has not steered its full members to do so. When compared for instance with Australia's investment in developing cricket in Papua New Guinea, the ECB have been a very passive influence in Europe. They have, at times, incorporated both Denmark and the Netherlands into domestic competitions and this has been a catalyst for development in those countries, but this has been motivated more by tournament structures than an active commitment to supporting their neighbours. Following the establishment of ICC Europe they have provided access to resources such as coaching materials which have been beneficial and supported some tournaments. But they have all too rarely looked beyond their own shores and have missed an opportunity to play a pivotal role in the region.

The MCC on the other hand has always had a more global outlook and the regular tours MCC made to the continent played a vital role in providing regular fixtures for cricketing teams in areas where local opposition was limited. Making a good impression on the MCC was a major factor in providing cohesion and purpose to cricket clubs across the continent, especially before the Second World War. But there is no doubt that the principal motive for such tours was to provide an enjoyable trip for MCC players rather than to leave a legacy in the countries in which they played. Their impact was indirect, when there was the potential to do so much more. For instance despite several requests from continental European boards the MCC never took the initiative to organise national tournaments in the pivotal decades before the Second World War. They played on the continent for fun, their serious cricket was against other Test nations. They were committed to the kinship the Commonwealth offered and looked to distant colonial outposts more naturally than lands across the North Sea.

However, this passive support became more active in the late 1980s when the European Cricket Federation was formed under the auspices of the MCC. The principle focus of the ECF was to provide a tournament structure for European associates and affiliates. At this time the only official tournament organised by the ICC was the ICC Trophy, held every four years, and this was limited to associate nations and therefore didn't include affiliate nations such as Italy. Between 1990 and the formation of ICC Europe in 1998 the ECF organised the European Cricketer Cup, the ECF Nations Cup and the ECF Indoor Nations Tournament. These were critical in consolidating cricket in countries across the continent, providing the focus to develop small groups of cricketers into something more formalised and ambitious. This provided a tournament framework that was later built on by ICC Europe, but it did not have any explicit objectives to develop cricket in the region.

ICC Europe

The politics, programmes and patronage of the ICC had more impact on some countries in continental Europe than others. The focus on high performance transformed the competitive opportunities, approach and ethics of the national squad in the Netherlands. But the majority of countries in the region fell below the elite performance line and for them decisions made in Dubai had little impact on their cricket, at least until the creation of the World Cricket League. However, the establishment of a regional office in Europe was to usher in an era of intervention and, in many cases, dependency that was to change the way cricket was organised in the whole region.

Introduced in 1997 the Europe office was tasked with delivering the objectives of the development programme in their region. This included providing a regional tournament structure and pathways to qualify for global tournaments, supporting members in boosting participation levels and the profile of the game, providing education programmes and promotional materials and supporting development of cricketing infrastructure and facilities. It was intended as an enabler of development, a framework of support that members could benefit from. The philosophy of ICC Europe has not been to proscribe policy or strategy to its members. But as in other walks of life those that hold the purse strings hold the power and countries have aligned their domestic plans with ICC priorities. After all, meeting ICC targets results in increased funding.

When the office was founded the amount and level of cricket being played on the continent was relatively modest and the lack of structure or cohesive strategy meant that development was solely dependent on the vision, commitment and resources of members. While some boards had sought to introduce cricket into schools and promote the game, for most the organisation of local and national leagues was the sole priority: a short-term imperative to ensure cricket was played. Some individuals may have had grander ambitions of development and long-term strategy but there had not been a shared vision or an organisation to provide direction and support implementation.

But 1997 was a propitious time for ICC Europe to be formed. The previous year the Netherlands had become the first continental country to qualify for a World Cup and Denmark were among the leading associates, showing that the region had two leading candidates for elite development. Other associate members in the region were Gibraltar, Belgium and Italy with Austria, Greece, Italy, Portugal, Spain and Switzerland the affiliates. But increasing levels of economic migration to the region, in particular from South Asia, was providing a stream of potential players and creating a groundswell of interest beyond existing members. The demographics of the continent were shifting rapidly and ICC Europe was in place to consolidate this interest into development of the game in the region.

The ICC Europe team consisted of a regional development manager supported by a number of development officers, who were assigned a number of member countries to work with directly. In addition there were officials responsible for umpiring and scoring and a back office providing administrative support and financial functions.

They provided support in the following areas:

Membership and Governance

The regional office is responsible for ensuring its members fulfil the ICC's membership criteria and makes recommendations to the ICC board to approve new members, promote a member to a new membership category or take action following any breaches of conduct or non-compliance of membership criteria.

The ICC has never had a stated strategy for prospective members. It has never set targets for numbers or global reach of new members and its support is limited to those countries that are applying for or have been granted membership status. In a European context this means that the regional development manager does not have a remit to proactively support cricket in all countries in the region. The process for admitting new members is essentially a reactive one. The ICC publish criteria for membership and if a prospective member can fulfil these they make an application to the regional office. The regional development manager then visits the country and compiles a report on whether the criteria have been met. If they haven't, feedback on the shortcomings is given. Approval of the regional office is required before a prospective member can make an official application to the ICC. This is then considered by committees before moving to the board for discussion and endorsement.

There are no initiatives or funding available to help prospective members meet the minimum criteria. However, until 2012 the requirements on new members were relatively modest and this enabled the regional offices to undertake an active recruitment drive. If a country recognised the laws of the ICC, had four senior teams, a ground and a sole governing body it could join the party. This low bar saw the cricketing map of Europe flood with colour as the cricketing communities that had sprung up in the 1990s were officially incorporated. By 2007 Sweden, Luxembourg, Malta, Cyprus, the Czech Republic, Finland, Norway, Croatia and Slovenia had been awarded affiliate status. Over the next six years they were joined by Bulgaria, Estonia, Hungary, Russia and Romania. Beyond continental Europe ICC Europe also welcomed Jersey, Guernsey, the Isle of Man and Turkey into its ranks.

This flood of new members had a significant impact on ICC Europe. For a start it provided a very quick and simple way of boosting participation levels, keeping their masters in Dubai happy. But it also provided a challenge to instil a development focus on such a widespread membership and incorporate them all into a regional tournament framework.

In theory the major development milestone for an affiliate member was to meet the criteria to become an associate member. This would provide a significant financial boost and increased opportunity, for example by enabling access to the ICC Trophy. However, while the ICC established a High Performance Programme to support development of the leading associates it has never had a strategy or parallel programme to support its members in getting promotion through its membership categories. Naturally the bar for an associate is much higher with a more challenging set of criteria to fulfil. This includes a greater number of teams, including for juniors and women, more advanced governance structures and infrastructure and established development frameworks such as education programmes. Achieving these far more stretching criteria with the limited funding available to affiliate members has proved very challenging indeed. However, both Italy and France managed to achieve promotion. The ICC centrally has focused on supporting members in being competitive on the global stage, rather than necessarily advancing as a cricketing nation through their membership hierarchy.

Shortly after the ICC celebrated its 100th member in 2008 its enthusiasm to continue its recruitment drive and increase its membership further began to wane. It crept up to 106 over the next few years, thanks largely to continued growth of the European cricket community with Romania, Russia and Serbia joining in 2012, 2013 and 2015 respectively. Globally the ICC only had half the members of FIFA and basketball so it could be seen to be job only half done. But rather than see the recent rise of members as the foundation for future growth the organisation began to worry that it had gone too far. Had it been too welcoming? What was the chance of cricket developing in the host of new affiliate nations under its stewardship? What was the return on investment for the membership grants it was issuing? Having asked themselves this last question they made it a requirement for new affiliates to secure $2,500 in non-ICC income. From this point the role of ICC Europe turned from a compliance-based relationship to a critical friend, with a feeling that being too directional may constrain innovation.

This nervousness translated into a new set of membership criteria that made it much more difficult for new members to join. They now needed eight senior teams, four junior teams, two grounds, a programme to develop women's cricket and a minimum of $2,500 in non-ICC income. These criteria were difficult to attain without support or funding from the ICC but that support and funding was only given once the criteria were met. The membership had reached three figures but had seemingly reached a zenith. In continental Europe there are countries where cricket is played who may have become members under the old system, but will now remain out in the cold due to the tougher criteria applied.

Inevitably with this stricter ethos the emphasis switched from welcoming new members to challenging compliance of existing ones. ICC Europe put greater scrutiny on its weaker members, that is to say those members who happily took the grant money but who lacked a structured approach to complying with what was expected of them. Failure to provide a team for regional tournaments was a common issue and was met with official warnings. Another contentious issue was non-compliance with governance requirements, such as being the sole and undisputed national body for cricket. After multiple warnings and direct interventions from ICC Europe Switzerland had their membership revoked. Turkey were suspended too.

Over the coming decade it is much more likely that ICC membership will contract than expand, both in Europe and across the world. While growing membership was clearly consistent with the 2011 strategy for a bigger global game it isn't a priority under the new mantra of contributing to cricket's global economy. The ICC want to spend money on countries they feel could be cricketing superpowers of the future, like USA and Nepal. They don't want to spend money on countries where cricket isn't known and is predominantly played by expats.

Participation

Participation levels on continental Europe were always going to increase from the 1990s due to economic migration trends bringing cricketers and those from a cricketing culture to the region. It should be remembered that the participation figures held by the ICC are submitted by their members and therefore do not give a figure for the continent as a whole.

Its recruitment drive had provided welcome spikes in an upward curve of participation numbers and ICC Europe focused on supporting members in building their own cricketing communities and reaching out to those hitherto unaware of the game. This objective was given renewed impetus with the launch of the ICC's Bigger, Better Global Game Strategy that included a target of a million more participants in associate and affiliate members by 2015. Every region was expected to deliver its fair share. The use of the term 'participants' was significant. Although the number of active cricketers on the continent was increasing due to economic migratory trends bringing cricketers to the region it was unrealistic to deliver such a dramatic increase in league players. For a start there were nowhere near enough grounds to accommodate such a rise! But 'participants' was defined as anyone introduced to the game. A child holding a bat for a matter of minutes as part of a school event counted, even if they never picked up a bat again. The more telling statistic therefore was the percentage of those new participants who became active cricketers and were integrated into the club structure. This was the nub of the challenge, but didn't deliver the eyecatching statistics the ICC sought for its press releases.

ICC Europe worked with its members to fund and organise participation initiatives, partnering where possible with clubs, schools and community groups. These were inspired by the development of simple, short formats of the game such as Kwik Cricket, Cage Cricket and Street20 that required minimal equipment and could be held almost anywhere. Experience in England had shown that they could also provide an important social role in bringing communities and faiths together through cricket, easing tensions and aiding social inclusion. Accessible and engaging, these formats showcased the excitement and fun of the game, aiming to inspire interest rather than develop technical skill. But it was recognised that running such initiatives would be wasted effort unless there was a pathway for those introduced through such an outreach event to become an active cricketer. The regional development officers worked with their members to ensure that clubs forged links with youth and community groups to maximise retention of players. In parallel there was an emphasis on increasing the number and quality of coaches and officials to build capability in each country, as well as improving infrastructure. An influx of players discovered through outreach schemes would soon leave the game if there wasn't the facilities and infrastructure to enable them to play.

Within the broad ambition to boost participation levels the ICC regional offices were directed to target their resources on particular countries and groups. With an eye on delivering a return on investment and maximising impact they focused schemes on members with the highest participation potential. In a European context this meant countries with large populations and significant untapped interest. The logic was clear, a participation event run in German cities with large immigrant communities would deliver more numbers than an equivalent scheme in Gibraltar or Malta. It was, in short, a results-driven initiative. As well as focusing on particular countries there was also a directive to target events at indigenous communities and females. In the ICC these groups are referred to as 'markets'.

Sustaining participation growth in a region with limited cricketing infrastructure was a significant challenge, both for the ICC and for member boards. In an attempt to overcome or at least mitigate the impacts of these constraints ICC Europe instigated educational programmes in multiple languages to support development of coaches, officials and instructors and sought where possible to enhance facilities. With precious few grounds across the region, particularly in the recently elected affiliate nations with no cricketing heritage, there was a reliance on indoor facilities and access to public parks and open spaces.

In recent years the ICC's participation statistics have illustrated the rapid growth in informal, unstructured cricket. While player numbers remained relatively static the numbers playing under the category of 'modified games' rose significantly. This statistical subplot was a sign that cricket on the continent was changing, and changing quickly. Recent immigrants to the region wanted to play cheap, quick, accessible cricket in the neighbourhoods in which they lived. With makeshift stumps and a tennis ball wrapped in tape they could play outside their homes, in a park or any piece of nearby open ground. While the amount of cricketers is increasing, the amount played in clubs under the auspices of national boards is decreasing.

Tournaments and Elite Performance

Although the MCC had helped develop and run some international tournaments in the region prior to the formation of ICC Europe opportunities for countries to play competitively remained few and far between. This meant that their ability to compete on the global stage was almost solely determined by the strength of the domestic league and the national board's ability to develop high quality players. As avoiding embarrassment and commercial ramifications in global tournaments was a key driver for the creation of the development programme, performance was naturally a priority for regional offices.

In its first decade ICC Europe focused on developing a regional tournament structure. The programme of tournaments naturally expanded as it incorporated its new members, developed the women's game and provided more opportunities at age group level. This structure became even more significant when regions were entrusted with providing a qualification pathway for global tournaments including the World Cup, World T20, Under-19 World Cup and the World Cricket League. Running these tournaments became the bread and butter for the office at Lord's.

By 2001 ICC Europe were running under-13, under-15, under-17, under-19 and under-23 tournaments along with a two-divisional European championship, a women's tournament and an indoor championship. These tournaments provided members a busy competitive schedule each year and a focus for their domestic development programme. By 2009 the regional men's tournament was comprised of five divisions and age group tournaments had been introduced for the women's game. With such an all-encompassing structure most countries had one or two representative teams competing in tournaments throughout the European season.

With over ten tournaments a year to organise the regional office was committing significant resource to preparing and checking venues, arranging logistics, providing officials, checking and validating player eligibility and resolving visa issues, let alone promoting and managing the tournaments themselves. An important element of each tournament was working with the host country to improve standards and facilities in order to leave a legacy for cricketing infrastructure across the continent.

In addition to regional tournaments ICC Europe also played a role in ensuring European members successfully hosted global tournaments such as the Intercontinental Cup and World Cricket League. The standards these tournaments required, both in terms of the grounds and supporting infrastructure, often meant considerable work and investment was required to ensure venues complied.This process played a crucial role in improving the standards of cricketing facilities across the region.

In addition to the tournament structure ICC Europe also focused on developing elite performance. This was the regional contribution to supporting the High Performance Programme's objectives to make teams more competitive on the global stage. They supported elite performance initiatives within member countries, through performance clinics and support for coaches. While their focus on participation was intended to broaden the base they also wanted to develop the elite players to win matches. A broad base rarely grabs a headline, but winning a global tournament does.

This onus on elite performance saw ICC Europe develop its own high performance academy at La Manga, Spain, where selected players benefitted from elite coaching, world-class facilities and professional fitness, strength and conditioning training. It was hoped that the participants would take these skills and approaches back to their countries to inspire greater professionalism in domestic leagues.

Under the 2011 strategy regional offices were instructed to target their performance frameworks and initiatives at the highest ranked nations in their region. The Key Performance Indicators for 2015 were to improve performances at 'major' global events and to be more competitive against full members. This represented a much narrower focus which for ICC Europe meant targeting funds and support at teams in the higher divisions of the World Cricket League, such as the Netherlands, Denmark and Italy. This naturally meant the withdrawal of much support provided to the lower ranked associates and affiliates. High performance was being measured by region, rather than within each member. This was a change in emphasis that would become a point of contention between ICC Europe and many of the member boards.

There was recognition in the development programme that sustaining a high level of on-field performance required good governance, structures and strategic planning in member boards. Reading between the lines it was clear that the ICC were unwilling to invest in developing elite performance of a player from one of its members if the benefit of that investment would be undermined by a lack of support and development within the domestic structure. Put another way they were challenging the over-reliance members had on ICC support. They sought to develop professional governance within member boards and encourage the development of domestic frameworks that focused on playing structures, selection processes and preparation for ICC events. They targeted improvements in player management, including contracts for leading players, and review of domestic structures to concentrate talent and improve performance levels. Again this emphasis clearly showed a narrowing of focus to the leading associate nations.

By 2011 the most commonly cited term in ICC press releases was 'meritocratic pathways'. In an ICC development context merit

Austrian openers, set to make short work of a tall order. June 2011. (Barry Chambers)

Sweden and Austria in front of an old Glaswegian Routemaster serving as a pavilion in the Czech Republic. (Czech Cricket)

One of the most intriguing cricketing backdrops on the continent, the old Routemaster cricket pavilion at the Vinor Cricket Ground, near Prague. (Czech Cricket)

Exuberant appeal by Croatian bowler, European Championships 2011. (Barry Chambers)

Denmark captain Michael Pedersen collects the trophy from ICC Europe's Richard Holdsworth. (Barry Chambers)

Victorious Danish squad, European Championships 2011. (Barry Chambers)

Veteran PJ Bakker claims a wicket for Holland, following his successful career for Hampshire. (Getty)

Sheep don't seem that impressed by a Danish extra cover drive. (Getty)

German batsman working to leg. (Getty)

Italian squad savouring success. (Getty)

Young Danish batting star Hamid Shah, right, prepares for his innings. He gained experience in the Irish league in 2016. (Getty)

Denmark's Freddie Klokker leads the charge. (Getty)

Indoor training session in France. With grounds and facilities scarce across the region sports centres are often a hive of cricketing activity. (Getty)

Dutch squad qualify for yet another World Cup, young batsman Rahil Ahmed holding the T20 Qualifier trophy aloft. (Getty)

Stuart Broad sinks to his knees as the Dutch claim a famous scalp at Lord's in 2009. The victory gave the Dutch squad a brief period of fame back home, appearing in magazines and on chat shows. (Getty)

Brian Mantle of the German Cricket Board runs a session for refugees new to the country, many of whom made the journey by foot from Afghanistan. (Getty)

Refugees waiting to be processed stage an impromptu game of cricket near Calais. Immigration trends are changing cricket in the region, boosting numbers considerably. (Getty)

Dutch squad in 2005. (Getty)

Italy recruit some locals into the slip cordon. (Barry Chambers)

A cricket clinic for schoolchildren in the Czech Republic. These are run across the region to boost interest and participation levels. (Getty)

The author with Danish talisman Freddie Klokker at European Division 1, Jersey. (Author)

Romania, one of the newest cricket nations in the region, celebrate a wicket. Thanks to a millionaire benefactor they are blessed with one of the finest grounds on the continent. (Getty)

Carst Posthuma was the first continental cricketer to play first-class cricket, playing alongside W.G. Grace for London County at the turn of the 20th century.

Swedish squad foreground, Alpine peaks background at the picturesque ground of Velden on the Austria/Slovenia border. Cricket became an officially recognised sport in Sweden in 2015 releasing significant government funding. (Barry Chambers)

translated as winning games in tournaments. Victories in tournaments meant promotion and promotion meant additional funding, further opportunities and in some circumstances the awarding of status. Winning could begin a virtuous cycle while losing could unravel years of hard work and commitment. This pressure was of course spared the full members. But I digress. Merit was also evaluated on a global basis which was to have significant ramifications for opportunities regionally. In the period 2011–15 the tournament structure in Europe was reframed to support qualification for global events. This meant regional qualification for four day, 50-over, 20-over and under-19 tournaments. Providing regional age group opportunities was no longer prioritised. Indeed, providing regional opportunities for countries not likely to qualify for global tournaments was not a priority. This recalibration of the performance focus of regional offices took several years to come to fruition. In 2016 the only ICC Europe tournaments were the Under-19 World Cup Qualifier – Europe division 2 and the ICC World Cricket League – Europe Qualifier Division 2.

Strategic Planning

Over time ICC Europe extended its ambitions from providing opportunities to its members to shaping their strategic planning. This was to be a far greater level of intervention than inviting teams to participate in a tournament. It was intended to challenge any complacency of member boards and ensure that national initiatives were aligned with global development objectives. ICC Europe's success was measured against a set of metrics covering the key performance indicators of performance, participation, promotion and infrastructure. Introducing a requirement for its members to develop, measure and report on annual development plans gave them this accountability.

This process presented both an opportunity and a challenge to member boards across the continent. It instilled the need for a focus on development within the boards and was the foundation for many successful initiatives across the region, particularly in building participation. But it also created potential tensions with clubs and cricketers within the country, who may take a different view of where the focus should lie and how money should be spent.

Development plans were drafted by the member boards themselves but with support from ICC Europe development officers who could challenge and cajole. Member boards who did not take development seriously would be challenged, especially in allocation of funding. The plans included stated and measurable targets, which meant the performance of boards could be monitored. While the regional development manager could only apply sanctions for breaches of membership requirements rather than failure to achieve targets, the requirement to submit development plans nevertheless provided an audit trail. As funding and support became more and more targeted countries with better development records and statistics to prove it were naturally in a stronger position. Development in the region was not being left to chance. Corporate concepts of accountability, audit trails and success indicators had been applied to continental cricket. To some extent this papered over the cracks of examples of poor administration and governance within member boards. There was a carrot and a stick.

As the plans where intended to deliver a common set of targets and were aligned with a common set of categories in the scorecard funding mechanism they were naturally all very similar. While differing legal frameworks and institutional processes necessitated some tailoring of national plans, overall development strategy in the region was homogenised. Climatic differences meant that while Finland had to focus on indoor tournaments Spain could plan for beach cricket festivals. The constraints faced by members often varied too. For example in some countries cricket could be introduced in any school that showed an interest. In others cricket had to be recognised as an authorised sport by the government before school programmes could be launched. These plans not only had to be approved by the regional development manager but also ratified at the annual general meetings of the member boards. The detail was often less important than the need to secure funding to keep individuals in jobs and enable cricket to survive. A consequence of this was that chairmen and professional staff at the board were often seen as 'the ICC's man' by clubs seeking greater autonomy, at times creating an 'us' and 'them' mentality.

While the introduction of annual plans made the organisation and development of cricket on the continent more structured and target driven it also had an unintended consequence from the ICC's perspective. Over time it encouraged a culture of dependency amongst some members. All corporate organisations seek to promote initiative and innovation amongst their employees or constituents. This is essential in driving progress from mere compliance. Member boards received funding from the ICC and dedicated consultants who could advise on, shape and help deliver strategies. If they were content with the role they needed only to implement and act as local arbiters of the laws and leagues. Much depended on the personalities, passion and commitment of those in key roles in their country. Some were more proactive than others.

Promotion

The promotion of cricket in continental Europe has always been challenging given the very low profile of the sport in a football-obsessed region. The KNCB had recognised this in establishing a committee to build the profile of the game in the country, and other countries with less structured governance did what they could with local press and promotional materials. ICC Europe has sought to promote the game through its own communications activities and through support to its members. Traditionally the focus of promotional efforts has been around tournaments to capitalise on the inherent interest in the success of a national team and tapping into national pride. ICC Europe has a communications officer who works with members to get as much coverage through as many media formats as possible. Coverage is then measured and analysed. Television, radio and newspaper coverage of cricket on the continent is very limited and is almost wholly reliant on a topical hook, such as a global event, a very high profile international cricket story or the success of a national team.

ICC Europe has sought to capitalise on the opportunities of new media to raise understanding and profile of the game on the continent. They have run training events for members on developing communications strategies making full use of platforms such as Facebook, Twitter and Instagram. They have also worked in partnership with media providers to increase the quality and quantity of cricket content online. This has included a quarterly e-zine with features, articles and video content of match highlights, development initiatives and country features. Together with a concerted effort by members new media has definitely helped energise the cricket community on the continent and played an important role in increasing participation levels by signposting cricketers to local clubs.

But while cricket's web presence in the region is growing it has been challenging to reach beyond existing players and followers to engage new audiences. The stark truth is that the majority of people on the continent are not aware that cricket is played in their country. If they have heard of cricket it is probably only through a vague connection with England and the notion of fair play. In recent years the development programme has taken the decision to target promotional efforts in markets with high potential. These include the USA, China and Nepal. Continental Europe has not been identified as a priority. Limited funds have been allocated to provide tournament coverage within the region through platforms like YouTube although real-time highlights on Facebook and Twitter have proved very popular.

Live coverage of matches through internet streaming has generated very encouraging audience figures, though many of these have come from Asian fans desperate for any coverage of cricket they can find. Coverage of Dutch international fixtures in 2012/13, funded by ICC Europe, provided an opportunity to engage audiences, attract sponsors and energise the cricket community. But even the modest costs of such productions has proved too much for already stretched budgets and this model for promotion has not yet been enthusiastically adopted by boards.

Members have been encouraged to build relationships with journalists to not only increase coverage of cricket on the continent but also to enhance the range of cricket stories publicised to cover its social context. Unfortunately most current content serves to further marginalise cricket by emphasising its foreignness or by making fun of its complex rules.

Governance and Administration

While ICC Europe have sought to provide structures and support to enable the objectives of the development programme to be achieved in Europe it is member boards that run cricket in their countries. There has been a tendency in the media and within the cricketing community on the continent to blame the ICC for any failings or shortcomings. Less scrutiny has been placed on the management, strategy and efficiency of the member boards themselves.

From ICC Europe's perspective the member boards are the delivery agents through which they progress their objectives. They therefore have a vested interest in member boards being run efficiently. They are also their paymasters and have a corporate responsibility both to ensure boards are complying with the requirements of membership and that there is a clear audit trail to demonstrate return on investment. There has been considerable comment and debate about the level of ICC funding in Europe, but very little is said about how effectively the money is spent.

In order to support good governance in its members ICC Europe runs regular sessions to improve skills, increase business acumen and implement best practice in recruitment and management practices. Cricket boards at associate and affiliate level are not established as businesses and are rarely run along corporate lines and yet they receive and administer funds. An example of this amateurism was seen in Ireland in the ODI quadrangular tournament they hosted in 2007. The Irish Cricket Union had marked the occasion with a dinner for its committee members, all sporting very smart ICU blazers. However, while they were dining the handful of spectators in the ground were forced to walk around the boundary because no chairs had been provided. This slapdash approach soon changed with the formation of Cricket Ireland, a professional organisation run by the very businesslike Warren Deutrum. An Irish example, but illustrative of an ingrained amateurism prevalent across Europe at the time.

I have very rarely seen the competence of national boards for carrying out such functions analysed or challenged. As a national sporting body their governance, ethics and performance will be audited but as their key sponsor the ICC have a right to be assured of fundamental corporate principles such as transparent decision-making, clear audit trails and demonstration of value for money.

Influencing the Influencers

While ICC Europe has been able to have a considerable influence on the strategy and development initiatives implemented by its members, the long-term success of these objectives is largely dependent on local support and champions for the game. It is difficult, indeed near impossible, to sustain growth in participation, performance and profile without improved facilities. While most countries in continental Europe have national and regional structures and programmes to promote sport it is difficult for member boards to secure funding and support for cricket when the sport has such a low profile. Even with all the will in the world a development plan with ambitious targets cannot be delivered without a ground or nets. Member boards spend a great deal of time building relationships with national sporting bodies and regional and local administrators to get support for improving infrastructure and facilities. ICC Europe recognise the extent of this challenge and support members in building these relationships in several ways. Firstly they invest time to present to and meet government organisations across the continent to help support members' objectives. Secondly they invite people in key positions of power and influence, such as town mayors and politicians, to high profile events to demonstrate the international profile of cricket and how it could benefit a local community. Many a project has been given the green light after an afternoon being wined and dined at a Lord's Test match.

Funding and Targeted Support

Traditionally the ICC provided a grant to its members depending on their membership category. This was a fixed annual amount irrespective of size, population, geographic location, exchange rate, performance or number of players/clubs. The funding was provided to fulfil membership criteria, such as the requirement for an office, a full-time member of staff and running a domestic league. It did not come with any performance-related caveats and was not designated for development. Members had autonomy on how it was spent.

This block funding model had several fundamental faults. Firstly it made no distinction of need or level of challenge. Tiny Gibraltar received the same funding as France and significantly more than an affiliate nation more than 20 times its size. Secondly there was no incentive to deliver results or mechanism to adjust the level of funding based on performance. Secondly European nations were at a distinct disadvantage with members in other parts of the world where money would go a lot further. The same issue was seen in the standardised allocation of the High Performance Programme grant. This enabled the Netherlands to contract three players while Kenya used the same money to professionalise 17 largely mediocre players.

Over time the ICC recognised the limitations of the model and sought to introduce a merit-based system and greater levels of accountability. To ensure greater accountability members were required to submit financial plans and reports annually, which were then assessed and validated by ICC Europe. This put a greater onus on members to demonstrate clear alignment between spend and delivery of priority objectives. Their wish for a merit-based system saw the replacement of block funding with the scorecard approach.

In 2013 the ICC reformed their funding model. This was part of a process to target funding at more competitive teams, introduce the principle of merit-based funding and reduce the proportion of grant members were spending on tournament participation. The contribution in direct grant was halved to $70,000 for associates and $10,000 for affiliates. The remainder of funding was allocated through a scorecard system that ranked countries across a range of criteria including performance, participation and infrastructure/facilities. For leading associates there was a third funding element through high performance grants and qualification bonuses for reaching global tournaments. A third of the scorecard rating was still allocated to performance, with other criteria being number of players, number of umpires/officials and number of grounds. Each country was ranked through a weighted average for each category with teams banded by ranking. In 2014 over 20 teams received no grant at all through this scorecard.

While in principle the scorecard funding was fairer than the traditional grant-based model, changes that were taking place in parallel meant that affiliates and lower ranked associates were facing significant cuts. For a start the overall funding for associates was recalibrated to target half at the top six associates that had ODI status and were part of the HPP. This obviously left a much lower share to be divided between the rest. This was compounded by the reduction in scope of global and regional tournaments that saw many teams fall out of tournament structures, which meant they automatically got the lowest weighting for performance on the scorecard without any chance to actually prove themselves on the field.

The next stage in this process was to remove the block grant altogether and make funding entirely dependent on two scorecards, one based on performance and another based on development criteria. In turn this meant that members no longer had to meet membership criteria such as having an office or a full-time member of staff. The performance-based scorecard only included teams that were in the World Cricket League, that had been reduced from eight to five divisions. In continental Europe this meant that only the Netherlands, Denmark and Italy received any performance-related funding. The development scorecard was weighted 70% on participation, 10% on infrastructure, officials and staff and 20% on the level of non-ICC income received. Teams were ranked in categories from A, $500,000, to N, $10,000. This had the effect of ensuring that the teams that needed the most support to improve in the development criteria got the least funding to achieve this.

These funding reforms had seen funding slashed across much of the continent and ICC Europe received a fierce backlash from embittered members. However, this was largely from members who had not been proactive in boosting participation numbers. The ICC argue that teams can increase their funding by delivering results. How they do this is far from clear.

In addition to core funding provided centrally ICC Europe had a regional budget to support targeted initiatives in Europe. This was aligned with the objectives and ambitions set out in annual development plans. Members could apply for funding to support initiatives such as events to boost participation, forging links with schools and projects to boost profile amongst women and indigenous communities. The vast majority of these applications were granted funding support. Progress and outcomes were closely monitored by development officers and failure to demonstrate successful outcomes and value for money generally meant a blacklisting for the next funding round.

The Light-Touch Model

With the decision to target the majority of associate and affiliate funding at the most competitive teams it was inevitable that the development programme would become more centralised and the control, resources and influence of the regional offices would diminish. In 2016 their funding and their role was considerably reduced. With the regional tournament structure stripped away, the removal of a regional budget for targeted support and loss of development officers supporting members ICC Europe's role has been considerably, to borrow a corporate phrase, streamlined. Their role now is limited to overseeing the regional pathways for global tournaments and offering a range of services that members can choose to pay for if they wish.

This withdrawal of support puts the onus on development in the region firmly back with the member boards themselves. They will get much less support, both financially and in access to specialist advice, and therefore will have to be far more proactive in building relationships with national and regional government, sponsors and sporting organisations. The ICC expect these bodies to be the principal funders of cricket development in the region as the ICC itself takes a back seat. The scorecard funding model provides them with a clear steer on what the ICC expect them to focus on, but there is no requirement to do so. The stripping away of tournaments for all but the leading sides is a clear indication that they are expected to focus on building domestic structures to support long-term, sustainable growth.

The question of return on investment for direct ICC involvement in Europe has always been a compelling and contentious one. Despite the introduction of success indicators by the development programme it has never been clear what level of impact ICC funding has achieved. It has definitely helped boost participation levels but beyond that it is arguable that other factors have had greater impact. Although seen as a percentage of the total revenue the sport generates the amount it has spent in developing cricket in Europe is minimal, nevertheless the cumulative cost of member grants, targeted funding, running tournaments and supporting a regional office are not inconsiderable. That this funding has helped cricket survive and grow in the region is undeniable. But whether this investment has made continental Europe a region that 'contributes to cricket's global economy', and furthermore whether this was ever a realistic ambition, remains a matter for debate.

* * * * *

The expansion of the ICC as an organisation and its flirtation with a commitment to development has been a significant influence on cricket on the continent today. But the scale and standard of cricket in the region has largely been determined by the number and geographic distribution of people who are aware of, like and play the game. As seen in part 1, despite being the first modern sport with an opportunity to capture the imagination of a continent before football and other challengers had taken root, cricket was never more than a minority sport played by passionate but largely isolated communities across the region. Despite the efforts and advocacy of many it never achieved the breakthrough it needed in becoming a mainstream sport in schools or part of the national sporting consciousness. It always remained an English sport adopted by some, rather than a universal game played by many. Even when a continental country has enjoyed high profile success, such as the Netherlands' defeat of England in the T20 World Cup, it has not led to a significant or sustained growth amongst the traditional demographic. Although T20 has been a popular format and enabled cricket to adapt to the time demands of modern life on the continent, it too hasn't achieved the hoped for breakthrough. Cricket wasn't part of European culture when pioneers first introduced it and it remains on the fringe of continental life.

But continental Europe is now multicultural and for many of its constituent cultures cricket is the predominant sport and integral to life. From the late 1960s the demographic of the continent changed as several waves of economic migrants arrived from southern Asia to find employment and make a new home. Those migrating to the Netherlands or Denmark would more than likely have become aware that cricket was played relatively quickly as although the profile of cricket was low the network of clubs, particularly in the main employment centres, was relatively extensive. Over time, and depending on how welcoming the clubs were to broadening their own demographic, they could become incorporated into the domestic player base and club scene. For those who emigrated to a country without a national cricket board, league or local clubs playing cricket would be more challenging and many would have left the game through lack of opportunity. But some would have continued to play wherever they could and with whatever equipment they could lay their hands on. Of these a small number might even have the drive to establish a club or a national board themselves.

For national cricket boards across the region this influx of immigrants from cricket-playing cultures was both an opportunity and a challenge. It was an opportunity to boost participation levels and the number and geographic spread of clubs, not to mention the overall standard of play and the quality of national and representative teams. But with limited facilities and grounds and in many cases a club culture that thrived on exclusivity it was also a challenge. Prior to the establishment of a regional office in the 1990s there was neither a requirement nor incentive for members to grow the game. Although club and national sides slowly became more multicultural, reflecting broader societal trends, this was often as much from colonial links and expats from non-Asian Test sides as from local communities.

By the eighties some players of Pakistani and Indian origin were representing continental European national teams having qualified through residency. But member boards tended to look to the traditional player base for national representation and for many years the ethnic composition of national teams did not reflect the composition of the leagues. In some cases this was because many cricketers from ethnic groups were playing recreational cricket outside the formal league structures from which representative sides were selected. In other cases there was a selection bias towards cricketers developed in the country, either to support development structures or to ensure that the national team was representative of and would be supported by the majority, indigenous ethnic group.

By the time ICC Europe was established in 1997 the size of ethnic communities in major cities had increased further through both further waves of migration as air-travel became cheaper and the job and labour market more international, and second generations who were born and raised in continental Europe. In some cases these players joined established clubs. But increasingly there was a trend for these communities to form their own clubs exclusively for players of a particular nationality. This was to contribute to what many have called the 'two cultures' of European cricket.

This demographic trend saw clubs form in parts of the region where cricket had never become established and therefore laid the foundation for the proliferation of new affiliate nations in Scandinavia, Central and Eastern Europe around the turn of the century. In most cases it was expat Englishmen or Australians that took the administrative lead in forming new national administrations, often helped by British embassies, but it was cricketers of Indian, Pakistani, Sri Lankan and Bangladeshi origin that provided the player base needed to meet the membership criteria.

When the ICC set targets for increasing participation levels and later made this a key determinant of funding levels member boards were able to reach out to these communities in their recruitment drive. This underpinned the steep curve of participation increase seen between 2002 and 2012. The advent of social media accelerated this process further by providing a simple, accessible means of matching those interested in cricket with clubs in their area. As awareness grew so did participation numbers, geographical spread and standards of play. This demographic change not only boosted player numbers but also increased the number of umpires, scorers and volunteers.

The ICC's participation statistics are not segmented by ethnic group but it is clear from the composition of leagues and national sides that the dramatic rise in participation levels in the region are the result of immigration from South Asia.

Furthermore the game on the continent is now predominantly played by cricketers of South Asian origin. Even in the Netherlands and Denmark where domestic cricket was predominantly played by native players until the late 20th century there has been a significant shift. Native players now only constitute somewhere between 30% and 45% of the domestic player base. Overall only one in ten cricketers in continental Europe are white. This profound cultural shift has naturally had a considerable impact on how the game is played and perceived in the region.

The level of integration of different ethnic groups into the cricketing fabric of continental countries has been variable, reflecting the inevitable prejudices and cultural tensions present in any multicultural society. In many cases traditional clubs have welcomed a more diverse membership and in so doing broadened their player base, improved performance and served as bridge between communities. However, cricket is a very strong and emotive cultural marker for South Asian countries and there are many examples across the region of clubs being established exclusively for a single ethnic group. They often have their ethnic origin in the club name and their kits mirror the colours of national teams like Pakistan and Sri Lanka.

Equally there are clubs that have sought to protect themselves from South Asian dominance. To a large extent this merely reflects the human desire to be drawn to those with similar backgrounds and beliefs. This is not a trend unique to continental Europe of course, and a similar pattern has been noted in urban centres in Britain, USA and Canada. But where it has happened this delineation on ethnic and cultural lines has caused tension within cricketing communities. For some this changing demographic has led to them drifting away from the game. In the Netherlands for instance some local players who were attracted to the game by its gentle grace, cordiality and sense of fair play have become disillusioned with what they perceive to be a more combative, competitive approach by Asian-dominated clubs and therefore have left the leagues to play recreational, Zami or Zomi cricket, the Dutch equivalent of the gentle games of English village greens.

Unfortunately the creation of clubs for specific ethnic groups has led to an undercurrent of 'two culture' tensions in some cricket communities. In the most part this is merely the expression of prejudices held by individuals translated to a cricketing context but has been exacerbated by several factors. Firstly there have been cases where clubs have been caught ball-tampering, abusing officials or playing unregistered players. These issues have not been exclusive to Pakistani clubs, but they have in general faced more disciplinary action than most. For those with a predisposition to blame a deterioration of standards and a change in culture on an evolving composition of cricket, such incidents are naturally grist to their mill. South Asian cricketers arriving in the region typically learned and played their formative cricket in unstructured settings and are not as familiar with rules and regulations as Europeans for whom routine and compliance are inculcated in early childhood. This of course doesn't excuse wilful violation of rules or unsportsmanlike behaviour, that can only ever be the fault of individuals, but it does perhaps help explain its prevalence.

Secondly, as well as racial differences, cricketers often come from a very different background. For instance it must be quite a culture shock for a French cricketer whose club is based in the picturesque grounds of a chateau to play in a deprived, down-trodden Parisian suburb. The opposition is likely to be speaking a foreign language and with the natural exuberance of the subcontinent may well appeal enthusiastically and often. This may not be considered in the spirit of the game by those who prefer a polite enquiry to a screaming, arms outstretched entreaty to the umpire for a delivery likely to miss another set of stumps. It may even be perceived as cheating. All these factors can create tensions as cricket on the continent shifts from a game played with traditional English sensibilities to one reflecting the more visceral game of the subcontinent.

With such a high proportion of cricketers in continental Europe being of South Asian origin it is not surprising that many in the region perceive it as a foreign sport. It can be argued that this has always been the case, but that some have found it easier to identify with an English sport than an Asian one. Member boards seek, or at least they should seek, to reach out to all communities to broaden the player base and ensure that as far as possible cricket reflects the ethnic composition of the city or country overall. But this is challenging if one particular ethnic group is dominant. Sadly there have been examples across the continent of parents withdrawing their children from events run by member boards or schools because on arriving to find virtually all children are of South Asian origin they decide it is 'not for them'. There is a risk that these attitudes, if prevalent, can reinforce the widely held belief that cricket is a foreign, rather than universal, sport. You would hope that all children would have equal access to all sports so that they could make their own mind up about which they wanted to play. Regrettably this isn't always the case.

The development of the women's game on the continent, which has been a great success in recent years, has demonstrated the impact of cultural factors on cricket development and attracting youth to the game. While many national boards have struggled to reach, engage and incorporate indigenous boys into their development programmes they have had much more success with girls. This is in part because some cultures in South Asia do not encourage girls to play sport. This has therefore naturally led to female teams largely being made up of indigenous players, which many parents feel more comfortable with and therefore give wholehearted support.

A predominantly ethnic player base has inevitably led to predominantly ethnic national teams, at age group and senior level. Despite the ICC introducing strict player eligibility rules that require players to fulfil nationality or residency criteria the ethnic composition of European national teams has proved an emotive and contentious issue. There are many teams in continental Europe that field teams entirely made up of players of South Asian origin. This is entirely natural given the ethnic composition of the leagues in those countries. However, it touches a nerve for many. Views range in quite a broad spectrum from those who couldn't care less as long as all players meet required eligibility criteria to those who feel such teams undermine international cricket.

The truth is that there are only a handful of nations in continental Europe that could field a competitive team consisting entirely or largely of indigenous players. Whether this is a damning indictment of development efforts in the region or just merely an indication of its stage of development, depends upon your viewpoint and your expectations. Firstly the composition of a national team only reveals the selection process at any given moment in time. Secondly the ethnicity of a player is secondary to where they learnt and developed their cricket.

The nature of the sporting psyche and a development and funding structure largely predicated on rewarding on-field success naturally leads to a winning-is-everything mentality in sporting tournaments, cricket included. This means that teams are encouraged to pick the best possible XI they can. For most teams in continental Europe this will mean picking expats who played at a competitive level before they emigrated to the region. It is these players who are most likely to be match-winners, secure promotion for the side and therefore access additional funding and further competitive opportunities. You can even argue that it is impossible to develop international class players with the facilities available in most continental countries. However, although this approach makes sense in preparing for a single tournament it may have unintended consequences for development more broadly. For instance if a national team consists entirely of aging expats this will seriously dent the morale of young players coming through the development programme who are denied an opportunity to play. It may also limit the extent to which the team engages the support of the cricketing community and the country as a whole, potentially compromising participation programmes, investment and sponsorship.

It is important to assess selection policy in the context of long-term planning. This can be illustrated through several different scenarios:

Scenario A

1. In year one of a tournament cycle a continental affiliate picks its strongest XI available, picking several aging expats who played at a high level in Pakistan and have recently qualified through residency. They are portly and unfit, but are match-winners on their day. The average age of the squad is 33. No players from the youth development programme are selected. Interest from national media is limited as there are no local players selected. The team win the tournament thanks to match-winning contributions from the aging expats. They get a funding boost of $20,000 for winning and are promoted to a further tournament in six months' time.

2. In year 2 the $20,000 is invested in a national performance centre, which serves as the base for the development programme. This includes a turf pitch, bowling machines and a programme of specialist performance and fitness sessions. One of the expats retires and becomes a coach at the national performance centre. Four young players from the under-19 squad are selected, two of whom are indigenous and all are born in the country. The team finish fourth in the next tournament and retain their place in the tournament.

3. In year 3 the affiliate wins a regional youth tournament thanks largely to the rise in performance levels due to the national performance centre. The $5,000 bonus for winning this tournament is invested in a pilot project introducing cricket into three schools in the neighbourhood. Two children from these projects join the development programme. A national newspaper runs a feature on the schools pilot and the expat coach of the national performance centre is interviewed on local television, raising the profile of cricket in the country.

Scenario B

1. In year 1 the person in charge of selection picks a team of his friends, who happen to be aging expats. There is no transparent process for talent identification or selection and many league players who had performed well and had hoped for selection feel disappointed. The squad is undoubtedly talented but is aging and unfit. After a strong start in the tournament the lack of fitness and athleticism tells and they miss out on promotion.

2. In year 2 there is no tournament for the national team. There is increasing dissatisfaction within the league that there is no fair and accountable selection process. With this lack of incentive for

good performances umpires report that the standard and intensity of play begins to drop.

3. In year 3 there is another international tournament and the same squad is selected as in year 1, despite some of the players being in bad form in the league. Once again the team perform well in patches but do not progress. Furthermore they begin to get a reputation among other teams that they are aging, unfit and not developing youth. This is seen by the ICC. The national sporting body also hears of this criticism and reduces its level of funding and support. Believing that there is no opportunity for international recognition, many of the best young players leave cricket to focus on other sports. This has an impact on the scorecard grant made available which then limits options for holding participation initiatives and developing a youth programme.

* * * * *

Many with an interest in European cricket make snap judgements just by viewing surnames on a scorecard. However, this only offers a blinkered view of the situation. For a start a surname gives no indication of where someone was born or where they learnt their cricket. It is unrealistic and frankly naïve to assume that Norway will be able to field a team of blonde, blue-eyed Vikings at this stage of their cricket development. But this doesn't mean that there is no virtue in cricket being played in Norway. As scenario A illustrates a positive development cycle can start by fielding a team of expats. Therefore criticism in year 1 would be unfounded. However, in scenario B it can be seen that without a development focus, reliance on aging expats can be damaging.

While some take an extreme view that a national team should be entirely composed of indigenous players most agree that the team should be as representative as possible in order to engage as many cricketers and potential cricketers in the country. The difficulty is with the interpretation of representative. Most national teams on the continent are representative of the cricket-playing community in the country. With cricket in most countries concentrated in particular ethnic communities it is unrealistic to make the national team reflective of demographic trends in the country overall.

Selection on racial grounds has been a contentious issue within Test-playing nations, with positive discrimination being applied in both South Africa and Zimbabwe to redress an historical imbalance. This is one of the stated reasons why Kevin Pietersen left South Africa to get greater opportunity in England. Teams in continental

Europe have taken different approaches. Most have just selected the best players whatever their ethnic origin and not worried about perceptions. But some have followed a policy of selecting indigenous players even when these are a minority within the cricket-playing community. This positive discrimination has been applied to ensure credibility. Some member boards and selectors simply don't want to have an expat-dominated team wearing national shirts. It follows of course that expats and cricketers from certain ethnic groups within those countries are marginalised.

There are other sporting examples in Europe where strong, truly representative national teams have developed from an initial expat base. Italian rugby has been integrated into the top tier regional tournaments in recent years, with the national team playing in the Six Nations and leading club sides in the Heineken Cup. This success was built upon a long-term policy of blending talented expats with emerging local talent. Once a virtuous cycle of rising profile and development is initiated the player base and talent pool naturally increased and became more diverse. If this cycle can be sustained over a long period the quality and diversity of players is such that selection based on merit will naturally align with a representative national team. What is critical in achieving this ambition is having a long-term development vision and not being judged too early in the process.

Striking a balance between a development focus and winning games is difficult. Japan applied a self-imposed rule that the national team must include a minimum of seven indigenous players. This was introduced to provide opportunities to and engage Japanese youth and make them feel cricket was their game and not a foreign sport just played by expats. However, this policy rendered them uncompetitive against expat-dominated teams in the WCL and after several years they fell out of the tournament. But despite this short-term setback this policy may yet pay dividends in the long term if Japanese youth identify with and adopt the sport. In Europe Italy imposed strict regulations on its clubs to select native players and the national team were all native Italians. This native team proved hopelessly uncompetitive in international tournaments which led to a switch in policy to play foreign-based cricketers with Italian passports along with the best of the South Asian players in domestic cricket.

* * * * *

Although national teams are the most visible outward projection of cricket in the region they represent only a tiny fraction of cricket played on the continent. The demographic trends and cultural shifts in the region have also had a significant impact on the way cricket is played and in turn this has had an impact on how cricket is run. Traditionally the often isolated cricketing communities on the continent had been based around a strong club culture. Often these were either founded by Englishmen or part of multi-sport clubs on a European model and therefore had constitutions, structured organisation, links to the local community and a development focus. The larger of these could run multiple teams at different age groups and consolidate and boost the profile of cricket in the area. The importance of a thriving network of well-run clubs to support healthy grass roots development has been seen in England, Ireland and Scotland. These clubs can ensure local implementation of national initiatives to boost participation, provide a talent flow into regional and national representative teams and ensure the game is played in the right spirit. Representation of clubs on national committees and boards ensured a consistent approach to and links between recreational, league and international cricket.

The influx of new players into the region from a different cultural background has had an impact on this club culture. Alongside traditional clubs run on this structured European model a plethora of new teams have sprung up across the region, formed by or incorporating players originating in South Asia. National boards generally apply rules of membership for clubs, ensuring that they meet certain criteria before they can enter official leagues. This has been done both to ensure clubs remain a catalyst for grass roots development and that they support the development initiatives of the national boards. However, the European club structure and ethos is not common on the subcontinent and it has been a challenge for boards to apply these principles consistently. Many expat players have complained about or resisted attempts to enforce structure and adherence to a national strategy. First and foremost they want to play and win. A more long-term approach or application of a development focus is, for many, an unnecessary distraction. Of course this sentiment can apply to cricketers from any ethnic background but is more likely for those who have played their formative cricket in a different cultural setting where cricket is played in a less structured and regulated environment.

National boards across the continent have been under pressure from ICC Europe to implement structured, long-term plans for development. But the majority of new participants in their countries have come from a culture where cricket below professional level is largely unstructured. Inevitably this has caused some tensions, some of which have had significant ramifications.

From a national board's perspective a network of strong clubs spread throughout the country can provide regional hubs for development. These clubs can take responsibility for raising the profile of cricket and boosting participation in the region, while developing talent for national development programmes. However, if the primary motivation of a player is to play as often as they can they may place more importance in being in the first XI than being part of a large club where competition for places may be stiffer. This motivation allied to a natural wish to play with friends from a similar background has meant a great proliferation of 'clubs' have been founded across the region. While on the one hand this provides an encouraging statistic for the expansion of club cricket it has made it more challenging to apply a common purpose and a unifying strategy within each country.

An example of this trend and the challenges it brings can be seen in Oslo. Despite limited playing numbers there are now a remarkable 57 clubs in the city, which possesses only four grounds! When a club has attracted more than 20 players it has tended to splinter into two different clubs. This ensures everyone gets a game and there is the added incentive of clubs getting grants directly from the government. One of the consequences of this trend is that clubs have not grown sufficiently to be able to finance and run youth teams. Senior players do not want to surrender their place in the team and therefore youth players get frozen out and denied opportunities to play. This is one of the major challenges facing the Norwegian Cricket Board who are struggling to implement their strategy for youth development due to the nature of how club cricket has developed in the country. But it isn't just the newer cricketing nations that face this challenge. Even in the Netherlands where many of the leading clubs were formed in the late 19th century the KNCB felt compelled to launch a club charter to encourage formation of youth teams and a development focus at club level.

One of the defining challenges for member boards in recent decades has been managing the tensions that have arisen between different and at times diverging objectives of the board and many of its cricketers. While boards look to develop a cricketing culture many of the players just want to play and resent being asked to contribute to achieving a longer-term ambition. For every continental cricketer that is enthused about playing their part in developing a cricketing nation and leaving a legacy for the next generation there will be those who take a self-centred attitude. Unless boards can get widespread support for a vision of development they are vulnerable. If they are not careful they can be stuck between an ICC rock and a hard place in the form of club opposition.

The majority of cricket administrations on the continent are run on a democratic membership model. Clubs pay membership subscriptions and in return they get a say on the policies and governance of cricket in the country. If they don't agree with how their money is spent they can challenge it. If they don't share the ambitions of the board they can vote them out. In practice this means that the organisation of cricket in each country is determined by what is important to its cricketers and not the strategic objectives of the ICC. But while the ICC sanctioned a considerable degree of intervention through its regional offices in shaping development plans and targeting funding at achieving its key success indicators it does not intervene in the governance of its member boards.

The governance and constitution of member boards does not make for engaging copy for the cricketing press and most cricket fans remain largely ignorant of the philosophical battle that has been waged across the continent over the last decade. For it has been a battle fought beyond the public eye, in boardrooms and committee meetings. On one side there are the champions of development. Their priority is to lay the foundations for growth. They aim to establish cricket as a recognised sport in their country, raise its profile, broaden its appeal and enthuse the younger generation. They dream of seeing their team play at a World Cup or in a Test match, with coverage on terrestrial television. They want cricket to be introduced to all schoolchildren and one day to be a professional sport. For the champions of development opportunities are to be seized upon and constraints to be overcome. But they are opposed by a group you could term the 'here and nows'. They want to play as much cricket as they can in the best conditions possible. They want to see the benefits themselves, not build for a utopian future built on an unrealistic dream. They want to play cricket in Europe but are not committed to the development of European cricket.

The fate of cricket in the region rests on who wins most support in these battles. Sadly the pattern in recent years is that the champions of development have been voted out in favour of those promising short-term benefits to clubs. In many countries the dreamers have either lost their mandate or remain under constant pressure and in turn the ICC are losing their agents of development. Some newly elected boards have withdrawn funding from development initiatives such as school programmes and participation schemes and instead targeted funding at clubs, to enable ground improvements or to reduce match fees paid by players. As a result across much of the continent cricket has become more insular and less ambitious. If you don't believe in a dream it certainly won't become a reality.

If this trend continues there is a risk that cricket on the continent will become increasingly unstructured. If the payment of match fees and avoiding irritating regulations become the most important issues for cricketers then many will simply leave formal leagues.

This will take them beyond the reach or influence of the national boards. Playing in tape ball cricket matches with friends may be more appealing than having to pay subs to club and commit to midweek training. It is not as fanciful as it may seem to envisage a future where the number of cricketers on the continent increases dramatically but that the number of clubs and formal leagues decrease.

* * * * *

Cricket has played an important role in integrating economic migrants from South Asia into European society and this valuable contribution of the sport has been recognised by governments. The sport has provided cohesion for communities and provided a positive outlet for cultural expression. Reflecting its importance, some governments on the continent have given funding to national cricket boards to provide opportunities for immigrants to play. This funding has helped improve infrastructure and facilities and pay for the additional equipment required for a much expanded player base. In Scandinavia these ethnic integration grants are considerable, dwarfing the funding provided by the ICC. This trend has extended to other ethnic groups too, with Roma children in the Balkans and the Moroccan communities in the Netherlands.

In the last few years cricket has provided solace, purpose and identify to thousands of refugees who have arrived in continental Europe after fleeing conflict in their homelands. Some boards have taken this humanitarian role to their hearts and worked tirelessly with limited resources to provide opportunities for refugees to play, helping build their confidence and provide some familiarity in an unfamiliar country. Cricket development officers across the region have been in to refugee camps to play their part.

Cricket isn't all about targets and development pathways. It is about having fun, building bonds of friendship and contributing to a team and a community.

* * * * *

Playing cricket on the continent isn't easy. In fact the one characteristic that all cricketers in the region share is the determination to overcome challenges. Many travel over 300 kilometres to play, spending longer in their cars than on the pitch. Driving past pristine football grounds they arrive at a public park, or a piece of rough ground too remote or uneven to attract developers. For that is where minority sports like cricket exist, in the margins. Do they have enough players or enough bats? Will there be enough teams to be able to run a league next season? Will they be able to retain access to the pathetic patch of grass they play on? These are the questions that exercise a continental cricketer's brain. It is a primeval state they exist in, just seeking to survive. But that gives them a shared bond with fellow survivors and that is what makes cricket in the region so special.

* * * * *

Albania

The only cricket match to be staged in Albania was inspired by the nation's love for Britain's cheeky, cherubic post-war comic actor Norman Wisdom. Under the regime of communist dictator Enver Hoxha Wisdom's slapstick capers were the only Western films allowed to be shown, elevating him to national hero status. So perhaps it was only natural that in 2015 a cricket match was organised to mark a hundred years since his birth on a pitch laid at a football stadium in Tirana. It can only be hoped that in reverence to their hero cricket will catch on in the country.

Andorra

This tiny precipitous principality wedged between France and Spain in the eastern Pyrenees appears an odd place to play cricket and oddly this is exactly why a match was played there in 2012. Always looking for an adventure and another country to tick off, the Dutch Odd Places Cricket Club contacted Britain's honorary counsel, Fiona Dean, to ask for her help in staging the country's first ever cricket match. With her assistance a match was organised on a football pitch at the town of Ordino, 1,300 metres above sea level, with the occasion making the front page of the local newspaper.

Austria

Cricket was first played in Austria after the founding of the Vienna Cricket Club in 1975 by Kerry Tattersall, a teacher at the city's Handelsakademie school. Two more clubs were founded in Vienna in the 1980s and in 1990 Austria played its first international tournament, the European Cricketer Cup, recording a maiden victory against Luxembourg. In 1992 Austria joined the ICC as an affiliate member.

Austria faced the limitations of grounds and facilities like every other emerging cricket nation in the region but in 1995 they came up with a bold, if a little barmy, idea to help raise the profile of the game. Wanting to host an international tournament and play a leading role in the efforts of the European Cricket Federation to spread the game but lacking a suitable venue they came up with an ingenious plan. They secured the use of a large ship moored in the mighty Danube River and this vessel played host to a European indoor tournament. The hosts were obviously inspired by their inspiration, making it to the final, where they lost to Greece.

Later that year the focus returned to more conventional cricketing settings when the first dedicated cricket ground in the country was opened in Seebarn, a short distance north of Vienna. This provided the country's cricketers with their first proper artificial wicket and niceties such as sight screens. In 1996 they won the European indoor championships held at Lord's and in the summer hosted France in a two-match series at Seebarn, the first international fixture played outdoors in the country. The following year Velden Cricket Club's ground was opened in Latschatch, which remains one of the most picturesque on the continent. By the new millennium there were around 400 active cricketers in the country representing 11 clubs.

In 2001 they were promoted from the ECC Trophy to the B division of the European championships but were unable to defeat any of the more established associate nations. Despite modest success in tournaments and a small player base Austria has produced two players of genuine quality. Leg-spinner Lakmal Kasturiarachchige had impressed in the European championships in 2002 and was considered one of the most promising young players in Europe, going on to attend the legendary Terry Jenner's leg-spin clinic at Lord's. Batsman Satyam Subhash, having played representative cricket for Austria from under-15 level, impressed sufficiently to be given a trial by Somerset.

After the restructure of ICC regional tournaments and a year break from European competition Austria finished third in European division 4 in 2009 and two years later won promotion to European T20 division 1. By 2013 they had been promoted to European division 1. However, they narrowly missed out on qualifying for division 6 of the World Cricket League. Their next ICC tournament will be WCL Europe division 1 in 2017 alongside Norway, France and Belgium. This will be another opportunity to qualify for the global WCL structure for the first time.

There are currently 400 cricketers and 16 cricket clubs in the country. The main competition is the 50-over Open League with a T20 tournament played in the summer and an international sixes tournament held at Velden. There is a national academy at the Markommenstrasse ground in Vienna, which is the focus for Austria's development programme.

Since 2000 a youth tournament has been organised in Vienna called the Future Schools Cup, featuring boys, and girls teams, between the ages of five and 14. In 2016 this featured teams from Germany, Czech Republic, Hungary and Slovakia.

The number of senior players has remained stable at around 200 since 2002 although the introduction of youth sections by several clubs has seen junior playing numbers rise tenfold. There has been a commitment to developing the number of coaches and umpires in the country but there are only four grounds, a constraint to further growth. Austria received a mere $15,000 in ICC funding in 2016.

Belgium

When Ken Farmiloe moved to Belgium from England in the late 1980s he was surprised by how good the standard of club cricket was. There was no formal league or organisational structure at this time although levels of participation had grown due to increased levels of immigration and the presence of organisations, institutions and multinational companies based in Brussels as the administrative centre of the EU. By the late 1980s several clubs had been established in Brussels and Mechelen and the Belgian Cricket Federation was established in 1990, becoming an affiliate member of the ICC a year later.

Although a representative team was selected to appear in the European Cricketer Cup in 1990, which led to the formation of a national team, there was little progress in developing the game beyond existing clubs and communities. Ken Farmiloe, playing his cricket in Antwerp, was asked to become the chairman in 2000 to give some strategic direction to the federation. Gradually the geographic spread of cricket within the country increased, with clubs established in Ghent, Ostende, Meise, Liege, Hassalt and Sint-Truiden. He placed the focus on youth and encouraged the development of youth sections in clubs, working closely with Martin O'Connor. There was growing interest amongst expat kids in Brussels and Antwerp and informal youth games were organised. This focus was replicated, albeit on a smaller scale, in Ghent and Ostende.

Although the BCF was becoming more ambitious there was, according to Ken Farmiloe, 'a limit to what we could do without more funding'. In order to overcome this constraint an application was made for elevation to associate member status, which brought with it a significant funding increase to $150,000 a year. ICC Europe were content that facilities and the structure of domestic cricket met the criteria, although there was a question mark over the performance levels of the national team. Nevertheless associate status was granted in 2005 and this provided funding to develop a national youth team structure that supported national team representation down to under-13 level in regional tournaments. Despite the fact that there isn't a particular emphasis on or much government support for sport in Belgian schools the BCF launched schools programmes in five cities. This boosted participation numbers but it proved challenging to convert these initiatives into more regular youth players in clubs. Courses were organised for PE teachers to teach cricket in their schools and many proved enthusiastic but the BCF lacked funding for school liaison and regional development officers to oversee this process.

Despite this challenge, through the commitment of BCF coach Faizal Mahmood 50 school visits across Belgium were organised in 2011 where over 2,000 children were introduced to the sport. In 2012 the board agreed that from 2015 it would be a requirement for all clubs in the country to have a junior section. There was however some opposition to this from clubs who saw it as an unnecessary expense.

With the financial pressures of running a development programme and funding national team tours at senior and age group level the board looked to complement the ICC grant with sponsorship. By 2011 the board were also focusing on developing the women's game, in line with objectives set by the ICC's development programme. The board managed to secure sponsorship from diamond companies based in Antwerp and also looked to innovative ways of generating revenue, such as hosting Bollywood film nights.

As well as funding difficulties a constant challenge for the board was the availability of grounds. In addition to the challenge of securing long-term availability of existing grounds it was also becoming difficult to find the additional grounds required to run an extended league with a growing player base. With cricket being very much a minority sport in the country and with a very low public profile it proved difficult to get the support and funding necessary to secure access for cricket over the claims of other sports or other land uses. This proved the case for the Antwerp club that lost its ground in Brunst. The club approached the sports minister and vice-mayor of Antwerp and invited him to Lord's for an ICC President's Day to watch a Test match. This had the desired effect with the mayor becoming a convert to cricket and promising his support. He authorised the handover of an existing football facility in the city to the cricket federation. This not only provided space for four grounds, senior and youth, but also practice facilities and office space.

The club raised revenue by renting the ground to an American football team in the winter and also received subsidies from the city when it became an accredited sporting club. City authorities in Bruges and Sint Trouton also provided land for grounds. A key element of securing this funding was to demonstrate how cricket could help social integration of different ethnic groups. The board supported clubs in developing their infrastructure through a grant process to provide matting and other equipment.

In parallel to investing in youth development and supporting clubs the BCF also looked to improve elite performance. A more structured selection process was introduced in the early 2000s and in 2002 an elite performance camp was held in Folkestone, Kent. An improvement in ranking was a key strategic objective and this was achieved under the stewardship of former England player, Jack Richards, who instilled a greater level of commitment and professionalism. He introduced weekly training sessions with the national squad and challenged anyone not showing sufficient commitment to improve. A regular training programme and additional preparation time to bond as a squad was a crucial factor in Belgium qualifying for the World Cricket League in 2012, taking the team from a regional to global tournament structure. Despite the challenge of the heat and unfamiliar conditions in Samoa they performed well with Faisal Khaliq and Abdul Rehman finishing joint second top wicket-takers. However, despite this bowling strength they could only finish fourth, outside the promotion places.

When the WCL was cut to six and then five divisions Belgium were unable to requalify though they will have a further opportunity next year in WCL Europe qualifier division 1. They proved reasonably competitive at regional level in T20 tournaments, finishing second to Norway in European division 2 in Essex in 2014. Their squad was captained by Brighton Watambwa who took 14 wickets in six Tests for Zimbabwe in the early 2000s. He had settled in Brussels after a spell in the USA.

In 2014 there was a takeover of the board and Sanjay Vaid became chairman. With financial pressures now even more pressing given the change from the block grant to the scorecard funding model the new board sought to align strategy and resource to the scorecard categories of increasing the number of participants, junior players and coaches. A schools tournament was held in 2014 and more are planned across a number of cities. In addition to the national league and T20 competition a sponsored T20 tournament, the Senior Citizens Memorial Tournament, has been formally included in the cricketing calendar.

Reflecting a broader trend on the continent in the last year, the federation and member clubs have been approached by an increasing number of new immigrants and refugees. In Antwerp large numbers of Afghan refugees have been turning up to training sessions from processing camps in the region. This has led to increased pressure on resources. There is also a rise in interest in the women's game despite only one club existing in the country. Investment in the women's game has been a contentious issue at annual general meetings due to the limited number of players in the country and the focus on a single club. But the BCF have encouraged clubs to develop women's teams and attracting more girls to the game is now a key part of the schools development programme. The youth programme has now been formalised through a BCF academy, that runs sessions for around 70 children of all age groups a year.

There are currently 21 clubs in the country with the greatest concentration in the traditional cricketing centres of Antwerp and Brussels but with an increasing number in the regions of Wallonia, Flanders and Limburg. There are just under 600 senior players and nearly 200 juniors. A critical constraint in increasing this further is the limited number of grounds. The schools programme and other initiatives saw over 5,000 introduced to the game in 2014 although there remains a challenge in translating this to senior player numbers. However, the further potential for growth is demonstrated by the increasing number playing informal, modified games. A focus on coach development saw the number of qualified coaches quadruple over the last decade with the number of umpires almost doubling over the same period.

The game is very much dominated by players of South Asian origin with many new clubs founded exclusively for particular ethnic groups. The key to promoting a greater level of ethnic diversity and more interest from indigenous players will be establishing a national schools programme and league. The board are targeting a return to the World Cricket League in order to qualify for performance funding from the ICC.

To mark the bicentenary of Waterloo a T20 game was played before the re-enactment of the battle.

Bosnia

Cricket is in an embryonic stage in the country. There are only two clubs but links are being made to other countries in the region. A Bosnian team toured the Czech Republic in 2014.

Bulgaria

The presence of cricket in Bulgaria is largely due to university professor Nikolai Kolev of the National Sports Academy. He has been a passionate advocate of minority sports in the country, introducing rugby and baseball in addition to cricket. In the late 20th century there were strict controls of what sports could be played in the former Eastern bloc. This prevented any non-traditional sports being imported and getting any official recognition or support. However, in 1999 the National Sports Academy signed the Bologna Agreement to permit new sports to be played. When some students approached

Professor Kolev, who lectured in rugby, football and tennis, with an interest in cricket he agreed to offer it as an optional discipline for students at the academy. To achieve this he sought support from ICC Europe and was given training materials and invited to the ICC conference to learn more about the sport. He also attended an indoor championship in Denmark to see how a cricket event was planned and run. Several cricket teams were founded and registered under Bulgarian law and the Bulgarian Cricket Federation was formed.

From its inception the federation sought to develop the game as a Bulgarian sport, focusing on youth development through sports and universities. Although there were some expat clubs, such as the Pakistani Bulgarian Cricket Club and a team of Indian medical students, Mr Kolev was committed to an indigenous development model. In 2003 the first national championships was held. This featured four clubs, including one from the Black Sea town of Varna. The following year a course was held to train local cricket coaches. 2004 also saw the Bulgarian national team compete for the first time, at the European Cricket Council Representative Championship held in Ljublana, Slovenia. With a very inexperienced and youthful side they were outclassed by opponents featuring wizened expats and were on the wrong end of some chastening results. In their first ever international Bulgaria conceded 322 in 35 overs against Switzerland, making a mere 66 in reply, only 42 of which came off the bat. It was an example of how boards who select native players, irrespective of their ability, can struggle to compete against sides that field experienced expat club cricketers. In this sense pride comes not from the result but in the commitment to playing native players, whatever the outcome.

The federation came under the wing of the Bulgarian Ministry for Sports that provided them with facilities at the National Sports Academy and limited funding to run a calendar of events. They joined as an affiliate member of the ICC in 2008, providing additional funding and making them eligible to play in official tournaments. In 2009 they warmed up for ICC division 5 by taking part in the Carmel Euro T20, held in Flintshire, Wales, where they faced the tiny Channel Island of Alderney in surely one of the most obscure international games ever played. At division 5 later that summer they won their first authorised international, beating Estonia, though they were indebted to expats Tewatia and Hanif for the victory. They finished joint fourth in the tournament, which was bottom of the bottom rung of the European tournament structure. Only three years later they played in their last official ICC tournament in European Championship division 3 Twenty20, held in Tallinn, Estonia. Once again they propped up the table, though they did defeat Estonia once again.

Bulgaria were one of the victims of the decision by ICC Europe to contract its tournament schedule. With the expansion of its membership the cost of running multiple leagues across multiple formats for men, women and age groups was significant but they also felt that teams in the lower leagues, like Bulgaria, were not competitive enough for international tournaments and should focus on developing domestic cricket, in the short term at least. What annoyed the boards who had been cut adrift was that there was no transparent process for how to re-qualify for the tournament structures, just a vague commitment that if standards rose they would be re-incorporated.

This meant that Bulgaria, like many other teams on the continent, either had to restrict their ambitions to domestic tournament structures or make their own arrangements for international fixtures. In truth Bulgaria had only had the briefest flirtation with officially sanctioned tournaments anyway, so merely returned to playing in unofficial tournaments. In 2013 the BCF took the initiative to form the Balkan Cricket Association to facilitate collaboration and organise tournaments between teams in the region. Greece, Serbia, Macedonia and Romania became members. The association runs senior and junior tournaments for both men and women, with countries taking it in turn to host. This model of regional collaboration is one of the ways countries can fill the vacuum of international fixtures left by the withdrawal of tournaments and support from the ICC. The close proximity keeps costs to a minimum and enables tournaments to be held over weekends, enabling players to fit cricket around work or study. This makes it far easier to incorporate into strategic planning within very tight budgets. It also enables the member countries to set their own priorities such as the development of native players, a shared ambition of countries in the region. The formation of the Balkan Cricket Association further strengthened the BCF's relationship with the Hellenic Cricket Federation, the most established cricketing centre in the region. Bulgaria also send an annual team to the International Schools Tournament in Corfu, where the idea for forming women's teams first emerged.

A key part of the federation's cricket development for 2020 that has emerged from the annual operational plans submitted to ICC Europe is a focus on schools and universities. They have established a Bulgarian Students Cricket Union that seeks to organise leagues and raise the profile of cricket in the country's universities. This has been successful and there is now a university tournament as part of the domestic calendar. The union also established the first European Universities Cricket Trophy under the auspices of the European University Sports Association. The university programme and mass participation initiatives were supported by targeted grants from ICC Europe.

In schools a programme called 'Cricket Friends' has been established in conjunction with the municipality of Sofia and is run on an annual basis to introduce cricket to teachers and children. There are plans to extend this programme to other cities. This forms part of a four-year national development strategy launched in 2014 in association with the Ministry of Sport to support a broader governmental ambition to increase levels of exercise amongst the population.

There are currently 15 cricket clubs in the country, several of which combine cricket with softball and baseball. Although concentrated in Sofia there are also clubs in Varna, Dupnitsa, Pravets, Gabrovo, Blagoevgrad, Botevgrad, and Razgrad with applications being processed for ones in Plovdiv and Pleven. In addition to support from the BCF clubs can apply to regional government for funding to run courses for children, promote exercise and achieve sporting excellence. Recognition in the Olympics would increase such funding considerably.

The domestic cricket calendar consists of an indoor championship played in winter and a national championship, T20 tournament, knockout cup, schools tournament and university tournament in the summer season. These are played across grounds in Sofia, Varna, Gabrovo and Blagoevgrad.

Supplementing the domestic structure Bulgaria is also becoming a destination for touring clubs, playing host to at least three touring sides a year and with established links to several clubs in the UK. In 2015 a partnership was formed with Yapham CC which includes not only bilateral tours but also joint training programmes and player exchanges.

For the Bulgarian Cricket Federation, rooted as it is in the National Cricket Academy, it is clear that development of cricket amongst native players is far more important than enabling expat players to play. The development programme is targeted directly at native players, through both schools and universities. This appears to align with government objectives unlike in many other countries in continental Europe where funding is provided to cricket because of its appeal to immigrant communities and its role in supporting social integration.

While this policy to focus on native players has been lauded by many it also has limited opportunities for the growing number of expats in the country. They may well participate in the leagues but with a few exceptions selection for the national team is drawn from native players, even if they are inferior in ability. This has led to some ill-feeling between the board and expat players. One such case is Saif Rehman, who represented Bulgaria in their first ever international and formerly a fixture in the national team, helping bring through a generation of native players before losing his place in the side to them. But it is for his contributions to cricket off the field that he has won wider acclaim. Rehman has done much to promote opportunities for those with disabilities, introducing table cricket to several institutions in the city, and with great success. Doctors have said table cricket has been instrumental in improving movement and mental stimulation.

The success of his table cricket sessions inspired him to introduce cricket to those with other disabilities. He formed a team for blind cricketers which led to the formation of the Bulgarian blind national team, which meets for regular training sessions in Sofia. When not supporting disability cricket he is a soap star and former semi-finalist in *Bulgaria's Got Talent*. As you do. It is heart-warming that a form of cricket can have such a positive impact in such an unlikely destination.

Since 2008 there has been a steady increase in participation levels with 330 senior cricketers in the country and 220 youth players. Bulgaria has almost 500 beginner level coaches as a result of its programme of seminars, though less than ten intermediate level coaches. This reflects the focus on engaging youth and building mass participation rather than developing elite performance. They currently receive $15,000 in ICC grant.

Croatia

As with much of the rest of the continent it was an influx of expats from cricket-playing cultures that provided the catalyst for the emergence of the sport in the country. But in Croatia it was historic emigration to Australia rather than economic migration from South Asia that provided the source. Following independence in the early 1990s children of Croatian emigrants returned to the country and brought a passion for cricket back with them. In 1998 two such Aussie-born Croats, Robert Dumancic and Ivan Bilic, missing playing cricket, heard of a cricket club over the border in Ljubljana, Slovenia and put together a ragtag team to play them. Despite the lack of experience in this makeshift squad they nevertheless returned from the game inspired to form a club in Zagreb. They did just that in 2000 although, lacking equipment and a ground, they were condemned to be permanently on tour over the border.

ICC Europe and the British embassy helped the fledgling club by providing equipment and without a second thought they accepted an invitation to play in the ECC Representative Festival alongside other fledgling European cricket nations. There they faced familiar opposition in the form of Slovenia along with Finland, Norway and hosts Austria. Their playing strength was significantly boosted with the addition of the Vujnovich brothers, who had played cricket to a high level in New Zealand. Their quality and experience helped Croatia finish second: a remarkable achievement for a country without a single cricket ground and where the only club had been founded only months before. This adventure helped unify the squad further and harden their resolve to establish cricket in the country. They joined the ICC as an affiliate nation in 2001 and Zagreb CC joined the Austrian league. This meant a drive of at least four hours to every game. The travel sapped the energy of the players and they only secured a single victory in their first two seasons.

Despite the enthusiasm of the players the future of Croatian cricket remained vulnerable until they could secure a ground. As ever in such a predicament a saviour is required and this came in the form of the generosity of the Frankopan family, who acquired a ground in the centre of Zagreb in 2002. This provided a home ground at last and never ones to rest on their laurels no sooner had it opened than Croatia's cricketers were hosting their first international tournament, the next instalment of the ECC Representatives Festival.

In 2004 in the new ICC Europe tournament framework they competed in and won European division 4 but found the level far more competitive in division 3 the next year and finished seventh out of nine teams. However, in the same tournament in 2007 they were champions which saw them take part in a historic match, the first official international hosted by Israel. They won that play-off in Tel Aviv and were promoted to division 2. But here their upward trajectory ceased as they came last. But even so it had been a quite dizzying decade. By 2009, not yet ten years after the formation of the first club in the country, they had played 40 internationals, winning 17. Their star players were the Vujnovich brothers and Christopher Pivac, without whom they would not have risen through the tournament structure to division 2.

The club in Zagreb was joined by the formation of a club in Split and the romantic resurgence of cricket on the island of Vis, where Englishman Sir William Hoste had introduced cricket in his brief term as governor in the Napoleonic era. The admiral's great-great niece, Dorothy Burrows, played a key role bringing together her fellow descendents of the sea-lord for a match against the club that bore his name. It was quite a logistical feat to coordinate, all the more so for an octogenarian. The MCC, always keen on a tour, especially to sunny climes with an imperial link, sent a team, featuring county stars Darren Bicknell and Rob Turner, to play Croatia at Vis's Plisko Polje Ground. They came bearing gifts in the form of a combined $3,750 grant from the MCC and ICC that was used to fund coaching courses.

However, despite the formation of an indoor league in 2010 the domestic structure of cricket in the country had not developed in parallel with advancement of the national team squad and they failed to meet the criteria to play in official ICC tournaments. This has meant that international representation has been limited to unsanctioned, regional tournaments over the last few years.

In 2010 the Croatian Cricket Federation produced a five-year strategic plan. This was intended to grow and raise the profile of cricket in the country and address the development issues and concerns raised by ICC Europe. The priorities were to ensure that the number of senior and junior clubs in the country increased to at least the minimum level required to fulfil affiliate membership criteria. The plan also targeted the development of a women's league, again a requirement of their ICC membership. In addition the plan pledged to form international youth teams at under-13 and under-15 level, to improve participation levels and governance at clubs, to ensure regular media coverage for cricket in the country and to attract greater levels of non-ICC income through sponsors and partners. Unsurprisingly these focus areas aligned very closely with ICC Europe priorities and the scorecard funding categories.

As part of the plan the federation set out the strengths and weaknesses of cricket in the country. The strengths were listed as a strong national team, passionate members and links to embassies while the weaknesses included an aging demographic within the player base, the limited number of clubs and regular players, the small expat community and the lack of media coverage. The threats to realising the ambitions set out in the plan are depressingly common across the region.

The dominance of football makes it very difficult for cricket to gain a foothold in the country and it remains a virtually unknown sport. Lack of facilities and funding was also highlighted as a significant constraint.

Croatia are not alone in needing to be increasingly innovative in generating income, with the plan starkly admitting that ICC income alone was insufficient to run the game. In recent years ICC Europe has put increasing pressure on federations and boards across the region to reduce their reliance on ICC grants, with the level of non-ICC income given a high weighting in the scorecard funding model. In Croatia fund-raising ideas included establishing a supporters' club home and abroad with an annual subscription fee to help fund educational initiatives, selling branded caps and kit, raffles and even opening a Cricket Bar in the capital to help fund the work of the federation. It was hoped that these initiatives would help increase funding from $80,000 in 2010 to over $150,000.

The plan to boost junior involvement naturally centred on increasing the access to cricket in schools, including the pilot of programmes to introduce cricket as part of teaching English. Securing cricket as a regular part of school curriculums was the ultimate ambition, although achieving this when cricket had such a low profile in the country was extremely challenging. There was also a realisation that children needed something to play for and strive towards, such as international representation, training programmes and events and hosting international tournaments. It was hoped that new clubs could be formed in Podravina, Vadar, Istria and Slavonia and ambitious targets were set for increasing the numbers of umpires, coaches and scorers. Croatia's strength of connections in other countries through its diaspora, especially in Australasia, was also targeted in the plan to build links with clubs and communities in Australia and New Zealand and to arrange exchange programmes for talented young Croatian players.

Achieving these ambitions was always going to be challenging given the constraints of limited funding and the game's very low public profile. The transformative progress aspired to in the plan has not materialised, although there has been some progress made. To fill the vacuum left by falling out of the official ICC tournament structure Croatia have participated in several bilateral tournaments at both senior and junior level. In 2010 the Budenec Cup was inaugurated, hosting junior teams from Hungary and Slovenia, while the senior team has played in the Euro T20 Cup and Tri Nations Cup. Domestically the federation have sought to extend the reach of cricket in the country, running cricket clinics in towns such as Bjelovar, Berek, Cazma and Kastela. This initiative has increased interest and playing numbers amongst youth and several tournaments have been established, including at Cazma school and an annual youth indoor tournament. They have been supported by the British embassy and by the Croatian Olympic Committee, of which the federation joined as a full member in 2010.

Although the number of clubs has not increased as hoped there has been some success in promoting Croatia as a cricket tourism destination. The federation have got support from the Tourism Committee of the Croatian Parliament to boost this further and in addition to touring clubs playing club sides the creation of the Vis Sixes has proved a popular annual tournament. Perth-born Michael Grzinic has been very influential both as a player and coach for the national team, but also in increasing the standard of coaching in the country and providing the drive to establish new tournaments and initiatives to support the domestic game. His illustrious fellow countryman, Simon Katich, one of a number of players of Croatian origin to have played Test cricket, has also played a role. He has lent his name to the domestic cup and is also the ambassador for the Mediterranean Cricket league, a new tournament launched in 2016 that featured teams from Ukraine, India, Romania and Montenegro. The federation also secured a coup in getting national football icon Luka Modric, of Real Madrid and formerly Tottenham Hotspur, quoted as being a fan of the game.

With considerably less immigration from southern Asia Croatia has not seen the growth in participation levels and clubs witnessed in Germany and elsewhere across the continent, and the core of Croatian cricket remains the community of Australasian expats of Croatian origin who have been the driving force both on and off the field. If the federation can successfully market the country as a cricket tourism destination and attract further sponsorship then it could roll out its youth development initiatives further. But it will need more clubs and a broader demographic draw if it is to make significant progress.

Cyprus

Unlike in nearby Corfu cricket was not introduced to Cyprus in the colonial era and therefore does not have such a long heritage on the island. However, cricket was played in British military bases in the immediate aftermath of the Second World War, as Britain continued its presence in the strategically located island. As in Germany it was the pitches at these British bases that enabled a civilian league to spring from military competitions. By the 1980s the island had become increasingly popular as a destination for sun-starved expats and the Moufflon club was established and integrated into the British Military Cricket League. By the end of the 20th century the number of residents aware of and wanting to play cricket increased further with economic migration from the subcontinent and the return of Cypriots who had fled during the unrest of the 1970s and had learnt cricket in Australia and South Africa. This enabled ICC membership criteria to be met and the Cyprus Cricket Association became an affiliate in 1999.

It took some time to develop a domestic structure and a league was not introduced until 2003. It was not until 2006 that the national team competed in an international tournament. The domestic league had increased to ten teams by 2007 and in 2009 the island hosted their first tournament, ICC Europe division 4, which they won. An under-15 international side was established and Cyprus competed in ICC Europe T20 division 2 in Belgium and Corfu in 2011 and 2012 respectively. With the contraction of the European tournament structure over the last five years Cyprus have had to focus on domestic and unsanctioned regional fixtures.

There are currently 15 clubs on the island, largely based in Nicosia or the traditional military and RAF bases. However, in the last few years a civilian team from Paphos in the west of the country has been formed along with a North Cyprus team based in Kyrenia. Several clubs are based either in a college or company and there are teams representing particular ethnic groups, such as Pakistanis, Sri Lankans and Bangladeshis. The domestic league has both a 40- and 20-over format and there is a women's competition. The growth in the number of clubs is constrained by the number of venues available. Cyprus does have an advantage in this regard thanks to the grounds at military bases, although tight security controls means all players require passes and prior permission to enter. There are five cricket venues on the island, one being at the UN airbase with stunning views of the Kyrenia mountains. The main base is the Happy Valley site, technically on British soil, which hosted European division 4 in 2009 and has three grounds.

Cyprus's political context has always had an impact on cricket in the country, from the military origin of its clubs and grounds to the diplomatically sensitive division between north and south. But cricket has been a unifying factor too. In 2015 a North Cyprus Cricket League was formed to complement the league south of the so-called 'green line'. A historic milestone was achieved when the North Cyprus Cricket Club was given permission to enter the buffer zone to play a fixture, the first time any sporting team had been allowed to do so. But unfortunately this has not led to a full integration of cricket on the island. Nevertheless there has been a drive to improve facilities in the north and attract Turkish Cypriots to the game.

The development of its own ground has been a priority for the CCA for many years and recently they acquired a long-term lease for a dedicated ground at Techni, a village located between Limassol and Larnaca. Following the removal of trees and flattening of the area, concrete pitches and a grass outfield are being laid. A dedicated facility open to civilians and not having to compete with rival sports will provide a central hub for cricket on the island. It is also intended as the base for national team training and youth development

An ongoing challenge for the CCA is boosting the cricketing player base in the context of an often transient population. Military postings are often limited to several years and the population of economic migrants can fluctuate too. This makes it difficult to create stability at both club and international level and some of the most talented players leave the island before they reach the four-year residency period. The CCA has also been unable to secure any formal recognition or support from the government, leaving them very reliant on an increasingly meagre grant from the ICC. Government endorsement is a necessary prerequisite to launch a coordinated schools programme that could in time reduce the dependency on players from the military and economic migrants. However, this constraint does not apply in private schools where progress has been made, allied to a recent push to increase the number of qualified coaches led by national team coach Graeme Rickman. There is undoubtedly potential to engage more locals through beach cricket formats, but the necessary promotion required to build profile and generate interest is an expense the CCA would struggle to afford. The CCA has established its own YouTube channel and produces a biannual online newsletter. Former Lancashire and Leicestershire batsman Andrea Agathangelou is of Cypriot descent but does not meet the qualification criteria set by the ICC.

Czech Republic

British embassies have played a critical role in the development of cricket across the world. It is almost an unwritten rule for ambassadors and diplomatic staff that they will lend a hand in sowing the seeds of cricket within their country of posting. So it was in Prague in 1997 that a member of staff from the British embassy arranged a fixture between interested expats and friends and colleagues from Passau and Vienna.

The interest grew from there and a ground was established in a park in the north-west of the city. From these humble origins cricket in the city grew with some interested locals taking part and a growing number of Asian expats discovering cricket was being played and taking part themselves. By 2005 there was sufficient interest to establish a league and in 2012 a new private ground in the north-eastern suburbs was acquired.

Cricket in the country remains centred on the capital, which now has four established clubs. However, the game is slowly spreading in the country and there is a team in Brno, in the south-eastern corner of the country, that is hoped can be a catalyst for growth of the game in that region. In addition to the ground in Viner a practice facility in the centre of Prague is being extended to act as a training hub and an opportunity to pique the interest of passers-by, particularly locals, through banners and a poster campaign.

With limited funding it has proved challenging to raise the profile of cricket and word of mouth remains the most effective recruitment tool. The federation has used Facebook and Twitter to raise awareness and has also worked with organisations such as the British Council to promote international tournaments. There has also been a targeted campaign to promote tournaments and the work of the federation in Irish pubs and Indian restaurants. Increasingly they are looking to focus on new media, such as online videos, to capture attention and imagination.

To date youth development has been focused on international schools in Prague, where cricket clinics and presentations are held. This has been quite successful with some children, including Czech nationals, joining local clubs and being integrated into leagues. There are plans to engage universities in the longer term. Although there have been some school visits in other parts of the country the lack of funding for a schools development officer has been a constraining factor, although the federation plan a training programme for Czech teachers to deliver cricket coaching themselves under supervision of the federation.

The league is currently played from May to July across 20- and 40-over formats but the intention is to extend the season to September. In the winter a six-a-side indoor tournament is played from January to March. The cricket calendar has also benefitted from increasingly frequent visits from touring clubs. The prospect of visiting a historic city and playing cricket into the bargain has made for an attractive proposition, with cheap, good beer and affordable flights and accommodation no doubt also proving a considerable draw. The federation hope that it can become an established destination for cricket tours and accommodate 20 visits a year.

A lack of knowledge of the game, limited funding for promotion and the difficulty of acquiring new grounds are the main challenges in establishing the game among the local culture. The small cricketing community and the sport's lack of profile also limits its appeal to sponsors. Availability of grounds is the most urgent problem with all league games currently played at Vinor, although two wickets at least enable games to be played in parallel. This is clearly a limiting factor in developing new clubs and expanding the league. However, there is a new ground being developed to the north of Prague and it is hoped that a permanent facility can be found in Brno too. A lifeline for Czech cricketers has come from increasing interest in cricket in neighbouring Germany. Friendly games have been played in Dresden, just two hours' drive from Prague, and clubs have also been able to organise competitive fixtures thanks to the development of the Berlin league.

As the Czech Republic is not incorporated into the regional tournament structure the federation have sought to foster collaboration with other countries to create an international calendar of tournaments to boost cricket in the region. They have taken an innovative approach, seeking to agree international breaks within the domestic schedules across a number of countries to enable tournaments to be organised. Through collaboration and coordination each country participating could help drive interest in these tournaments through social media to create a real buzz. But as Dan Casey, former Secretary of Czech Cricket points out, such aspirations are hard to realise, when all those involved juggle cricket with work and family commitments.

> 'The problem is, of course, that we're dealing with a lot of people all over Europe who are in a similar position – they would love to improve things, but they all have their own work or family concerns to look after too, so taking on the organisation of such tournaments can be tricky. In my experience one of the problems is being over-ambitious, rather than focusing on delivering something simple and effective.
>
> 'We are lucky we have an attractive location to host a tournament. Central Europe is a popular destination and prices are low. But unfortunately we all have correspondingly low salaries, which makes it difficult to commit to travelling for more than one tournament every year because without financial support all these costs come out of the players' own pockets. We have a strong relationship with Poland and Hungary and there is a shared commitment to playing regularly. There are a lot of potential opponents around Europe so there are lots of opportunities.'

There is an appreciation that if the game is to grow significantly in the country it will have to attract local players. While increased Indian immigration in recent years has helped boost player numbers this has not been sufficient to transform the club scene or raise the profile. There have been some notable successes in finding and developing local players, with the prime example being female left-arm seamer Magda Pokludova, who played several games for Somerset ladies. Lucas Fencl, who turned to cricket from softball, became the first native Czech cricketer to score a century.

But with a small community it has been difficult to grab the attention of the government or the media to help develop the game. The ICC have provided grant funding to help promote the game among natives and it is hoped that having a Czech ambassador for the game would engage the media and break down preconceptions that it is a foreign sport. Becoming an Olympic sport would help provide the legitimacy and endorsement required to make a genuine breakthrough. Having cricket shown on free to air television would be a significant factor in raising levels of interest. It can currently be viewed, albeit occasionally and only ever as a gap filler for other sports, on Eurosport. It is currently perceived either as a genteel English sport, or a game played by Indians.

The aspiration in the medium term is to increase the player base to around 500 active cricketers, with a greater geographical distribution in the country and access to more grounds and facilities. The importance of creating interest in the national team, through participation in well promoted tournaments, is acknowledged. By 2020 it is hoped there will be a ten-team league and cricket played regularly in ten schools.

An unusual sight in Czech cricket is an old routemaster bus that is parked by the boundary and used as a mobile pavilion. Having a long and distinguished career of service in Glasgow it was bought by the father of Czech cricketer, Ben Soucek, who having enjoyed many a holiday in the bus in his youth decided to renovate it for yet another lease of life. Though now thousands of miles away the bus still declares its destination as 'Renfrew Ferry'.

Denmark

Unlike their Scandinavian and north European neighbours Denmark already had an established cricketing community at the birth of the modern era. Although not a mainstream sport the number of cricketers had been relatively consistent in a range between 2,000 and 2,500 since the 1950s. They were one of the strongest non-Test teams in the world and had come close to qualifying for a World Cup through the ICC Trophy. The recent history of cricket in the country has been defined by an opportunity and a challenge. The opportunity came in the form of the ICC's development programme that sought to bridge the gap between the leading associates and lower ranked Test teams. The challenge was to make a sport steeped in tradition and old world values relevant and appealing to younger generations and a changing demographic.

In the 1980s Denmark had a strong national team that were very nearly the equal of the Dutch. In fact the quality of domestically produced players was similar and quite often it was only the inclusion of players with first-class experience in Test nations that had settled in the country as player-coaches that gave the Dutchmen the edge. The Danish pace bowling attack was formidable and proved a handful for any international team, let alone continental neighbours. In Ole Mortensen, Henrik Sorensen and Soren Vestergaard they possessed three bowlers good enough to play county cricket. When Australia toured Denmark in 1989 Mortensen and Sorensen bundled them out for 191 with only Tom Moody scoring a 50. But Denmark's batting was much weaker and only three batsmen made double figures as they lost to the Australians by 45 runs. But this was no humiliation and the game attracted 4,000 spectators. Denmark were competitive against one of the world's best teams, were attracting Test sides to the country and boasted a number of players good enough to have professional careers across the North Sea. Their calibre was demonstrated in that same year when they defeated Italy by 409 runs in a 40-over match.

The *annus mirabilis* in 1989 saw Denmark enter the 1990s with confidence. Their domestic league was producing some players of country calibre and they were on the cusp of qualifying for global tournaments. However, the ICC Trophy only came around every four years and it always seemed a case of nearly but not quite for the Danes. If they had got the wins needed to qualify for a World Cup the profile and the press coverage of the global stage could have ignited interest in the game back home and turned Denmark from a capable cricketing nation to a prospective full member. In retrospect it is clear that the nineties were a critical period for Danish cricket. They simply had to capitalise on the advantages that a long-established cricket culture and national league provided before other associate nations closed the gap. They had a head start, but they didn't grasp the opportunity.

Despite the disappointment of not qualifying for the 1996 World Cup, a breakthrough tournament for the global game, and having to watch at home as the Dutch enjoyed the Bollywood glamour and global publicity of the Indian hosted event, Danish cricket did secure something of a coup in 1999 by being incorporated into the English county season. This provided an opportunity for the national team to get more experience against quality opposition and also helped raise the profile of cricket in the country. Unfortunately in the six years they competed they failed to progress past the first round, limiting them to a single fixture a year.

If 1989 was an *annus mirabilis* in Danish cricket 2005 was definitely one to forget. In early May Northamptonshire visited Brondby for the first round of the Cheltenham and Gloucester Cup. It was a Tuesday, so little chance of attracting a crowd as large as that in 1989 and the damp conditions didn't help. In fact the Danish authorities had strongly advised against hosting the game so early in the Danish season. In the event water had seeped under the covers and Denmark were routed for 56 when put in to bat. South African seamer Charl Pietersen took seven wickets for ten runs. No Dane made double figures and only 32 runs came off the bat. The county side chased down the target in less than 17 overs with two wickets falling. It was a humiliating defeat and although they could cite the unluckiness of losing the toss in such conditions it spelled the ignominious end to Denmark's inclusion in county cricket. But it was only the start of what would become a defining year for Danish cricket.

In July the Danes travelled to Ireland to compete in the ICC Trophy. As a European team they were more familiar with conditions than many of their international challengers. Furthermore the ICC had enlarged the World Cup to 16 teams, meaning the leading five teams would qualify, joining Kenya. For Denmark, who had regularly been in the top four over the last few decades, this was the opportunity to finally make the World Cup. Although their bowling greats had long since retired the team included former Hampshire seamer Tom Hansen and the batting was strengthened by Freddie Klokker, who would go on to become the first Dane to score a county championship century. They finished fourth in their group which was not enough to qualify automatically but offered them another chance through a play-off. In a twist of fate it was to be against traditional foes and local rivals, the Netherlands. They were outgunned and outclassed with their bowling attack unable to tie down Dutch stars Bas Zuiderent and Daan van Bunge, who each made centuries and saw the men in orange post 314. In reply only Klokker made a half-century and the Danes limped to 225 all out.

It was yet another near miss and just as the team were coming to terms with narrowly missing out on another World Cup they were hit with a body blow by the ICC. The governing body chose this moment to select teams for the full roll-out of its High Performance Programme. The five qualifiers, along with Kenya, would be given ODI status in the lead-up to the World Cup, along with a significant funding boost and elite development support from the ICC. In effect a sub-category of membership had been created above the associates. Denmark, for so long an associate heavyweight, had been condemned to the chasing pack. With more opportunities and more funding the Netherlands were set to pull away from Denmark, establishing themselves as a team on the global stage, on an ICC-prepared path to professionalisation, playing first-class international matches through the Intercontinental Cup. Denmark meanwhile were left to lick their wounds and contemplate what the future held. They now not only had to close the gap on Test nations but a gap had appeared between them and the leading associates.

Since the era-defining setbacks of 2005 Denmark have sought to regain their position as a leading associate through climbing their way up the World Cricket League and improving performances in T20. But a combination of factors has made this challenging. Firstly there has been a significant improvement in the quality of sides in other regions, particularly in Asia, meaning Denmark are not as competitive as they once were. Secondly the availability of talented expat players and those who learnt their cricket in a Test nation but qualify through a passport has been a much more significant factor than the quality of domestic leagues. The Danes have selected only from their national leagues, in contrast to the Italians for example, who have regularly selected first-class cricketers from Australia and South Africa with Italian passports, and have not had the benefit of a team like the UAE who can select players with first-class experience in the subcontinent. Thirdly Denmark has not benefitted from the funding or support in elite development enjoyed by countries in the High Performance Programme, nor for that matter a regular programme of international fixtures to steadily improve performance and professionalism. Collectively these factors have eroded a traditional advantage the Danes had.

At the ICC Trophy in 2009, rebranded as the World Cup Qualifier, Denmark came last out of 12 teams. Such is the ICC's merit-based development pathway that every loss brings with it a further lessening of opportunity. Denmark's poor performance in 2009 saw them miss out on the regular fixtures provided to leading associates through the World Cricket League Championship. In the 50-over format they were limited to annual or biennial World Cricket League divisions, thereby increasing the gap further from those who finished above them in the 2009 tournament. It is difficult in these circumstances to arrest a cycle of decline and in 2014 Denmark failed to qualify for the World Cup Qualifier. This disappointment was matched in the T20 format where in the same year they failed to qualify for the global T20 qualifier. In the space of a decade Denmark have gone from a World Cup contender to failing to qualify for the qualifiers. They are currently in World Cricket League Four, the second lowest rung of international cricket.

The reasons for this decline are largely due to the factors outlined above. Other countries have fielded stronger teams; they have progressed while Denmark have stagnated. It is not that Denmark has failed to produce talented players in the modern era. Freddie Klokker is arguably the most talented keeper-batsman ever produced in continental Europe. He has two county championship hundreds and averages close to 40 in the World Cricket League. In European division 1 in 2013, a T20 tournament, he scored 464 runs in just seven games, averaging 77. His 129 not out against Guernsey in that competition was one of the best innings ever seen in a European tournament across any format. His runs have often carried the team. Another quality player is captain Michael Pedersen, who showed great promise as a teenager as an MCC Young Cricketer. He hasn't perhaps got the weight of runs his talent deserves in international cricket but has proved an astute captain. Other leading players have been fast bowling all-rounder Aftab Ahmed, leg-spinner Bobby Chawla and left-arm spinner Basit Shah. The Danish league continues to develop gifted players, with Hamid Shah and Saif Ahmed stars of the future. But there has been too much pressure on one or two individuals to perform.

During the period of rise and decline from the late 80s to the present day Danish cricket has changed in composition and character, reflecting general demographic trends in the region. In the second game of the Australia series in 1989 the top scorer for Denmark was Aftab Ahmed, making an impressive 77 against a strong bowling attack. He was one of two Pakistani-born players in the team, along with Atif Butt. In European division 1 in 2015 eight of Denmark's starting XI were of Pakistani origin, though most were born in Denmark and had progressed through the Danish youth set-up. This national team selection reflects an ethnic shift in the domestic game, where over recent decades an increasing proportion of players come from a subcontinent background. By the early 1990s an all-Pakistani club, Norrebro, was challenging for the league and Aftab Ahmed was the top domestic batsman. Another Pakistani club, Ishoj, won five of the six youth tournaments in 1993. Although the number of players in Denmark has remained relatively stable the number of native Danes playing the game has decreased despite efforts by the DCF and clubs.

Most of the players in the current Danish team are of Pakistani origin and they have a role model to aspire to in assistant coach Amjad Khan. Born in Copenhagen in 1980, he was brought up with his father and uncles talking about cricket and would watch games on television. But as a boy he preferred football and was on his way to training when he happened to walk past some cricketers practising. Intrigued, he asked if he could join in and was soon identified as the most promising young talent in Denmark. He was already the quickest bowler in the country at the age of 16 and made his international debut at 17. He had planned to become a lawyer and after school took his exams. But his coach, Ole Mortensen, recommended the young star to his old county chum John Wright, who invited him over for a trial at Kent. He played second XI cricket in 2000 and in 2001 made his first-class debut, taking the wicket of Pakistani great Saeed Anwar, albeit only after he had caressed a double century. In his first full season in 2002 he took 63 wickets which put him firmly on England's radar. His form then dipped for a few seasons but he got British citizenship in 2006. After recovering from a serious knee injury he made his debut for England, taking 1-111 against the West Indies in Port of Spain. He also played a T20I on the same tour. That was to be the sum total of his England career, though he was to have a successful, if injury-interrupted, county career, taking 347 wickets in 108 games.

But county cricket's gain was to be Denmark's loss. After taking 16 wickets at an average of under 16 in the 2001 ICC Trophy he did not represent his country again for another 13 years. Whether his quality and pace could have made the difference in Denmark's near misses in that period we will never know, but it certainly would have helped. Returning to Denmark after his county career Amjad is resuming training for a belated start to his legal career, while also serving as strike bowler and assistant coach for the national team. He is leading bowling workshops while also using experience from his county career to help players with the psychological elements of the game. On the field he has lost a few yards of pace but is still penetrative with the ball and is a handy batsman in the lower middle order. But he puts just as much emphasis on his role in developing match awareness and composure under pressure on the field, helping head coach, former Ireland international, Jeremy Bray, instill a more professional approach.

With a generation of players recently retired, including Carsten Pedersen and the Hedegaard brothers, and Klokker and Amjad the wrong side of 30, the DCF are investing in youth development. The aim is to develop a generation of home-grown players from a mix of ethnic backgrounds that can lead Denmark up the World Cricket League and back into global tournaments. The focal point for this development programme is the Viborg Academy, a residential college where young people combine education with sports development. In 2014 the DCF concluded an agreement with the academy to add cricket to its roster of sports. Promising cricketers join the academy at 14 or 15 years of age and in addition to their education go through a cricket development programme run by Danish coaches Martin Hedegaard and Amjad Khan. This consists of three training sessions a week and fixtures on the weekend. The Viborg scholars are also integrated into the elite development training camps for the national and age group squads. The intention is to mirror the professional development pathways at English counties and groom the next generation of Danish international cricketers. At Viborg young cricketers train with emerging stars of more popular and high profile sports like handball, providing an insight into the level of professionalism, dedication and fitness required to succeed in sport at the top level.

Michael Pedersen

Michael Pedersen and his older brother Carsten have been the batting bulwarks of Danish cricket in the modern era. They were introduced to the game by a neighbour who badgered the boys to come down to the nets to try the game, which just goes to show that word of mouth can be a powerful promotional tool for the game on the continent. Quickly identified as a talented prospect he was selected for the Danish under-15 side in 1999 and moved up through the age group squads until making his full international debut in 2005. It was a proud and joyful moment for him, especially joining a team captained by his brother, but a sad day for Danish cricket as they were skittled for 56 by Northamptonshire, ending their inclusion in county cricket.

Following the ICC Trophy in 2005 Pedersen joined the MCC Young Cricketers where he played alongside friend and Danish team-mate Freddie Klokker and other young associate stars including Wilson, O'Brien and van Bunge. On his second year on the staff he hit form, scoring a century in the second XI championship and averaging just under 40 and a county career looked within reach. However, some niggling injuries and a loss of form saw his average slip down to 23 in 2007. He returned to Denmark, club cricket and an increasingly busy international schedule incorporating the World Cricket League, regional tournaments and qualification tournaments for both the World Cup and World T20. Along with Klokker he has been ever present for the Danes in the WCL, scoring over 700 runs in 27 appearances. Surprisingly, given his talent and calm assurance at the crease, he has only scored a single century, making 121 against the Netherlands at the World Cup Qualifier in 2009.

However, playing for his country, he has often had to lead a recovery after a clatter of wickets and has proved a useful foil for Klokker, the country's batting dynamo and match-winner. His angular off-spin has also proved a useful addition to the attack.

In 2011 he replaced Klokker as Denmark captain and remains in that role. One of the most erudite and cerebral cricketers on the continent, he has played an important role in guiding the team through a transitional period with an ever greater emphasis on youth. He plays his league cricket with Skanderborg, alongside Klokker and fellow national team players Rizwan and Kamran Mahmood.

* * * * *

Freddie Klokker, as well as being the talismanic star of the national team and a qualified groundsman, is employed by the federation as a development officer. This involves running participation initiatives and coaching clinics in schools, building links between schools and clubs and implementing Danish cricket's development pathway. The federation provides clubs with promotional and training materials to run cricket sessions in schools. The concept is to link up with three schools during the pre-season, organise a number of visits and then organise inter-school tournaments. A grant is given by the federation for prizes. While Klokker oversees this programme in Copenhagen, Lars Hedegaard does in Jutland. Last year a major new initiative was launched called the Master Club Programme. The objective is for a network of clubs across the country to promote cricket in their regions, increasing the profile of the sport in their communities and the level of participation. Regular regional seminars are held to share best practice and discuss solutions to common challenges. This has resulted in the adoption of innovative schemes, such as clubs using mobile apps to engage with youth players, establishment of volunteer networks and promotional plans run in partnership with local media. One of the objectives is to make cricket club culture more accessible and exciting for young people. Some clubs have even given youth players the chance to edit their websites, to make the content more appealing to their peers. To support their Master Clubs the DCF have produced videos and online resources on topics such as leadership, player retention and marketing. There are six clubs in the first phase of the Master Club Programme that will run for three years.

In addition to strengthening the role of clubs as regional ambassadors for the game the DCF are also focusing on the recreational game. The 'Open Cricket' strategy aims to attract the increasing number of people playing tape-ball cricket in urban areas into the broader cricketing community, increasing the number of players and providing recruitment for clubs. There are currently over 40 clubs in the country, with a concentration in the Copenhagen area but also in the Jutland region. There is steady interest in forming new clubs, especially from Pakistani communities although many older clubs in rural Jutland have disappeared.

Estonia

Most countries outside the Test world are indebted to a pioneer for having the vision, determination and perhaps even eccentricity to sow a cricketing seed in virgin soil. Estonia has one of the most intriguing. In 1996 Jason Barry, a club cricketer from Leicestershire, embarked on a cricket tour with a difference, aiming to play cricket in over a hundred countries to raise money for charity. After several years he had notched up 128 and raised well over $100,000 for charity. Having wielded the willow in some of the most exotic locations in the world, he chose to settle in Estonia around the turn of the millennium, a country extricating itself from Soviet grip. As well as being an adventurer he also had an entrepreneurial streak and he brought this to cricket in the country too. While most cricket on the continent started at a military base or in the corner of a public park cricket in Estonia was to make its name on ice. Apparently inspired by local ice fishermen, Barry wondered whether the frozen lakes surrounding the capital of Tallinn could make for cricket grounds that could help cricket fanatics get through the long, cold and boring Baltic winters.

In 1998 an Estonian businessman returned from a trip to Australia transfixed by cricket and determined to play a game in his homeland. He arranged a fixture with a team from an Indian restaurant in the city and this kick-started cricket in the city. Before long the games moved from a football pitch to a patch of grass in the middle of the Hippodrome, a racecourse known for a slightly less golden version of Ben Hur style chariot racing. With local cricket established and Estonia becoming more accessible to the West the Hippodrome became a somewhat unlikely destination for end-of-season cricket tours. The charm and fairy-tale architecture of Tallinn's old town, cheap flights and even cheaper beer made it an ideal, albeit quirky, choice for teams looking for an end-of-season diversion. In 2003 the Estonian team went on tour themselves, to the Helsinki Sixes and came runners-up. They returned fired by a desire to formalise the development of cricket and formed the Estonian Cricket Association in 2004, with Barry at the forefront. The aims at the outset were to get more Estonian nationals playing and to introduce cricket into schools.

With a view to grabbing some headlines for the game, extending the domestic season and generating some revenue to fund development Barry launched the concept of ice cricket. Although played in St Moritz, Switzerland, since 1988, the Estonian version did away with matting, placing the focus very much on fun with balancing rather than cricketing skills coming to the fore. The concept was targeted at club and pub teams, principally from the UK, who were looking for an end-of-season social. If the ice was not thick enough to be played on the venue was switched to an ice rink in a former Soviet missile factory on the outskirts of the city. The ECA offered package tours in conjunction with local hotels which made ice cricket a very innovative form of cricket tourism. Along with the sheer silliness of the concept and the affordability and quirkiness of Tallinn as a destination the genius of the concept was offering amateur, often overweight and almost certainly hung-over cricketers the chance to say they played against a national team. The Estonian team participated in each tournament, sporting their official national team tracksuits. After a few years this international element was enhanced further as tournaments were branded as ice cricket World Cups. Around the cricket teams could choose other activities, such as shooting or historic excursions and the proceedings ended with boozy prize-giving ceremonies hosted in medieval cloisters in the old town.

The profits from ice cricket were reinvested into facilities and youth development initiatives, such as introductory courses in schools. The slippery shenanigans also helped boost the profile of Estonia as a cricketing and tourism destination on social media. Momentum built and high profile visits from the MCC and Lord's Taverners saw donations of kit and equipment that were provided to clubs and local schools. By 2006 Estonia were hosting around 20 teams a year at the Hippodrome and running a busy programme of ice cricket. The local player base grew to around 30, with several Estonian players taking up the game in earnest. This enabled a four-team domestic league to be established in 2007. By the end of the noughties the cricket calendar had grown to around 60 features a year comprising the league, visits by touring teams, bilateral international fixtures against other cricket teams in the Baltic region and the Helsinki Sixes.

Estonia became an affiliate member of the ICC in 2008, providing targeted support, a much needed boost in revenue and an invitation to play in officially sanctioned tournaments. Their official international bow was at European division 5 held in Greece in 2009, where the team won a single game. They fared better in the reconfigured tournament schedule in 2010 by coming runner-up in division 3. The core of the national team were expats, with the big-hitting Aussie Tim Heath and Sri Lankan fast bowler Murali to the fore. But they won admiration and plaudits for ensuring Estonians were integrated in to the team too, such as Vaik and Bihanovs. Despite modest success on the field Estonia were not lacking in ambition and developed their facilities sufficiently to host an international tournament for the first time in the summer of 2012. Not only that but they secured a headline-grabbing coup when Shane Warne accepted an invitation to attend the opening day, tweeting his support for the Estonian team. This unlikely visit was set up by a betting company who sponsored the national team, for whom Warne was an ambassador. However, while this connection provided the glitz of Shane Warne and the glamour of his then partner Liz Hurley it also brought the ECA into trouble with the ICC for breaching advertising regulations.

Off the pitch Estonia sought to fulfil the objectives they had set out in their application to become affiliate members. This focused primarily on boosting participation levels and, ambitiously, to make cricket an Estonian sport. Starting in 2008 the ECA set up a programme of cricket roadshows around Tallinn and introduced cricket into several schools to form an inter-school competition. In addition the ECA looked to establish cricket beyond the capital, with Tartu, the second city in the country, hosting its first game in

2011. In the last few years cricket has also been introduced to Parnu and Nava.

The challenges in developing the game further in the country are the relatively short season, the availability of grounds, a lack of funding and a relatively small number of over-burdened volunteers trying to run the game. Although they have had more success than many other countries in getting native players into the national team, to act as role models for development of the game as a local sport, the general perception remains that cricket is a foreign sport. If the sport is to achieve wider acknowledgement and acceptance ongoing engagement with schools will be crucial. Five-week training programmes have been piloted in schools, featuring trilingual materials and training aids. However, for these pilots to be rolled out across the country the ECA will need to get endorsement and funding from national and local governments and this could well be contingent on cricket being recognised as an Olympic sport.

Cricket is struggling to match the appeal of baseball where daily games are shown on ESPN compared to just a handful of cricket games a year shown on Eurosport 2, a subscription channel. Baseball is seen as a faster-paced and more interesting game than cricket and the failure of the ICC, to date at least, in getting coverage of cricket World Cups shown in more countries has put the ECA at a distinct disadvantage. However, there has been some television and print media coverage, generally focused on national team tours and, above all else, victories. The ECA hope that the stated ambition to have an all Estonian XI representing the country in the future will engage the press and the country at large.

There are currently five clubs in the country across Tallinn, Tartu and Saaremaa. They play in 35- and 20-over leagues, with an indoor league played in the winter and a super eight tournament held in Tallinn. There is also a women's league. In the absence of official ICC tournaments the national team play in annual, unofficial tournaments, including the Baltic Cup against Latvia.

Finland

The origins of cricket in Finland go back further than you might expect. It was included as a demonstration sport during the 1952 Olympics with British embassy staff playing a game against British sailors. This proved a false dawn but in the early 1970s British and Australian residents of Helsinki formed the Helsinki Cricket Club. However, for several decades the club was the only cricketing presence in the country and relied on either foreign tours or the odd visiting team for fixtures. In the early 1990s things began to change as immigration from South Asia, as well as second generation Finns returning from cricket-playing countries, brought more cricketers to the country. Informal cricket sprung up in public parks in the capital and irregular games started in Lahti and Turku too. In 1996 the weight of numbers and level of interest was sufficient to start a national league and there were four clubs in the country by 1999 when the Finnish Cricket Association was founded. This was sufficient to meet ICC affiliate criteria and Finland joined as a member in 2000.

ICC membership provided legitimacy for the association and helped secure government endorsement. In 2000 the country played its first international matches, against nearby Estonia, with the two countries forging close links and playing each other regularly ever since. It was an encouraging start with the Finns amassing 333-9. This series provided the impetus for the development of a national team on a more formal setting in 2001, whereafter they regularly competed in ICC Europe tournaments. A key figure in the development of the game in Finland has been Andrew Armitage who moved to the country from England in 1988 and has been heavily involved both as a player and administrator ever since, firstly helping form clubs and later the Finnish Cricket Association. He has also played a leading role at the ICC, being the representative for affiliate members in committee meetings.

An Armitage anecdote about playing cricket in Finland even inspired the writing of a book. Fielding during a game at Ruskeasuo Park he looked on in wonder as an elk burst through the adjoining forest and on to the ground. Play had to be suspended for five minutes until the beast cantered past midwicket and back into the trees. This made writer Charlie Connelly chuckle sufficiently to write *Elk Stopped Play*, the *Wisden* collection of tales from beyond the Test world.

By 2003 there were around 350 players in the country, with around 70 Finnish citizens. Two clubs, MTS and the Finnish Naval Academy CC, were entirely composed of native players. By 2007 there were ten clubs in the country and the FCA created a club development forum to provide guidance, improve governance and encourage the formation of new clubs. In Finland as in much of northern Europe there is considerable government support for sports clubs but also a considerable amount of red tape to register and benefit from funding. The association had been able to access government funding in 2006 as the number of players and clubs had crossed the threshold for support. This meant cricket was one of the sports that could benefit from a share of national lottery funding, though naturally cricket had to be content with a much smaller slice of the pie than more established sports.

The main challenge for the FCA was developing a permanent base for cricket in the country. Although cricket was being played by an increasing number of teams and players there were no dedicated grounds, making cricket a squatter and only able to play at the whim of local councils or landowners. They also recognised that it was near impossible to improve the standard of play to enable Finland to compete internationally if it continued to be played on rough patches of land. So the search began for a national ground and this meant finding an influential champion for the game. Through a work contact the mayor of Kerava, a small town close to Helsinki, was invited to Lord's for the ICC Europe President's Day and was sufficiently impressed and charmed to offer his support for the FCA in their search for a ground. He made available an area of land from a former farm next to the ring road on the outskirts of the city. Work began in 2009 with a significant amount of work required to level the ground and provide drainage. With a lack of funding and relying largely on dedicated but busy volunteers it took five years to make the dream come true but on 10 June 2014 the national cricket ground finally opened.

The opening of the national ground in Kerava was marked by a historic opening match against the MCC, who included former England captain Mike Brearley in their ranks. The ground includes nets and a pavilion and includes several wonderfully eccentric touches, such as the 'Not so Long Room'. The ground hosts all Finnish international and league matches and is the focal point for cricket in the country. The opening in 2014 marked the culmination of the first phase of Finnish cricket's development plan and it is hoped that Kerava can become a hub for development across the country, providing all cricketers in Finland with excellent facilities and a permanent home.

There are now over 20 registered cricket clubs in the country and the game is played by 22 different nationalities, with almost a third of players Finnish. The Oulu club, 500km north of the capital and on the cusp of the Arctic circle, is thought to be one of the northernmost in the world.

Given the northern climes indoor facilities play a vital role and youth programmes and national team camps are held in the corner of a vast indoor hall, vying for space with football and other more recognised sports. A dedicated indoor facility for cricket would provide an all-year hub to complement the national ground at Kerava and build on sessions held at the Finnish National Elite Performance Centre.

One of the routes to engaging more native players in the country is by forging links with the traditional, baseball-like game of *pesapallo*. The game requires similar skills in ball striking and hand to eye coordination and the association hope that this familiarity could lead to *pesapallo* players taking up cricket. There is also the tantalising prospect of sharing the many *pesapallo* grounds, to increase the number of areas where cricket can be played. But *pesapallo* is itself now a minority sport and its administrators see cricket more as a threat than an opportunity. Nevertheless, it is a route the association continue to explore. The government has set an objective for Finland to become the world's most active nation by 2020 and the FCA are looking to play their role in achieving this aspiration, tapping into government funding along the way. The role of cricket in developing physical fitness, mental agility and team ethics is one of the key pillars of the FCA's schools programme. They are providing training sessions for teachers and also seeking to incorporate cricket into the teaching of English in schools. It is hoped that a network of teachers teaching cricket in schools can generate sufficient interest for inter-school tournaments to be played. In addition Finland is one of the countries in Europe that have embraced the Street20 format to boost interest and participation.

Finland has been influential in developing regional tournaments in the Baltic and Scandinavia, with particularly close links to Estonia and Sweden. The Helsinki Sixes draws teams from across the region. But it is an even more novel format that is really sparking media interest. Cage cricket recently featured on Finnish television in a primetime slot with a staggering 800,000 viewers from a population of a five and a half million. This has seen a flood of interest in the sport and the FCA hope this can translate into a boost in participation and further media interest.

With cricket firmly established in Helsinki, Turku and Tampere the association are targeting growth in Lahti, Oulu and Jyvaskala.

France

With its large population, rich sporting heritage, relative affluence, growing ethnic diversity and close proximity to England across La Manche, France has great potential as an emerging cricketing nation. But somehow, despite periodic signs of promise, it has never come close to reaching this potential. It possesses some of the best, and certainly some of the most picturesque, cricket grounds on the continent at the Chateau de Thoiry and Saumur, but the challenge of coordinating cricket over such a large country on a limited budget along with sporadic periods of political infighting has meant France has remained a promising potential market for cricket rather than an emerging regional power in the game.

The founding of France Cricket in 1997 was intended to put the development of cricket in the region on a more professional footing, incorporating the large number of economic migrants into the formal set-up and placing a long overdue emphasis on youth development.

Elevation to associate membership followed in 1998 providing a further funding boost, although this was tempered by a cut in state funding for the sport in the first decade of the new millennium. France had always been a very popular destination for touring teams and the number of established clubs across the country, many with grounds the envy of others in the region, meant that recreational cricket was relatively strong and secure. The challenge for France Cricket was to promote and cultivate cricket amongst native players to take cricket beyond merely expat residents playing in the country, and to put in place a pathway to identify and develop talent to enable France to blossom from a regional team to an emerging force on the international stage.

There are two different cricketing cultures in the country. In Paris and the Ille de France it is an Asian game, with a fiercely competitive club scene and a smash-every-ball-for-six mentality inspired by the pyrotechnics of Shahid Afridi. In the south-west the game is gentler and more genteel, a taste of home for the many English expats who play there. There is more of a recreational focus to the cricket and generally more of an inclusive club culture with a greater emphasis on youth. This clash of cultures and philosophies has been the backdrop to a power struggle within French cricket that has determined the strategy of administrators and the future of the game.

In the late noughties former chairman Mark Moodley set out a new strategic direction for the governing body, placing a greater emphasis on youth development and seeking to introduce a greater degree of professionalism, both in domestic structures and for the national team. Moodley had emigrated from England, was a leading figure in the traditional Chateau de Thoiry club and sought to be a unifier of cricket in the country.

With support from ICC Europe, France Cricket embarked upon an ambitious development plan to work with schools to increase awareness and participation levels and provide a more sustainable base for future growth of the game. This initiative included a programme of school visits, courses to train teachers and the provision of training equipment and promotional materials. This led to a formal agreement, backed by the ICC, between France Cricket and the body responsible for primary education to introduce basic cricket skills to children. Several local government departments included cricket on their syllabus. However, although this led to more than 20,000 children being introduced to the game this did not translate as hoped to a significant boost in playing numbers in clubs. One of the reasons for this was that clubs were often situated in parts of the city that were run down and had an overwhelmingly immigrant population. Even if children were inspired by the game in schools, they and their parents may not have been comfortable in joining such clubs. This made integration challenging.

This reflects a broader issue across the continent. Member boards are encouraged to run such initiatives to boost participation numbers in the ICC's annual report, but the percentage of these taking up the game regularly is depressingly low. In France, as in many other countries, this is largely due to the complete absence of a cricketing culture. There are a lot of other sports and activities that children can do instead, and in the most part they have chosen to do so. When cultural issues and prejudices are also considered it is clear that it is relatively easy to draft a development pathway for young players but far harder to successfully implement it, particularly on a limited budget.

To improve performances of the national team the Moodley administration first looked to professionalise the management and development of talent across the country. This was to ensure that players throughout France, whether they played in the Paris leagues or the south-west, had an equal chance of making the national team and that this ambition could inspire young players to commit to the game. As the French league is run on a regional basis a series was introduced to get the elite squads from each region to play each other and for this to inform national selection. There was also an aspiration to provide a pathway from national age group squads to the senior team. These reforms were intended to move away from an amateur form of selection based on word of mouth, picking friends and dominance of particular clubs.

The next stage was to make the national team more professional with the aim of qualifying for global tournaments and increasing funding in the process, which could then be channelled back into development and thereby create a virtuous cycle. Firstly it was acknowledged that the pitches and facilities in France were not good enough to develop the level of technique and talent necessary to challenge the leading teams in Europe and be successful on the global stage. To resolve this rather fundamental constraint France Cricket established a partnership with Kent County Cricket Club, across the Channel. Under this arrangement leading youth players in the country, such as talented young leg-spinner Zika Ali, were to join the Kent Academy in Canterbury with some French national team players joining local clubs to play in the Kent league. It was hoped that access to professional coaching and experience on grass wickets would improve techniques and temperament and, perhaps most importantly, instil a professional approach. At a team level it enabled the national squad to hold warm-up training camps in preparation for European tournaments, which were increasingly being held either in English counties or in the Channel Islands. At this time France Cricket also secured something of a coup in bringing Richie Benaud, the legendary Australian commentator with French ancestry, to lead a leg spin masterclass in France. A gimmick perhaps, but it certainly helped get cricket in the news.

It was through this link with Kent that seamer Simon Cook became national team coach. He aimed to instil a professional approach, improve techniques by focusing training on grass wickets and instil an ethic of fitness and preparation. However, his appointment coincided with a change of management and leadership in French cricket which was to see a different philosophy adopted. The clubs in the Ille de France wanted funding to be targeted at improving and developing facilities in Paris. They secured the votes necessary to claim control of the board and the development structures put in place were not given the time to bear fruit. In recent years France have not been able to translate talent into success on the field and an elevation from regional to global tournaments. The squad under Cook that competed in the European T20 qualifier in 2013 had a good mix of youth and experience, ethnic backgrounds and representation from clubs across the country. Better tactics and a quicker start to the tournament could have seen them make the hoped for breakthrough. During the tournament several players were forced to vacate their rooms to make way for officials from the federation and Cook took understandable umbrage at the president and the van driver shouting at the players from the sidelines.

Qualification for the World Cricket League has eluded them several times. Under the new board the team has become predominantly Asian, with players selected from the premier league, played exclusively in Paris. In 2014 the team under Dutch coach Tim de Leede lost every game they played in Jersey, including the play-off for World Cricket League 6.

A comparison of France with Jersey and Guernsey is helpful in illustrating the challenges faced in overseeing the development of a sport over such a large geographical area. To some extent it has been an advantage to the Channel Island teams that they have a limited player base competing in a small area. It enables the concentration of talent and makes it easier to develop an elite squad that can be competitive in regional and international tournaments. Along with the availability of grounds these issues have been major constraining factors in France progressing as a cricketing nation.

In 2012 the MCC crossed the Channel to commemorate cricket's Olympic debut back in 1900 when the Devon County Wanderers defeated French-based British scholars by 158 runs. The MCC won the rematch too.

Perhaps unsurprisingly the greatest concentration of cricket in the country is in the most international city, Paris. The elite domestic tournament, known as the Premier Ligue, consists entirely of clubs from the Paris region. In practical terms this is an advantage as it keeps travel times and logistical challenges to a minimum. In truth a truly national league, with teams having to travel between Paris and Marseille, would not be workable. Below the premier league is the League Nationale, which is comprised of several regional leagues. There is then a third division at the bottom of the league structure. In addition to the national structure there are separate regional leagues in the south-west and north-west. Paris is the only region to have a sufficient number of youth teams to organise a youth league, although inter-region games at youth level are played each year in other parts of the country.

Under Moodley this commitment to youth development extended to influencing club culture and national team selection. All clubs in the Premier Ligue had to field a youth team and challenge matches were organised to enable the country's most talented young players to test themselves against the senior team. This policy saw a much greater progression of players from youth teams to the senior side and a reduced reliance on aging expats in the squad. Mike Selig ran youth training to ensure this progression continued. But the emphasis on youth wasn't supported by all.

With development objectives so difficult to achieve in a country without a cricketing culture and with a collective commitment required to a long-term view on return on investment it is perhaps unsurprising that many cricketers in a country like France take a more personal and pragmatic view of how funding should be spent. A club cricketer playing week in week out on a poor pitch with little or no facilities may well see improvements in infrastructure as a more pressing concern than inspiring the next generation. This was the context for a power struggle that saw the development-focused board under former chairman Mark Moodley voted out. Rory Gribbell, a promising fast bowler who left the national team set-up in the aftermarth of the takeover, explained his concerns:

'Following the takeover the focus on youth and coaching development ended. The board focused exclusively on domestic cricket around the Paris region. Whereas in 2012 the majority of the national side had come through the youth set-up and there was inter-regional selection tournaments, now players are selected exclusively from the Paris region and the board show very little interest in any clubs outside the Ille de France.

'The board also essentially stopped communicating with anyone but the Paris-based clubs. They are short of money and so are issuing hefty fines for minor infractions which has led some clubs to leave the official leagues.'

This insight into the issues and power politics within French cricket illustrates a broader division within continental cricket communities between those who support a long-term development focus however hard, or even unlikely, that might be to achieve and those who just want to facilitate cricket amongst those who currently play. Depending on your viewpoint this is either a diminution of responsibility or perfectly pragmatic logic. If the Parisian-focused leadership continues it is likely that the game in the rest of the country will be limited to recreational cricket played between established clubs.

The gamble must be that a focus on the concentration of the talent in Paris and diverting of funds from the school programme into elite development of France's leading players will lead to on-field success that will in turn see an increase in ICC funding through qualification for global tournaments.

On a more positive note there have been some notable successes in developing the women's game. Many teams at under-15 level are mixed and more clubs have formed women's teams, leading to the formation of a national tournament for women. Two of the most promising native players to emerge have been women. Cindy Paquin and Laura Codrons were rated so highly that they were selected for the boys' teams by France Cricket, a move that led to France getting a slapped wrist from the ICC and withdrawing from two tournaments. France has embraced an innovative approach to funding women's cricket with the squad financed through crowd funding. However, this has not been given much support by the new board.

There are 1,200 registered players in the country and more than 60 clubs have access to their own grounds. These statistics are the envy of most countries in the region and suggest that if a truly national strategic plan can be created and implemented by a board focused on laying the foundations to capitalise on long-term opportunities the future could be promising. For now though it remains a cricketing country of stark contrasts. The grounds at Chantilly and Thoiry are amongst the best on the continent. And yet many of the best players in the country play at Dreux, where the pitch backs on to a disused mental asylum. With the focus of the new board almost exclusively on the capital and the national team almost all Asian, there is a danger that the sport is perceived as just a Parisian sport and only played by a particular ethnic group. There is undoubted potential but for now France is taking the back seat and it is Germany where momentum is starting to build.

Germany

Germany has been one of the success stories of continental cricket over the last few years. But they have hit the headlines not through an eye-catching on-field performance but rather an extraordinary expansion of the domestic game and an inspiring example of the social role cricket can play. Germany has been one of the most popular destinations on the continent for economic migrants and the Deutsche Cricket Bund, with a very limited budget, has enabled thousands to play the game they love and settle in a new country. Through intelligent use of social media and tireless efforts of administrators the DCB has processed a deluge of requests from cricketers across the country to be matched to or form a club. On a weekly basis news is broken on Twitter and Facebook of yet another club being formed and another pin in the increasingly pin-pricked cricketing map of Germany. Only the most hardened cynics, and there are a vocal few who think that only native Germans taking up the game is a positive news story, can fail to be inspired.

Germany has been the destination for thousands of refugees that have fled to Europe to escape warzones and civil strife in Africa and the Middle East. Many arrive in the country after perilous journeys walking thousands of miles over several months from countries like Afghanistan. Their families spend life savings smuggling them out and those that arrive in the sprawling immigrant camps have stories defined by tragedy and barely comprehensible fear. Through cricket they have begun to rebuild their lives, confidence and sense of being. The images of these refugees playing cricket in German gymnasiums, joy radiating from their smiles and their very souls, is truly life-affirming. Cricket is about scorecards, statistics and square drives but at its core it is a social event, a way of people bonding over a shared pleasure. Seen in this context the work of the DCB goes far beyond ICC objectives to boost participation levels. It is a reminder that behind every statistic is a human story. Cricket can bring joy and togetherness to all who play it, whatever their ethnic origin or ability and increasing the number of cricketers on the continent is undoubtedly a positive social trend. The DCB's efforts have not gone unnoticed, with their work with refugees covered by leading newspapers and news channels across the world and German authorities recognising and appreciating the role cricket has played in integrating new arrivals into German society. A bite-size BBC documentary on the issue was one of the most watched videos on their website.

One such human story is that of Arif Jamal. Like many of his countrymen Jamal made the perilous journey from Afghanistan to Germany to find a better, safer life. He was placed in a children's home, thousands of miles from his family in an alien land. But cricket has given him the direction and hope he needed. With the help of the federation Jamal now plays for the German under-19 team and is a part-time youth development officer. Participation levels in Germany have doubled in the last five years and there are now more cricketers in Germany than Denmark. But cricket's association with immigration and refugees has not brought tragedy as well as hope. Far right groups, who resent the mass migration of recent years, are thought to be behind the recent vandalism of pitches in Bonn and Cologne.

It will take several years to appreciate what the impact of this rapid increase of cricketers will be on the development of Germany as a cricket nation. It is not clear for instance whether cricket will be a sport limited to particular ethnic groups, albeit those growing rapidly in number, or if it will raise the profile of the game and support cricket breaking through into Germany's sporting consciousness. What is clear, however, is that cricket has become a much more common sight in Germany than it has ever been before, with the DCB recently celebrating its 100th member club. Participation levels in Germany had doubled from just over 200 in 1970 to 460 in 1990. But this still represented a very low participation base. However, in the last few years participation has snowballed. If recent levels of growth are sustained Germany is set to overtake the Netherlands as the largest cricketing community in continental Europe. Of course the largest doesn't necessarily equate to the most successful on the field and it is likely to take some years and a significant funding boost for the DCB to translate soaring participation levels into sustained success internationally.

Unfortunately for the DCB the timing of this incredible recruitment drive has coincided with the virtual withdrawal of ICC support from all but the strongest of its regional members. It therefore faces a significant challenge in overseeing and facilitating cricket across a considerable geographic area on a very modest budget. The scorecard funding mechanism accounts for growth in participation numbers and so they will be set for increased grant funding but the level is still much less than comparable governing bodies receive. Help could come in the form of government funding. If participation figures hit 10,000 the DCB will have reached the threshold for support from the German Olympic committee. This recognition and endorsement could in turn help generate more funding through sponsorship.

The boost in participation has necessitated changes to the domestic structure. The national league is sub-divided into six regions, with teams playing in the Bundesliga (1st division) and Regionaliga (2nd division). Alongside this is a national T20 tournament that now comprises over 100 teams. In order to ensure a concentration of talent and to enable the country's best players to face each other the DCB have launched a super series, with the best players from each region playing each other. The logic is that as the player base continues to broaden the standard of the super series will increase in parallel, enabling a systematic selection policy for the national team, increased standards and, in theory at least, a more competitive national team capable of beating the best in the region. A further benefit of the super series is that it ensures that the best players benefit from the best grounds and facilities in the country.

But organising a national, regional and elite league structure in a country as fond of regulations as Germany is a challenge for the DCB. Ensuring all clubs adhere to a common set of laws and support national objectives with a limited number of paid staff has proved difficult. The DCB face a constant challenge from clubs not wanting to pay match fees or comply with other conditions applied for the greater good. This makes them vulnerable to breakaway leagues and rival governing bodies. An entrepreneur with a silver tongue, the promise of glamour and glory and free matches without irksome requirements will tempt many. They can attract sponsors too and in 2015 a rival league was established made up exclusively of Pakistani clubs. In parallel there was a move to oust the DCB with a view to split ICC revenue directly between clubs and withdraw funding from development initiatives. But this storm was weathered and several teams came back. Being in the fold has its advantages, such as being eligible for selection for the national team. There are now 205 teams playing in official leagues, up from 70 five years ago.

League cricket in Berlin was humorously brought to life by German national player and former DCB media officer Andre Leslie's book *Batting in Berlin*. His account of bringing together a team from a disparate group of cricketers made up of a handful of locals and expats from various countries who had come to Berlin with jobs for varying lengths of time gives a flavour of what club cricket is like in the region as a whole. But although he illustrates the challenges, common to most cricketers on the continent, of the long commute to grounds that don't have changing rooms and clubs struggling to consistently field teams amongst a transient player base, there is definitely a feeling that this is more than compensated by the comradery of playing a minority sport and the opportunity in such a small pond to be a big fish and win the national league, perhaps even qualify for the national team.

Since Leslie's book was published many more clubs have joined leagues, though this has had a greater impact in other regions rather than in the capital Berlin. But this has undoubtedly increased standards overall, with the level of play in the super series now very high. With discipline, commitment and funding for development of the elite squad it is likely that Germany will quickly climb global rankings and the rungs of the World Cricket League ladder.

At international level Germany has often flattered to deceive, with obvious talent being compromised by a lack of preparation, consistency of selection and training. Not to mention availability of leading players due to work commitments and visa issues. But they have certainly had their moments. In 1997 in the Nations Cup in Switzerland they smashed the hosts for 467-1 in 50 overs, with a 349-run stand between Shamaz Khan and Abdul Bhatti, with the former making an undefeated double century. It wasn't an ODI of course, as only certain countries are allowed to play those, but if it were he would have beaten Sachin Tendulkar to the feat. They have performed quite well, albeit fitfully, in ICC tournaments and qualified for World Cricket League 7 in 2011. They performed well in the Kuwait-hosted tournament, finishing third, and climbing into the top 40 ranked teams in the world. They competed in WCL7 again in 2013, this time in Botswana, but did not register a win and were relegated. The contraction of the WCL means they need to requalify through regional tournaments.

Success on the international stage will surely come but for now the focus is squarely on development. While the energies of the DCB have been largely on incorporating new players and founding new clubs they are also looking to develop youth. Cricket is taught in 40 schools in Germany, mainly in after-school clubs run by volunteers. As in other countries there has not been the hoped for success in incorporating these players into local clubs. Supporting this school focus the DCB also ran Street20 events with support from ICC Europe, boosting participation levels and making cricket visible in town centres and public places. In higher education there have been some successes, helped by the international student base of German universities. There are five German universities in the national league. The DCB have insisted that clubs in their elite division field youth teams. ICC Europe strongly encouraged this reform but it was not popular with all clubs and was difficult to push through. However, this has provided impetus for improving standards in national age group teams and progression of talented young players into the senior team. It is an example of the tensions that often arise between a cricket board implementing a long-term vision but clubs focusing on the current season and the current team. This culture change needs to be effected slowly over time.

A poignant image of Germany's sporting past and future can be seen on summer weekends at the Kornerplatz, Berlin, where cricket is played in the shadow of the stadium that hosted the 1936 Olympics. Hitler did all he could to snub cricket out in the country. He was also not a huge advocate of multiculturalism, to put it mildly. So it is a proud testament to the new Germany that this remains a sporting centre with a far more inclusive philosophy. But in 2011 play at this historic ground, that had hosted cricket for 60 years, was temporarily suspended as the local authority had removed the artificial pitch. The reason, it transpired, was that the authorities were concerned about compensation payments should passers-by be struck by the ball. Thankfully a concerted social media campaign, backed by the *Times* newspaper, led to the pitch being re-laid and league games re-commencing.

Their recent work with refugees has given German cricket a huge boost in profile and this should lead to more funding and support from national and federal governments as well as the ICC. It is clear that this level of growth cannot be sustained without a significant increase in funding. If a big sponsor can be found, they qualify for national sport funding and get more support from the ICC, they can increase staffing resource and enhance current initiatives. A future challenge will be demonstrating the universal appeal of the game to increase interest and participation amongst native players.

In 2006 Germany won an ICC Global Development award for establishing an under-17 women's tournament in Oldenburg. This led to the formation of a German women's team and club and regional tournaments. In 2015 a super series was established, mirroring the elite development pathway introduced for men.

In the summer of 2016 Germany won division 2 in Sweden and were promoted to division 1 in 2017 from which they will hope to re-qualify for the WCL. It is likely that the significant boost in player numbers alied to the concentration of talent in the elite league will see them challenge Denmark and The Netherlands as the strongest European team in the coming years. Attracting native German talent remains challenging.

Gibraltar

The heyday of Gibraltar cricket on the international stage is over as the growth of cricket in the rest of the region and the introduction of a meritocratic tournament structure has marginalised the team from the rock. Cricket in Gibraltar in truth has closer parallels with Jersey, Guernsey and the Isle of Man than its continental neighbours. Cricket is firmly established, fully incorporated into schools and remains an important part of island life. However, the player base is tiny with very little opportunity to expand. It remains a popular port of call for touring teams, as it has done ever since British presence was established. Occasionally Gibraltar produces players of genuine calibre, such as Kieren Ferrary, who has been selected in ICC Europe talent development programmes.

Unfortunately political tensions and the wish to retain exclusivity has meant that Gibraltar hasn't played a development role in the growth of the game on the Iberian peninsula. Although there are fixtures with British expat clubs in southern Spain there has never been a coordinated joint development programme to enable Spain and Portugal to benefit from coaching strength on the rock. Hopefully this will change in the future.

Greece

Cricket has a long heritage in Corfu. Games have been played in the Esplanade since the early 18th century and the ground is one of the prettiest in Europe, flanked by a Venetian promenade of bustling cafes and the island's main museum, located in the architecturally admirable former governor's house. The island is popular with British tourists and when the cavernous ferries dock in town sunburnt Britishers take a seat next to the boundary and write excitable postcards to friends and relatives back home of the quintessential English scene they are witnessing in this exotic clime. It is certainly a romantic story and a wonderful setting and the Hellenic Cricket Federation (HCF), based in Corfu, understand its importance all too well. Along with cheap flights, Greek food and hospitality and of course the sunshine their historic ground has made Corfu a very popular touring destination for teams, particularly from England. This has provided opposition and impetus for local cricket and ensured that in Corfu at least cricket enjoys a high profile, both amongst the public and in the media. It has visibility, a very rare commodity for cricket in the region.

The HCF has sought to capitalise on these strengths by branding Corfu as a cricket tourism destination. In addition to club tours they are also increasingly looking to host international tournaments. They have not invested in the facilities to enable them to host university or county sides from England, but there is potential for this. The clement weather would cater for pre-season camps in April at a fraction of the cost of going to the West Indies or South Africa. But Mr Nikitas, president of the HCF, is shrewd and has ensured that the federation has strong relations with local politicians and that the importance of cricket to the island's tourism is appreciated. This in turn brings funding and access to facilities. But although cricket has more influence in Corfu than in much of the continent it still ranks below income generation and town planning. A while ago much of the leg-side of the ground was lost to increase the size of the city centre car park. This means boundary riders have to skip across tarmac weaving between parked cars. I can speak from personal experience in saying this makes for an interesting challenge for commentators.

Due to the historic presence of cricket on the island Corfu makes for a natural regional hub for the game. The HCF is a key part of the Balkan Cricket Federation and regularly host neighbouring countries such as Bulgaria and Romania. In particular they have been very influential in the development of women's cricket in the region, though this remains in its infancy. It has helped that the owner of one of the island's biggest hotel complexes is a friend of the federation, has built a cricket pitch within the grounds and offers preferential rates. This is the venue for the HCF's International Schools Tournament that has been running since 2009, drawing teams from England, India, South Africa and Bulgaria to name but a few. This generates income for the federation, brings tourists to the island and serves as a focus for the development of the Greek youth teams.

On Corfu itself there are well established links to schools and regular engagement through the HCF's development officers. However, the federation have not to date been particularly proactive in developing cricket in the rest of Greece. There have been development visits and participation events held in Athens and Thessaloniki which have seen cricket introduced to several schools. But continuity has been a real problem despite the federation holding coaching clinics for PE teachers to keep cricket going in these outposts.

There have been a few players drawn from the rest of Greece playing at youth level, generally those of half-English descent, but the national team remains Corfu-based, with selection based on the Corfu league. This is partly due to limitations of resource to implement a sustained development programme on the mainland but it also reflects a desire to retain a native focus rather than a reliance on expats. This philosophy has to some extent been necessitated by Greek law that strictly limits the number of foreign players participating in amateur sport.

In the 2000s they sought to strengthen their national team by complementing the best local players with players of Greek origin from South Africa and Australasia, many of which had played to grade cricket standard. This injection of talent saw Greece become more competitive, rising to division 2 of the ICC regional tournament structure. However, having selected a player who had not met residency criteria required by the ICC they were fined and demoted two divisions. This angered the federation who were critical of the reliance of other teams on expats from southern Asia. The emphasis of coaching on the island is on developing sound technique and they have lost out to power hitting teams with much less of a cricketing pedigree. Most teams in Europe, at whatever standard, have a few wannabe Afridis in the ranks who can flay an attack to all parts on their day. Against such bellicose batting finding the gaps and rotating the strike is often not enough.

The most high profile player to represent Greece was former South Africa wicketkeeper and Hampshire stalwart Nic Pothas who played and coached the team for several years, although surprisingly made precious few runs. He left to become director of cricket in Guernsey. Greece are currently outside the official ICC tournament structure. In October 2015 they embarked on a tour to Pakistan playing against good level regional opposition. It is hoped this can lead to future bilateral tournaments.

In Athens the growing South Asian immigrant community are making informal, eight-over-a-side games in parks a regular sight in the city. But legal restrictions mean they can't join clubs. For the near future, therefore, Corfu is likely to remain the centre of Greek cricket.

Hungary

Hungarian cricket is very much in its infancy but it got a mention in the *Wisden* compendium of global cricket, *Elk Stopped Play*. This was due to the planned development of one of the most intriguing and innovative cricket grounds in the world. With the only ground in the country a rough piece of ground used by the country's only club, the Magyar Cricket Club founded in 1991 in Budapest, there was an urgent need to develop more facilities to support domestic cricket. English expat Andy Grieve found an unusual venue in the form of an old quarry in the town of Iszkaszentgyorgy, 80km from the capital. This plot was purchased in June 2011 and preparations began to turn it into a national cricket ground. The so-called St Georges Oval was to be the world's first eco cricketing venue, made entirely of recycled materials and running exclusively on solar power. Spectators were to have an elevated view, picnicking from a grass verge on top of the quarry cliffs. It was hoped that this would host both league and international fixtures and there were even plans for a national development programme to be run from a local castle. Unfortunately the dream died when an investor pulled out and the land was used for golf and growing vegetables.

The Hungarian Cricket Association was formed in 2007 and a six-team league established. Despite not yet achieving affiliate status of the ICC they continued to develop, with the national team winning the Euro T20 tournament in Macedonia. In 2011 they took a further step forward by establishing a new ground in Budapest, the Szodiglet Oval. This helped them finally secure affiliate status in 2012. Although the cricket community is largely composed of expats, with an Afghan team established in Debrecen, there has been a focus on developing interest amongst the native population. In addition to the national team, that comprises a mix of ethnicities, there is also a national squad exclusively for native players. Fixtures are organised against other native squads across the region.

The idea is to give native players a chance to represent their country when they may not be as talented as expats who have learnt their cricket elsewhere. It also helps demonstrate to the government and media that it can be a local game, not just a game played by Asian communities. There are over 200 native cricketers in the country and weekly practice sessions are run, supporting an international programme.

There are youth development programmes in Budapest, Bekescaba, Pecs, Sarbogard and Szolonok and a women's national team has been established. The Danube Benders, a club comprised solely of native cricketers, toured England in 2013. They were captained by leading player Claudia Balogh.

Iceland

How many people have had a passion for cricket ignited in them after an afternoon watching a Test at Lord's? Quite a few you would imagine. That was certainly the case for Ragnar Kristinsson who returned to Iceland after what was clearly an inspiring day at the Home of Cricket to establish the Kylfan Cricket Club in Reykjavik. A year later, in 2000, another club was formed in Stykkisholmer and the two clubs met to decide the Iceland Championships. Shortly afterwards they faced international competition for the first time in the form of a stag party of a Manchester barrister. Several years later a team that included *Test Match Special* eccentric Henry Blofeld toured the country. Although requiring significant development to meet the criteria for affiliate membership ICC Europe have been supportive, funding installation of an artificial pitch. The Iceland team are due to tour the Czech Republic in 2017.

Italy

In 1993 the MCC toured Italy to mark the 200th anniversary of the first recorded game in the country. This was the brainchild of Simone Gambino, who you've already been introduced to, who as a passionate and well-connected Anglophile conceived the perfect opposition to mark the first game by the crew of HMS *Agamemnon* in Naples. But over the following two decades it was influence from the east rather than the west that would define cricket in the country. A steady influx of economic migrants from Bangladesh, Sri Lanka and Pakistan brought cricket to Italy, especially in industrial towns in the north of the country, such as Treviso where there is a large Bangladeshi community serving the ship salvage industry. The large number of Sri Lankan immigrants, reflected in scorecards of Italy games, was further supported by a link-up between the Cesena Cricket Club and the Sri Lankan Cricket board.

This trend forced Gambino to ease the policy he introduced in the eighties to have a minimum number of nine Italians in club sides. It simply wasn't sustainable and didn't reflect the ethnic make-up of the country's cricketing community. On the back of this migratory trend the Italian cricket league has increased to more than 30 teams, split across three divisions.

The cricketing capital of Italy is Bologna, known as Bologna the fat, for the quality of its local cuisine. It is thought that cricket is more popular there than in other cities like Milan, Rome and Turin simply because football has not taken such a vice-like grip on its citizens, giving other sports a chance to gain a foothold. It is a university town, the equivalent of Oxford or Cambridge, and perhaps cricket's gentler pace and cerebral challenge is well suited to the Bolognese. It is the only city in the country that has a number of different grounds and therefore the only viable location to host international tournaments. The best ground is undoubtedly at the Pionoro club, pleasantly situated amongst the slopes of the Apennine Hills, a short drive from the city. It is dedicated exclusively to cricket and in this is a rarity on the continent. This means it doesn't have to vie with other sports and therefore serves as the de facto home of Italian cricket. Other famous clubs are Capannelle in Rome and Cesena.

Italy has a higher profile on the international stage than its continental neighbours, with the exception of the Netherlands and Denmark, due to a selection policy that puts the onus on Italian passport holders rather than players who learn their cricket in the country. Italy would almost certainly not have qualified for division three of the World Cricket League or played in global T20 qualifiers if they only selected the best eligible players from the domestic league. The federation has taken the view that the national team will get more support if it mainly features players of Italian ethnicity, irrespective of where they learnt their cricket. Allied to this has been a conviction that the only way to raise the profile of cricket in the country and enthuse the native population to take up the game is if the national team is successful. This policy has been criticised by many who feel that the national team is not representative of the strength of Italy as a cricketing nation.

This focus on the national team coincided with the international career of Joe Scuderi who took up coaching responsibilities after retiring as a player. The former Australian under-19 cricketer and Lancashire all-rounder divided his time between Italy and Lancashire as he made the progression from player to coach. Under his stewardship Italy have selected an Australian international, in Michael Di Venuto, and players with first-class experience in Test-playing countries including Gareth Berg and Andy Northcote. They have played alongside talented players in the domestic league, most of whom such as Samantha de Mel and Dinidu Marage are of South Asian origin. This blend has made Italy the third highest ranked team in the region and a fixture in international tournaments such as the World Cricket League. Time together as a squad has often been an issue with players based across the world and this has perhaps been a factor in them just falling short of qualifying for the World Cup Qualifying Series or the Intercontinental Cup.

In recent years they have sought to focus more on youth development and it is hoped that this will produce talented local players who can step into the shoes of veterans like Alessandro Bonora. In 1996 there were only two under-16 teams in the country and now there are over 40, competing in a junior championship. Kwik Cricket programmes have now been introduced into 50 schools and it is hoped this will increase to 60 by 2020. These initiatives are helping improve Italy's performance in age group tournaments but they remain much less competitive at this level than at senior level, where the foreign-based players have led to an elevated ranking. It is clear that at youth level they have a long way to go to match countries with longer development programmes in place, such as the Netherlands, Denmark and even the Channel Islands. One promising player to emerge is talented seam bowler Luis Di Giglio who has been incorporated into the national squad and has played a few games at major tournaments. His sister, Leonella, has played for the ladies' team and is now a qualified scorer in international tournaments. Although Italy possess several high quality coaches such as the award-winning Kelum Perrera the national coaching structure has to improve to develop young talent that can match rivals in northern Europe.

The domestic league has been extended in recent years following the formation of new clubs, many of which are dominated by particular ethnic groups. The top division, Serie A, includes leading clubs such as Pionoro, Trentino, Bologna and Capannelle. It is from these clubs that locally based national players are selected. In 2003 a Serie B was created followed by the introduction of Serie C in 2007. There remains very little cricket played south of Rome and extending the reach of the sport across the whole country remains one of the challenges for the federation.

Seeking to close the gap in quality between the players in the domestic league and the foreign-based passport holders that make up the core of the national team, the federation established a High Performance Programme. This programme provides leading domestic players with specialised coaching and high performance clinics to raise standards. A programme of 'A' team fixtures was also established to help prepare players for the transition to international cricket.

The most promising native player to emerge in recent years is 17-year-old Letizia Vania, from Treviso. A gifted seam bowler, she won the player of the tournament award when Italy won a women's tournament held in Jersey in 2015. There is now a structured development plan for women's cricket and the formation of more women's teams. The federation organises regional high performance camps at senior, youth and women's level.

Availability of grounds is a significant constraint to the further development of cricket in the country, especially away from Bologna. The federation are focusing on this challenge in order to create facilities that can form regional hubs, bringing together club cricket and development programmes in schools. They are currently bidding for government funding to lay a turf wicket at the Pionoro ground. This will help improve techniques and prepare national teams playing tournaments on grass wickets, where traditionally they have struggled to adjust.

Italy have also supported the establishment of a Vatican cricket team. Their pontifical neighbours decided to form the St Peter's Cricket Club in late 2013, selecting players from the 300 or so priests and seminarians drawn from across the world. The instigator of the team, Father Theodore Mascarenhas, an Indian priest and handy off-break bowler, wants to combine his passion for the game with using cricket as a way of building bridges between faiths. As well as fixtures against the Church of England the club seeks fixtures against Muslim, Hindu, Sikh and Buddhist teams. There are also plans to form a female team drawn from Rome's convents. The team play on an astroturf pitch in Rome and have had support from the Australian and British ambassadors to the Holy See.

Street cricket played with a tape ball by immigrant communities is an increasingly common sight across the country. Sometimes these informal games are played for money and occasionally have caused feuds that have led to violence. The publication in 2013 of a book entitled 'the game of the new Italians' shows that cricket is seen as a significant element of the changing social and cultural dynamics in the country. If the federation can incorporate these players into its league structure it could have one of the largest cricketing populations in the region, although such an influx would put additional pressure on grounds.

Latvia

Cricket was brought to Latvia by a common route, British embassy staff. They played informal games in Riga in 1998 and the following year a club was established by Indian residents of the city. They quickly established links with Estonia where cricket was also being established at a similar time. There has been close collaboration ever since. Like Tallinn, Riga has an appeal as a quirky touring location and the Latvian Cricket Federation, formed in 2005, regularly hosts visiting sides. The weather only permits a short season, from April to July, and this is certainly a constraining factor as is the lack of official recognition or endorsement to fund development initiatives or promotion.

The main focus for the national team is the annual Baltic Cup, played against Lithuania and Estonia. Under their captain Piyush Bagpayee, who moved to the country from Gwalior, India, Latvia won the cup in 2013 and 2014. They have also played games against Russia and Finland, as well as club sides from the UK and Norway. The team is largely comprised of economic migrants from the subcontinent along with students at the Riga medical school with much less of a focus on developing native interest than in neighbouring Estonia. The three clubs in the country are Riga, Kwibir and Turiba with Riga historically dominant. An indoor league and national team training is held at the Zelta Bowling Centre. It was hoped that availability of cricket on Eurosport 2 would increase awareness of the game beyond the expat community but the player base remains limited.

The main cricketing centre in the country is not the capital Riga but the town of Tukums, 45 minutes to the west of Riga with a modest population of 20,000.

Lithuania

The first game played in the country was organised by the British embassy and took place in the grounds of the Lithuanian military academy. A cricket federation was established in 2007. Although most of the players in the country are expats a driving force for establishing cricket in Lithuania has been artist Darius Myksys, who developed a love for the game after living for many years in London and returned to his homeland determined to introduce it. He used his influence to establish a cricket ground at the Gelezinio Vilko sports club and also introduced the game to a school in Vilnius. The team play against their near neighbours in the Baltic Cup.

Luxembourg

As one of the centres of the European community it was natural that the city would attract enough people from cricket-playing backgrounds to sustain a cricketing community. In the 1970s the Optimist Cricket Club was formed and in 1978 a beneficent mayor provided a ground in Walferdange. In the early 1980s the tongue-in- cheekily titled Communist Cricket Club was formed and together with the Optimists they supplied players for a Luxembourg team that competed in European tournaments. In the 1990s international bi-lateral matches began against France and Belgium and the Optimists joined the Belgian league. The Luxembourg Cricket Federation was established in 1994 and ran a national league. Once players had met residency criteria Luxembourg were able to compete in ICC tournaments, though with very modest success. There is at least a three figure player base now though given the size of the country the potential for growth is limited.

Malta

Cricket in Malta has strong parallels with that in Corfu and Gibraltar. Strong British links have provided a legacy of facilities and the Mediterranean setting means it is a popular destination for touring teams. It hosts over 20 teams a summer, providing opposition and focus for the relatively small native cricketing community. It has previously competed in ICC tournaments, most recently in ICC Europe division 4 in 2012, but is now below the formal tournament structure with little chance of being reincorporated. Instead the Malta team have participated in some informal regional tournaments, such as the Central Europe Cup in 2015. The main challenges are finding additional grounds to relieve pressure on the Marsa Oval and inspiring a new generation of Maltese to take up the game.

Monaco

Perhaps surprisingly the tiny, princely enclave between France and Italy does possess a cricket club, though the availability and price of land means they have to play their games over the border in the mountains north of Nice. Although they possess players there is no supporting organisation or infrastructure, such as coaching or links with schools. This means they are likely to remain just a cricket team rather than anything more structured and ambitious.

Montenegro

With a starring role in a James Bond film helping to market modest Montenegro as an Adriatic playground for the rich and famous the town of Tivat is seeking to mirror the appeal and emulate the success of Monte Carlo. This has brought superyachts to the country and with them expat boathands keen to play some cricket. Some of these have formed the Porto Montenegro Cricket Club and somehow convinced former international goalkeeper and Premier League star Sasa Ilic to be their wicketkeeper. The club have played against a touring Welsh team and are seeking fixtures against Croatian clubs.

Netherlands

The Dutch qualified for the World Cup for the first time in 1996 and it was an opportune time to raise their profile on the global stage.

The sport was on the cusp of a transformation that would see money flood into the game, the ICC professionalise and development taken seriously for the first time in the game's long history. The Dutch were a talented side, as was evident from victories against England in 1989 and 1993 and the West Indies in 1991. They were one of the leading teams in the ICC Trophy and one of the few who were not reliant on expat players. Dutch clubs were comparatively rich, there were plenty of grounds and the introduction of professional player-coaches had supplemented domestic talent with quality imports with experience of first-class cricket.

In Paul-Jan Bakker and Roland Lefebvre the Dutch possessed two stars talented enough to have successful professional careers in England while other local products of a golden era included all-rounders Tim de Leede and Steven Lubbers and classy stroke-maker Klaas-Jan van Noortwijk. But this talent was the product of an amateur age and against professional opposition the Dutch struggled, losing all five of their games on their World Cup bow. The KNCB and the Dutch fans, who always lend colour, enthusiasm and joy to tournaments, enjoyed a fairy-tale adventure on the global stage. But fairy tales are stories of the fantastical and unexpected. The Dutch wanted to get a standing invite to the party and this meant adopting a more professional approach in an increasingly professional sport.

Tim de Leede

Tim de Leede holds almost every Dutch international record going. In a record 236 international appearances for his country he took 216 wickets and scored over 4,700 runs, more wickets and runs than any of his countrymen.

Born in 1968 in Leidschendam to a cricketing father, de Leede quickly emerged as one of the country's most promising young prospects and broke into the national under-19 squad when only 16. Four years later he was part of a 'young associates' team that competed at the Youth World Cup, playing alongside Trevor Penney, perhaps one of the greatest fielders ever to play the game, and future Test captain Aminul Islam. He made his full international debut in 1990 on a tour to the UAE and finally hung up his boots in 2007, the World Cup as his swansong. His highest score was 114 against the MCC in 1994 and his best bowling 4-20 against Denmark in 1998. A skilful medium-pace bowler and powerful batsman he became one of the beating hearts of the team, always relishing a challenge and never over-awed by the opposition, however famous or formidable.

His first major international tournament was the ICC Trophy in 1990. He was one of a talented generation emerging in the late 1980s, when Dutch cricket was at its peak, and would play alongside the likes of Lefebvre, the van Troost brothers and Jeroen Smits for much of his career. He played in three World Cups and included batsman of the calibre of Tendulkar and Hayden amongst his scalps. Altogether he played in 29 ODIs, many of which came late is his career when the Netherlands were awarded ODI status under the HPP. His averages of 17 with the bat and 34 for the ball do not do justice to his talent.

His 17-year international career (23 if you include age-group cricket) spanned different eras of the game in the Netherlands. Beginning in very much an amateur age with only occasional international matches by the 2007 World Cup, he was the veteran of a team being groomed by the ICC on a path to professionalisation. In Amstelveen in 2006 he smashed a half-century against Sri Lanka in an ODI. That day he batted alongside 16-year-old prodigy, Alexei Kervezee, who made an accomplished 47 on debut. There was a 22-year age difference but both delighted the crowd.

Though flirting with a county career in the early 90s, trialling for Surrey, Sussex and Northamptonshire, he has dedicated his career to his country and the Voorburg club, alongside running a sports shop. After retiring as a player he has moved seamlessly into coaching, heading the Voorburg Academy and becoming a short-term coach for France in 2015. He has also been a selector for the KNCB and helped develop young cricketers in the country. His son, Bas, is one of the brightest young prospects in the country. He is backed by many as a strong contender to become a future coach of the national team.

Nolan Clarke

Nolan Clarke may not be a household name in cricket. In fact few outside Holland have probably even heard of him. But he holds a world record. For in 1996 Clarke represented Holland at the World Cup at the age of 47 to help his adopted country compete on the global stage. The Barbadian cricketer, first came to the country as a coach in the mid-70s. Having made his first-class debut in 1970 at the age of 21 he was bemused, but ultimately accepted, when offered a position as a coach in Holland.

In his first year in Deventer he enjoyed the cricket, though felt it lacked the intensity he was used to in the West Indies. He drifted out of the game in the late 70s but a chance meeting in New Orleans saw him return to Holland to coach at Hercules and then Quick. He was soon one of the leading batsmen in the country and made his debut for the Netherlands in 1989 at the age of 41. It was a debut to remember as he made 77 in a victory over England. He was to get 99 caps for the Netherlands overall, one of a number of expat players, including Peter Cantrell and Fabian Aponso, who joined the home-grown players, a long career for a debutant in his forties. He scored over 3,000 runs at an average of 38, placing him high in the Dutch batting pantheon.

He hung up his boots at the age of 49 but returned aged 56 for the VVV club and scored close to 800 runs! An eccentric character and flamboyant dresser, Clarke remains a fervent supporter of Dutch cricket ever ready with an anecdote and technical advice to anyone willing to lend their ear.

* * * * *

They failed to qualify for the 1999 World Cup but in 2001 they won the ICC Trophy in Canada to qualify as leading associate in the 2003 World Cup. This time they broke their duck with a resounding victory over Namibia, with centuries for Kloppenburg and van Noortwijk. In this tournament they didn't play any foreign player-coaches and only one player, Adeel Raja, was born outside the country. It was a team with a blend of experience and young talent, such as Sussex stroke-maker Bas Zuiderent, powerful batsman Daan van Bunge and seamer Edgar Schiferli.

But it was two years later at the ICC Trophy in Ireland that the Netherlands secured two of the most significant victories in their cricketing history. In defeating both Denmark and the UAE the Dutch secured qualification for their third World Cup. The timing was crucial, for it was on the basis of rankings in this tournament that the ICC selected teams for its High Performance Programme. The Dutch were bestowed with ODI status, secured additional funding and were guided through a process of professionalisation.

So it was that in 2006 the Dutch hosted Sri Lanka in an ODI at the VRA ground, Amsterdam, on the fringes of the verdant expanse of the Amsterdam Bos. For the KNCB and Dutch players it was a seminal moment, playing their first ever official ODI outside of a World Cup and hosting a leading international team on home soil with equal status. They hoped it would be the first of many and help put cricket firmly on the country's sporting map. It was a blisteringly hot day, the pitch was a road and Sri Lanka made batting look easy: ridiculously easy in fact, amassing a then world record 443-9. The scorecard that day makes interesting reading, for it marked a change in selection philosophy of the KNCB. While five years before ten of the team had been born in Holland, in this debut home ODI five were born abroad. This reflected modern demographic trends, but it also revealed a steely pragmatism in selection. The Dutch were going to play the best team available to justify this new found faith of the ICC and the opportunities it brought. Thus was planted a seed that was to grow into an issue of contention in Dutch cricket. Two of these foreign-born players would be instrumental in bringing greater professionalism to the national team over the years to come.

Throughout their history the KNCB had always admired the starch-collared amateur ideals of the MCC. This extended to national team tours where the players tried hard for their country on the field but off it enjoyed a drink and a jape. They relied on talent and big game temperament, rather than professional routines, modern training methods and the rather horribly phrased 'one-percenters' of modern cricket. It was, you could say, more the cricket of Tiger Moth fly-bys than professional dieticians. But Peter Borren was to change that. A New Zealander of Dutch heritage, Borren had represented his home country at under-19 level but had emigrated to Holland in his early twenties. His debut was inauspicious, being smashed for 94 off his ten overs and making just two with the bat. But he would develop into a match-winning cricketer and an innovative and inspirational captain. He instilled a fierce determination to win and professional attitude that not all Dutch cricketers have lived up to. Another making his ODI debut that day was Ryan ten Doeschate, a South African with a Dutch passport who had played several seasons in the domestic league as a stepping stone to a career in country cricket. His preparation, determination and professionalism was a wake-up call to others in the squad. If you wanted a career in cricket you had to work very, very hard for it. He certainly did, averaging 142 in first-class cricket and 67 in ODIs for the Dutch.

Back in the 1990s Dutch players predominantly played for their clubs with international games being the rare exception. ICC Trophies and World Cups were only played very four years and other than an annual game against Denmark and the odd warm-up tour that was about it. There was little time together as a national team. But that all changed under the High Performance Programme. In 2007 Peter Borren barely had time to play for his club. In February he played in World Cricket League 1 in Kenya, in March the World Cup, the Intercontinental Cup in Canada in June, a Quadrangular ODI tournament in Ireland in July and another Intercontinental Cup game in August. It wasn't of course as many games as full members were assured of through the Future Tours Programme but it was nevertheless a busy programme. Towards the end of the decade this intensified further with the addition of the T20 format at international level. The game was changing for the select few in the national team, while remaining as ever it was for the vast majority.

Although they had qualified for two successive World Cups the Netherlands had made little impact, failing to get a full member scalp or progress from the group stages. In 2007 Ireland had defeated Pakistan and won themselves a global profile in the process. However, in the opening game of the World T20 in 2009 the Netherlands shocked hosts England at Lord's and put Dutch cricket on the front and back pages of newspapers across the world.

The heroes were home-grown stalwart Tom de Grooth with 49 from 30 balls and a typically reliable contribution with bat and ball by Ryan ten Doeschate. Overnight the Dutch became the cricket world's favourite underdog and the team's heroics even earned them fleeting celebrity back home. But while they had charmed the world, back in the Netherlands they had to face up to some hard truths. There was a risk that the glitz of the global stage could mask some worrying trends in domestic cricket.

Participation numbers in Holland had reduced markedly since the mid-80s. Current levels are worryingly close to the 5,000 minimum required to receive the annual 250,000 Euro funding from the Netherlands Olympic Committee. Native players now made up only half the player base. Only 18 of the 48 clubs had any youth teams and there were less than 1,000 youth cricketers in the country; 60% of players in under-11 teams were lost to the game by the age of 18. The extension of hockey and football seasons had encroached into the cricketing summer and most children told to focus on a sport naturally favoured one with a million players and career prospects over a minority sport their friends didn't play. Although the KNCB had a healthy operating budget of two million euros this was predominantly focused on the national team, to meet the aspirations of the High Performance Programme. Little was allocated to recreational cricket or the lower leagues. Many clubs felt they had to make too many concessions to support the board's aspirations for the national team and that the league was being marginalised in a single-minded pursuit of glory.

This was the backdrop to the appointment of Richard Cox as CEO in December 2009. He sought to bring greater professionalism to the by now antiquated Dutch set-up by shifting responsibilities from the board to staff in the KNCB office, with board members adopting more of an advisory role. The close of the amateur era appeared to be symbolised by the end of a 79-year print run for the subscription magazine *Cricket,* whose membership had fallen to 600. Cox identified five key target areas: youth cricket, financial stability, sponsorship, staff responsibilities and coach development.

The Dutch lions youth teams had failed to win a tournament since 2004. They were consistently outclassed by Ireland and Scotland, who the Dutch saw as their natural comparitors, and even the Channel Island teams were beginning to close the gap. This stemmed a flow of talented players into the national team which had caused the selectors to broaden their horizons. Jeroen Smits, high performance advisor to the board after hanging up his gloves, bizarrely and disrespectfully referred to as John Smid in Matthew Hayden's autobiography, had been scouting for players with Dutch passports on the other side of the world. It was a policy that had a worrying echo of Italian selection strategy. He brought future Australia A batsman Tom Cooper to the Netherlands in apparent contravention of league rules. This policy was criticised by the clubs but they themselves had to shoulder some of the blame for not placing enough emphasis on youth. Many clubs had no youth teams at all, while others struggled to field teams.

In a positive move the KNCB revived committees for youth and women's cricket. The former consulted clubs and created a strategy called 'Developing cricket together', which targeted a doubling of youth players in five years. Five clubs across the country commenced a programme to build links with schools in their regions. The board also felt there needed to be a culture change in Dutch clubs who were not being proactive enough in attracting youth in their areas or promoting the game. To address this they introduced a club charter that set out a number of criteria for clubs to progress towards elite status. To achieve this objective clubs had to have both youth and women's team as well as a development plan and integration with their local community. It didn't prove popular with clubs and was replaced with the less proscriptive 'club support' programme.

The KNCB themselves introduced development officers in three regions to support the clubs and oversee a development pathway for young talent. Coach Peter Drinnen and high performance director Roland Lefebvre took a more hands-on approach too, developing personal development plans and a more competitive schedule for the

Lions programme. Just as in the early days of Dutch cricket being shown up against an English side was a major motivation to improve so the KNCB felt the pressure to perform well against other teams in the HPP. Additional funding enabled a few players to be contracted and they were given defined development responsibilities. Women's cricket, after a long period of decline, also revived and under the captaincy of Helmien Rambaldo the Dutch Lionesses won four titles in 2011, in European and ECB tournaments.

In 2010 a new elite division, the Topklasse, was introduced with the intention of increasing standards through a concentration of talent. In the same year the Dutch were integrated into the ECB's 40-over domestic competition, in effect withdrawing the national team squad from domestic cricket to play a higher standard against county opposition in England. To further support elite development the Netherlands were granted TAPP funding by the ICC to create elite regional squads and secure ODI fixtures with full members. This was all part of achieving their HPP objective of developing a national team that could compete on the global stage. The inference being that the Dutch league was not of the requisite standard to produce players of the required calibre.

The development of regional squads, the Hurricanes and Seafarers, was intended to be part of a joint collaboration with Scotland and Ireland, their fellow HPP countries in the region. Regional teams from each country, professionally run with franchise style branding, would compete in a tournament that it was hoped would be given List A status, perhaps even become professionalised once established.

However, Ireland decided to have their own inter-provincial tournament leaving the Dutch to partner the Scots in what would become the North Sea Pro Series. The tournament is still running, though it hasn't achieved the status or generated the interest that was envisaged. The idea was that the regional squads would create a bridge between club cricket and the national team, serving as a finishing school for young talent to toughen them up for the challenge of facing the world's leading teams. To ensure players were available for an increasingly busy international schedule the KNCB introduced retainer contracts, awarded to a squad of 16. Later five players, including captain Peter Borren and wicketkeeper-batsman Wes Barresi were given full-time contracts. These reforms were resented by some clubs who saw their star players, many of whom they paid decent salaries, miss much of the league through representative cricket.

In addition to the part professionalisation of the national squad this further injection of funding enabled the KNCB office to expand to 11 paid staff, including regional development officers. A very successful initiative launched in this period was the bilingual schools project. This saw 1,000 children across 27 schools introduced to the game, with regional coaching clinics for teachers, four regional tournaments and a national final. This award-winning programme was run alongside Street20, promoting social inclusion through cricket, and cage cricket bringing cricket to deprived communities in urban areas.

This represented a concerted, coordinated effort to place the emphasis on youth and broaden the player base. Whether it was the coincidence of good timing or a result of a more structured youth programme the Dutch youth teams had a successful year in 2012. Players such as van Meekeren, Kingma, Rahil Ahmed and Sebastian Braat emerged and for the first time in years there was genuine excitement about a new generation of young talent that could prosper on the international stage. The KNCB kept a close eye on their young charges and provided some funding to enable them to attend cricket academies overseas during the winter to further aid their development.

By 2013 these reforms were beginning to make an impact. The team were now beating counties in the Pro 40 tournament, there was young home-grown talent being introduced to the national team and progress was being made in reviving women's cricket. They had finally secured a sponsor too, with major Dutch bank ABN-AMRO providing funding for an international programme and facilities in exchange for market penetration in the Gulf and Asia and the visibility of sponsorship at the World Cup. It was through this partnership that the Netherlands secured an ODI with South Africa on home soil. It was part of a plan to establish Amsterdam as a preparation base for Test teams touring England.

They could acclimatise, train and use games against the Dutch as warm-up fixtures. The HPP associates had not secured the number of fixtures against full members the development programme had hoped, despite this being a key element of TAPP funding grants, and proposals by Cox and other CEOs to incorporate the ODI associates into the Future Tours Programme came to naught. Unfortunately, despite bringing arguably the world's best team to town the press in the Netherlands paid little notice and it didn't raise the profile of the game as hoped. Eric Szwarcynski was unluckily and heartbreakingly run out two short of a maiden ODI hundred in a comfortable victory for the tourists.

Mudassar Bukhari

Penetrative seam bowler and lower order batsman Mudassar Bukhari was one of the first players of South Asian origin to establish himself in the national side. He was therefore a trail-blazer, along with Adel Raja and Mohammed Kashif, for Asian cricketers in the country. Arriving in the country from Pakistan as a teenager he played youth team cricket in 2000 and joined the Asian club before progressing to the VVV club in Amsterdam.

He made his international debut against Canada in June 2007 and over the next few years established himself as the principal strike bowler. While certainly not quick he was capable of finding late movement and in close to a decade of international cricket has rarely been taken apart. His aggressive, if at times frenetic, batting has also proved useful. As one of the players awarded a central contract he has travelled the world representing his country and is one of the few Dutch players to have played over 100 List A games. He is perhaps unlucky not to have been given a chance in a franchise tournament such as the Bangladesh Premier League. He has a combined haul of 100 wickets in ODIs and T20Is.

At times he has struggled to reach the levels of fitness and professionalism demanded by national team coaches but is now one of the elder statesmen of the side, providing experience to a talented young seam attack including Vivian Kingma and Paul van Meekeren. He plays his club cricket for Dosti and has been very influential in the creation and promotion of a Dutch version of the Pakistan Champions League. Bukhari announced his retirement from international cricket in September 2016, finishing as the highest wicket taker for Holland with 245 scalps.

* * * * *

Although Dutch cricket was beginning to develop, further progress was contingent on retaining the increased levels of ICC funding available to HPP countries. This meant securing a place at the next World Cup, in itself a necessary prerequisite to attract sponsors. The quickest, most secure route to the 2015 World Cup was by finishing in the top two of the World Cricket League Championship. The Netherlands performed well in this tournament, but a controversial abandonment against Canada in King City, an incident that had Dutch cricket journalist Bertus de Jong foaming at the mouth in rage, saw the Dutch finish fourth, behind Ireland and Afghanistan. This meant they had to qualify through the World Cup Qualifier, held in New Zealand in January 2014. They started the tournament as favourites but were to have a disaster. Having already lost to Namibia they were humiliated by Kenya who flayed the Dutch attack to all parts in chasing down their total of 265 in less than 36 overs to move above them into the final stages of the tournament. Captain Peter Borren was dumbstruck and the cricket community back home dumbfounded. They had not only failed to qualify for the World Cup for the first time in the new millennium but lost their ODI status and High Performance Programme funding in the process. Borren spoke candidly about how a single bad day in the field had undermined a decade's process. The interview made for brutal viewing: the emotion, disappointment and anger etched into his face.

The spring of 2014 was a time of uncertainty and anxiety in Dutch cricket. With a reduction in funding it wasn't clear whether the progress towards professionalisation they had embarked on since 2010 could be sustained. Would the KNCB have to cut staff and what would this mean for development initiatives? Could they still afford to have contracted players? Would the North Sea Pro Series initiative, that was intended to be the first phase in securing a List A domestic tournament, be scrapped? With these questions in their minds and after their ODI careers had been abruptly ended the team prepared for the World T20 in Bangladesh. To accommodate more associate teams the tournament now had a preliminary phase. Recalling the heroics of 2009 the Dutch stunned Ireland by chasing down 190 in just 14.2 overs. They had done to Ireland what Kenya had done to them earlier in the year. It was undoubtedly one of the most exciting games in the tournament and saw the Netherlands progress to the Super 10 stage where they were in a winning position against South Africa only to blow it, but finished on a high with another victory over England. They were rewarded a few months later with T20I status. They could once again seek games against the full members.

Although the World T20 was a resounding success the Netherlands did not leave the tournament without controversy. Tim Gruijters, a talented off-spinning all-rounder, had been selected in the original squad. However, when Tom Cooper became available after his team were knocked out of the Sheffield Shield competition in Australia he replaced Gruijters, who was said to have a back injury. Gruijters posted a YouTube video on the internet claiming the KNCB forced him to have a scan and that the injury was a historic one that he had always played with and that the management had bent the rules to make sure their star player was available. The KNCB refuted this and were cleared of any wrongdoing by the ICC. Nevertheless it did little to dissuade many Dutch cricket supporters that the national team was buying success through imported players. Gruijters remains out of the national team but won coach of the year in the KNCB's 2015 awards.

By the end of 2014 the financial impact of losing ODI status and not qualifying for the World Cup was clearer. The ending of TAPP funding and the withdrawal of ABN-AMRO as sponsor had reduced the budget by $800,000. The ambitious target to double youth playing numbers had not been met, though years of decline had at least been stemmed by a modest increase. A new target was set for a 10% increase year on year but this has not been met either. In January 2015 Richard Cox left as CEO and wasn't replaced. Later that month the team won World Cricket League 2 in Namibia, securing promotion back to the World Cricket League Championship and the Intercontinental Cup. In the tournament seamer Ashan Malik recorded the rather improbable figures of five wickets for seven runs. It signalled an impressive recovery for the Dutch after losing their ODI status a year earlier and confirmed them once again as one of the leading associate nations in the world, albeit a little poorer than they were.

In late 2015 there was a shake-up in the KNCB with Betty Timmer voted in as chairman, with a team including Steven Lubbers and Rod Lyall. This new board promised a greater emphasis on youth. Meanwhile national selectors continued to bolster the quality of the squad with imported players. Former South African off-spinner and power hitter Roelof van der Merwe was selected for the World T20. The Dutch defeated Ireland but this time failed to get out of the preliminary phase, with Bangladesh progressing from their group. Since they were awarded T20I status the Dutch have played six T20Is outside global tournaments, four against Nepal and one each against the UAE and Scotland.

With the exception of the World Cup Qualifier debacle in 2014 Anton Roux has been a successful coach since replacing Peter Drinnen. Success in T20 is now being replicated in longer formats, with the Netherlands second in the Intercontinental Cup and leading the World Cricket League Championship. Unfortunately for the Dutch the ICC have taken the decision to focus funding on the top two associates, with Ireland and Afghanistan now elevated from the World Cricket League Championship to the ODI ranking table. However, continued good form in the WCLC could see the Netherlands qualify for the next World Cup and reclaim their much cherished ODI status. They could even play Tests if proposals planned for 2019 come into effect. This would enable them to maximise potential revenue from the scorecard and performance grant. This could potentially see the professionalisation of the national squad but this would be contingent on securing a regular programme of fixtures against the world's leading teams.

Despite the implementation of positive initiatives such as the bilingual schools programme and Street20 Dutch cricket still faces the same challenges identified in 2010. While its eastern neighbour Germany is likely to reach 10,000 players in the near future the KNCB have struggled to get playing numbers back up to 1980 levels, let alone into five figures. Cricket has been introduced to around 500 schools in one form or another but these initiatives are not leading to a broadening of the player base. There are fewer than 50 clubs in the country, less than half the number in Germany, and every year or so another goes. Not all clubs registered participate in tournaments and getting clubs to field youth teams is a perennial challenge.

The shift, if it does come, is more likely to come from the inclusion in formal leagues of recreational cricketers playing tape ball cricket. It may even be that official player numbers reduce as players choose to play recreational cricket rather than face the costs and comply with the regulations of the league. Cricket is very much the junior partner in multi-sports clubs and finding it increasingly difficult to protect a full length season and retain access to facilities in the face of more popular, more profitable sports. Cricket still has powerful, well connected champions that give the sport more influence than its minority status warrants.

This year saw the launch of the Pakistan Champions League Holland, backed by Bukhari and other high profile Pakistani cricketers in the country. The six-team T20 format mirrors Pakistani city franchises and includes leading domestic players of Asian origin such as Rahil Ahmed and the Zulfiqur triplets and has a sponsor in SR Professionals. The KNCB have offered notional support, though have not allowed their contracted players to feature. Whether this leads to other such tournaments and a challenge to the KNCB's league structure remains to be seen. It serves as a reminder though that players want to play cricket that is relevant and exciting to them.

On a positive note there have been signs that cricket is starting to spread out once again from the Randstad, the urban area on the western coast stretching from Amsterdam to Rotterdam. In 1990 there were 20 clubs outside this urban belt but by 2008 this had reduced to eight. However, since 2009 new clubs have formed in Heerenveen and Zwolle with the Friesland club, in the far north, recently reforming after 100 years. The board is keen for clubs to build links with local municipalities. A good example of this is Schiedam where cricket plays an integral role in the town's tourism promotion and an annual cricket week is held, attracting teams from across the continent. The Netherlands have also played a useful role in supporting less established cricket nations in the region, through tournaments like the Continental T20.

Two of the most promising young players in the country are women. Miranda Veringmeier, who made her ODI debut at 15, was recently selected as one of the associate stars to join a Big Bash franchise and this season is playing for Worcestershire. Meanwhile stylish batter Sterre Kalis has joined Essex.

National coach Anton Roux left for Otago in August 2016 and popular national team manager Ed Van Nierop was not retained. National team stalwart Mudassar Bukhari has also announced his international retirement making it a period of change for the men in orange. They are, however, very well placed in the World Cricket League Championship and in Van Meekeren, Malik and Kingma have a very talented, home-grown seam bowling attack.

Norway

On the outskirts of Oslo as you peel off the ring-road is a light industrial estate with row upon row of grey 70s-style office blocks and warehouses. One of these used to house one of the country's largest printing presses. But these days the whirr of print and whiff of ink has been replaced by the sound of crisply struck drives and an aroma of perspiration. For this is the rather unlikely setting for Norway's Cricket Academy. The facility cost around half a million euros to build and houses two nets, all the latest training aids, a gym and seminar room. In freezing winter evenings when the light is low and the snow knee deep the city's cricket clubs converge on the academy to hone their skills. It has become the bustling hub of Norwegian cricket, providing all-year facilities in a country where the season is curtailed by a harsh northern climate and where over 90% of the clubs do not have a home ground. It also serves as the high performance centre for the Norwegian Cricket Board. The national team trains in the nets, leading players go through their personal fitness plans in the gym and coaches and the high performance director assess progress on the country's strategic development plan. And virtually none of the thousands of motorists driving past every day even know what cricket is.

Despite its rather quirky setting the academy is one of the best facilities of its kind in Europe. While other continental cricketing nations have to book an hour or two at a multi-sport venue for training, making do with a roped-off corner of a football pitch, Norway's promising young cricketers have access to a dedicated, state of the art facility. For a minority sport it was an impressive coup that has given Norwegian cricket the opportunity to elevate the sport to another level and become one of the strongest cricket nations in the region. As anyone who has ordered a beer in Oslo will attest, Norway is an expensive nation and the grant they received from the

ICC wouldn't even cover a fraction of the cost. Instead the funding came from the government who acknowledge the critical role cricket is playing in integrating ethnic minority groups into an increasingly cosmopolitan culture. It is government money provided to achieve social objectives that is laying the foundation for cricketing success.

Cricket in the country began when the first wave of economic migrants arrived from the subcontinent in the 1960s. The Oslo Cricket Club was formed by Pakistani players in 1972 and was soon followed by the Indian-founded Kampen Cricket club. But there were several factors that limited growth of the game. Firstly there were no grounds available and because the football season extends through the summer opportunities to borrow a place to play were few and far between. Further to the south in say England or the Netherlands, sportsmen can play football in the winter and switch to cricket in the summer.

This seasonality has helped cricket both attract players looking for a summer sport and benefit from space and facilities in football's off season. But Norway doesn't have this advantage and the Europe-wide problem of attracting footballers to the sport is exacerbated by direct scheduling clashes. In 1996 the Oslo Sports Council provided a ground. Interest in the game developed as the Indian and Pakistani communities grew and cricket was available through Asian TV channels. By the early 2000s there were 14 clubs in the city. But they all had to use one ground, which made for a very congested fixture list. And when the ground became waterlogged all cricket in the country was suspended.

In 2000 Norway became an affiliate member of the ICC and won the first international tournament they played, the five nations tournament in Vienna. They went on to consolidate their position as Europe's strongest affiliate nation and were promoted to European division 1 in 2006. This represented very quick progress considering the country only got its first dedicated cricket ground two years earlier, in the Oslo suburb of Stovnor. In 2007 the cricket board was formally recognised by the Norwegian Sports Council. Sport receives a high level of government funding and support in Norway and this formal adoption was a critical point in the development of the sport because it meant the board could put in place more ambitious plans than would be possible under the meagre grant from the ICC.

The Norwegian Cricket Board has an office adjoining the 25,000-seater national football stadium in Oslo. They share a corridor and canteen with other minority sports, while the football federation and Olympic body have a capacious office upstairs. There are two desks, a trophy cabinet, boxes of promotional leaflets, a few national team shirts and a bookshelf with folders of league regulations and umpire contact details. It is the epicentre of administration and quite a contrast from the academy a 15-minute drive away. All sports have access to communal lawyers and accountants, not to mention a subsidised canteen. And what are the problems solved from those desks? The bread and butter is disciplinary issues in the league, visa issues on international tours and compiling statistics on participation levels for the ICC scorecard.

There are now 57 clubs in Oslo. While that might sound extremely encouraging it is actually far too many and one of the main challenges for the board. The pattern of cricket in the city has been that when a club gets more than 22 players it fragments in two. The benefits, from a players' perspective, are threefold. Firstly a registered club receives funding directly from the local government. Secondly with fewer players there is a greater chance of being a kingpin in the club and being the star player. Thirdly if there are only 11 players you are guaranteed to get in the starting line-up. From the board's perspective this trend has made it very difficult to implement their development plan. Clubs are a key vehicle for developing youth players but if they keep splintering they don't have the funding, capability or infrastructure to sustain a youth team. This proliferation of teams also puts considerable pressure on the four available grounds. Scheduling games becomes virtually impossible, especially if played across multiple formats. Talent doesn't concentrate in such a fragmented structure, making talent identification and development difficult. Currently the league structure, that features four divisions and a masters cup, only covers the Oslo area although there are clubs in Bergen, Trondheim and Tromso. Evening leagues are held at under-15 and under-19 level, though the board struggle to convince clubs to establish youth sections.

Norway became a force to be reckoned with in regional tournaments under the stewardship of Ralph Dellor, a much respected voice of both *Test Match Special* and *Match of the Day* who became one of the most respected and influential cricket coaches in Europe. He became coach in 2003 and soon identified the talent within the cricketing community, bringing a much more professional approach to training and fitness. He had an immediate impact with Norway winning the ECC affiliates championship in 2003 and again in 2005. This ensured that when a divisional structure was created in 2006 Norway leapfrogged many more established countries in the region. In 2008 they were promoted to European division 1 and qualified for division 5 of the World Cricket League. This capped a remarkable rise through the rankings under Dellor and saw Norway elevated from regional to international tournaments. Discipline and a professional approach to training were instrumental and Dellor harnessed the natural talents of players like Shabbas Butt, Zaheer Ashiq and Aamir Waheed.

However, they found the going much harder in the World Cricket League and suffered the humiliation of three successive relegations from division 5 in 2008 to division 8 in 2012. In division 8 in Samoa they finished fifth which meant a return to regional qualification pools. Dellor's good work had seemingly been undone and Norway had failed to prepare adequately or adjust to conditions outside Europe. The talent was still there but the team struggled to perform consistently over 50 overs, with players seemingly content with boundary-laden cameos rather than patient, match-winning innings. The fitness of an aging squad was also a problem. In response selection in recent years has focused more on younger, fitter players. The recent focus on T20 format for lower ranked ICC members has suited Norway who certainly have more power than patience, reflecting the mindset of idols such as Afridi and Akmal. In the shortest format they play in European division 1 and in 2014 defeated France to qualify for World Cricket League 6, held in Essex in September 2015. They performed well to finish fourth. Unfortunately the WCL was contracted once again to the original five divisions, so Norway will have to qualify again through regional pathway events.

Norway has been one of the teams criticised for an over-reliance on expats from the subcontinent. But with domestic cricket in the country only played by these ethnic groups it is unrealistic to expect Norway to play native players in the near future. The initial focus of the board is to attract second generation players from these communities, born and learning their cricket in the country. This can help get the sport more established which can then be the foundation for attracting greater ethnic diversity to the game, including native Norwegians. The board have struggled to get clubs to focus on youth development. The majority of clubs would rather see money spent on ground improvements than developing the next generation. The tension between the short-term focus of clubs and the long-term strategy of the board is central to the story of Norwegian cricket.

The board have a strategic plan for 2025 that puts the onus on youth development. The first phase is to introduce cricket into schools and provide training and support for PE teachers to teach and promote the game. It is hoped that this will lead to six partnership pilots between schools and their local clubs. Once this is in place the intention is to hold a national cricket week for children under 13 and establish leagues at under-10, under-13, under-15 and under-19 level. To address the significant constraint of the number and quality of grounds the board are targeting the development of a national ground, capable of hosting international tournaments, by 2020.

Following the success of the national academy they plan to establish three more indoor cricket facilities.

While Oslo teams struggle for grounds clubs elsewhere in the country struggle for games. The board offer financial compensation for clubs travelling to the capital but currently those in Tromso, Bergen and Trondheim are isolated. This makes them vulnerable to losing players and interest. It is hoped that Trondheim, on the north-west coast, can become a second cricketing centre. The board are speaking with the local club, the municipal authorities and schools in the town to develop a coordinated project to launch cricket as a local sport. They are hoping that by working with media partners they can plan a high profile launch and generate considerable interest and enthusiasm that can form and sustain a cricketing community and a local league. If this is successful it could become a model for setting up regional hubs. Regional leagues would then feed into a national championship to ensure a concentration of the country's leading talent.

Norway's cricketers are clearly well connected back in Pakistan as bowling star Mohammad Asif was lured over to play league cricket in Oslo as part of his preparations to return to international cricket after his ban.

Poland

The development of cricket in Poland, or at least the desire to develop it beyond games between a handful of clubs, came a little late to benefit from the more inclusive development approach of the ICC. While countries with a similar level of cricketing interest and infrastructure were able to meet affiliate criteria in the first decade of the 21st century, once these criteria were strengthened it became difficult for others to join. Therefore Poland is one of the countries out on a cricketing limb, without guaranteed funding, recognition or regional support.

Warsaw Cricket Club was founded in 1994, bringing together expats from Commonwealth countries who had migrated to the city for employment. They play at the Panorama Country Club, an old-world, old-school-tie venue that provides an idyllic location for cricket.

It is also situated opposite a nudist beach, which keeps the umpires' eyes sharp. As with many cricket clubs in the region Warsaw CC struggled to establish a settled player base with many cricketers on short-term contracts leaving just as they had become established. Around the turn of the millennium other clubs formed in Gorzow and Skwierzyna and domestic games could be played. The best players from these clubs that met ICC residency qualifications formed a quasi-national team, known as the Polonia Cricket Club.

In 2002 the Poland team competed against the Czech Republic and Slovakia in a tri-nations tournament in Prague. A more formal league was in place by 2012 with clubs in Lodz, Lublin, Wroclaw and Krakow. Cricket in Poland took a significant step forward when a new ground was developed in the Warsaw suburb of Stare Berbice. This has given the cricket community a firmer foundation. Poland has hosted a tri-series tournament at their new ground and regularly participate in regional tournaments, with particularly strong links to the Czech federation.

The Warsaw Hussars club have been very active in the development of 'native' international teams in the region. These allow indigenous players of any ability to represent their country without the pressure of needing to outperform experienced expats to make the national team.

Portugal

The wine trade brought cricket to Portugal where it was played as the most gentlemanly of English pursuits by English traders, both in Porto and Lisbon. Local players were excluded from the fun. Although it never secured a foothold amongst local players the annual match between the two cities ranks as one of the oldest cricketing rivalries in the region. The composition of modern Portuguese cricket is much more cosmopolitan, through a mixture of migratory trends and political upheaval following the 1974 revolution. Following the break-up of its empire people returned to Portugal from newly independent territories like Goa and Mozambique, that had cricketing heritage. Together with economic migrants from the subcontinent this provided a relatively large population in the urban centres who came from a cricketing background, and therefore the opportunity to develop cricket in the country.

The cricket association of Portugal was formed in 1994 and became an affiliate member of the ICC in 1996. The team performed well in regional tournaments in the late nineties and won the 2001 ECC Trophy, bringing them to the front of the chasing pack closing the gap on more established associate nations such as France and Germany. But unfortunately enthusiasm faded and performance suffered and Portugal slipped further and further down the regional rankings during the noughties. The one positive in this period was their strong performances in indoor tournaments.

Cricket in the country is centred in Lisbon which has a local league comprising of between three and seven clubs. Retaining players amongst an itinerant migrant community is a constant challenge. The Lisbon league has been expanded to incorporate clubs from the Algarve and Almoster. Availability of grounds has been a constant source of anxiety for Portuguese cricketers. The traditional home was at the Lisbon Casuals ground but when this was modernised and privatised access became too expensive for most of the players to afford. Thankfully a new site was found and there is now a dedicated cricket ground in the village of Albergaria. The highlight of the calendar though remains the Kendall Cup, between the Lisbon and Porto clubs.

Having been one of the countries warned by the ICC that they must participate in regional tournaments, Portugal played in Euro division 2 T20 in 2012 after being conspicuous by their absence for several years. Ironically they are now one of the teams that has fallen off the bottom of the regional tournament structure. Strangely there has not been close collaboration with Spain or any effort to establish an Iberian regional tournament mirroring the initiative shown in central Europe and the Baltics.

Romania

The story of Romanian cricket would make for an entertaining Hollywood script: an improbable tale of passion and beneficence. IT millionaire Gabriel Marin, a very talented handball player which is a popular sport in the country, sent his son Radu to a private boarding school in Switzerland. He just happened to choose Zuoz college where cricket has been long established and Radu became a convert to the sport. Radu badgered his father to buy a Sky TV box to watch the World Cup in 2007. Gabriel became even more hooked than his son, flying across the world to watch the Ashes and the IPL. He returned to Romania pledging five million euros to establish cricket in the country. At the time there were just a handful of expats playing for the Transylvania Cricket Club that had been formed in 2006, playing occasional matches at the national rugby stadium. Marin teamed up with the Transylvanian Club and helped set up Cricket Romania and using his business acumen established the organisation on a corporate model. His aspirations were far from modest and he had the financial muscle to turn his dream into a reality.

He bought a huge plot at the village of Moara Vlasiei and employed British groundsman Alan Lewis to design and build the best cricket ground on the continent. Featuring a turf wicket, a club house and an indoor training facility, it is the envy of cricketers across the region and an incredible base from which to grow the sport. It is the only turf wicket in eastern Europe. Soon clubs in Timisoara, Constanta, Iasi and Cluj were founded, providing opposition for Bucharest and spreading cricket across the country. There has been some success engaging locals in the game, partly because of the similarity of cricket with a traditional rounders-like game called *oina*. With similar skills required many *oina* players found they could strike a cricket ball a long way. The Timisoara Lions team is comprised exclusively of native players and it is a condition of the national league that clubs must field two native players.

A programme has been launched that has introduced cricket to 300 Romanian children in 20 schools and a Kwik Cricket inter-school league has been established. Romania were granted affiliate status in 2013 but the timing was unfortunate for their international aspirations as the ICC were contracting their regional tournament structure. Instead they play in Balkan tournaments and along with Greece and Bulgaria are primarily focused on developing native players rather than incorporating expats. In Moara Vlasiei they possess a facility that can serve as a base for developing the game in the region. There are currently eight clubs and 200 cricketers, with five other grounds sustaining cricket across the country. Coach and scorer schemes are regularly run to build capacity in the domestic game.

Russia

Cricket was played in St Petersburg in the 1870s and 1880s with British diplomats, merchants and managers of textile mills playing the game. There was sufficient interest for a four-team league to be established in 1895. But the Bolsheviks considered the game the epitome of bourgeois and the game was discouraged. After the revolution the British residents fled the city and cricket died out. The game revived in the mid-nineties when occasional matches were played between expats. In the absence of cricket equipment in sports shops broomhandles were used for wickets. In 1997 significant interest was generated by a match between Indian and Pakistani teams to commemorate the 50th anniversary of independence in 1947. This sporadic cricket was organised into a league in 2000, the organisation of which led to the formation of Cricket Russia in 2004. This comes under the auspices of the Multisport Association of Russia that oversees the running of sports which are not incorporated into the Olympics.

Cricket in the country is indebted to a more popular sport for one of its two principal venues, with cricket played at the Moscow State University Baseball Stadium. This has an artificial outfield and is the focal point for cricket in the country. The second ground is at the ISKRA Sports complex, though this has a shale outfield. In St Petersburg cricket was played in the former parade ground for the tsar's imperial guard and, following eviction from there, in the Tavrichesky Garden using metal chair legs for stumps.

Russia gained affiliate membership in 2012 and there are currently eight senior men's teams and two women's teams. Domestic cricket is played in 30- and 20-over formats. There is also an under-16 league playing ten-over matches. The official league is played exclusively in Moscow although recreational cricket is played in St Petersburg. An academy was established in 2012 to develop the game amongst native players, with over 130 boys, men and girls receiving tuition and coaching. Coaching materials have been translated into Russian for this programme.

The first foreign team to tour was our old friends the Carmel and District Cricket Club, who visited in 2007. The following year a Russian national team competed in the Euro T20 tournament in Wales and a six-nation tournament in the Czech Republic. They have also competed in tournaments in Bulgaria and Macedonia. In 2012 the national team included four native players.

Although Russia were accepted as an ICC affiliate member Cricket Russia have faced a challenge to their legitimacy from a breakaway league run by the so-called Board of Control for Cricket in Russia. While Cricket Russia has sought to generate interest and participation from native Russians, targeting the conversion of softball players, the rival Board of Control is focused purely on organising leagues for Asian expats. These leagues attract investment and some players in Russia are making a decent living from the game.

Cricket Russia have developed a Russian cricket academy in the Moscow suburb of Karacharavo and recently covered the astro-surface in sand to host a Moscow Beach Cup. This is yet another example of innovation generating interest and a potential source of revenue through cricket tourism. In the north a version of the game has developed called Cossach Wicket that combines cricket and a traditional game called *chizh* and is played with a single stump and a tape ball. Five hundred players have been introduced to this distinctly Russian form of the game.

Serbia

Serbia's cricketing pioneers, sensing perhaps that they were making history, chose a historical landmark as their first 'ground'. In 2007 cricket began in Belgrade on a grassed area below the Kalemegdan fortress using a baseball bat and a tennis ball. This group of native enthusiasts, joined by an Indian friend, soon attracted interest and more players. They were spotted by the British embassy who gave them a Kwik Cricket set enabling them to retire the baseball bat. The group soon swelled to 30, 20 of whom were locals, and they began playing tape ball cricket in ten-over games before deciding to put cricket in the city on a more formal footing, forming two clubs, Stari Grad and Mirijevo. The following year a team was established in Cacak in the west of the country and in 2009 the Serbian Cricket Federation was founded. They established a national 40- and 20-over league and the Carmel Cricket Club, who love nothing better than finding new opposition on the continent, became the first foreign opposition. The federation has been recognised by the Serbian Sports Administration and receives financial support from the Ministry of Youth and Sports.

ICC Europe provided modest support to the fledgling organisation, sending a coaching course on CD together with some kit. After the national league had been played for six seasons and cricket had become established they gained affiliate membership in 2015.

The main ground in the country is located in an airfield in a suburb of Belgrade. It has an artificial pitch laid over concrete and boasts outdoor nets. The second ground is based at Dunav Football Club, using a flicx pitch. There are eight clubs in the country with the leading four playing in 20- and 40-over tournaments, with a B division just playing T20. A cup competition was introduced in 2014 and an indoor league is played in the winter. There has been some success introducing cricket into schools in Belgrade and the association are looking to organise regular tournaments at under-14 and under-16 level. One club, Bodrog Deers, have an under-14 team which are drawn from the local Roma population. An annual tournament is played for students at the University of Belgrade. Three clubs have women's teams.

Serbia has succeeded where many others have failed in getting coverage of the game in the local media. The initiatives of the federation and the results of league games are covered in daily sports newspaper *Sportski Zurnal*. This has helped raise the profile of the game and also serves as an incentive to the players to commit to a game as it has achieved recognition in broader society. The federation's charity work and in particular their programmes to get Roma children playing the sport have been covered extensively on national television. They run a 'Street20 for Street Children' programme in collaboration with children's charities and have also held cricket camps endorsed by the United Nations in towns with tensions between Serb, Albanian and Roma populations. One of the reasons for the high level of media interest is that cricket is predominantly played by native Serbians with the country having a very small expat population. This has limited player numbers but increased profile. Cricket players have been in to immigration centres to organise tape ball cricket games for Afghan and Pakistani refugees.

There is a women's team playing in the second division of the local league, mainly drawn from philosophy scholars from Belgrade University. There is not yet enough players to form a league but half of youth players in the country are girls.

Serbia play against other European affiliates in the EuroT20, Continental Cup and Tri Nations tournament. Typical opponents are Hungary, Bulgaria and Romania. The federation are seeking to emulate the success of rugby league that now boasts 20 clubs and 1,000 local players since starting in 2001. The fulcrum of cricket in the country is Vladimir Ninkovic who in addition to playing and promoting the game is also a cricket commentator on Eurosport.

Slovakia

At the dawn of the new millennium there were some occasional, informal fixtures played between expat cricketers in Bratislava and teams from Prague. But cricket was only formalised when Vladimir Chudachik returned to his homeland from England, where he had fallen in love with the game and dabbled in club cricket in Gloucestershire. Finding no trace of cricket whatsoever he set out on a one-man mission to establish cricket in Slovakia. He persuaded some football-playing friends in his home village of Hajske, 45 miles east of Bratislava, to form a club and the local football club allowed him use of their ground. He enlisted the help of cricket clubs in Vienna and Prague and decided to put the emphasis on youth. His old club Frampton CC sent over some kit and he set up training sessions for children and seniors.

In 2003 the team toured Austria and Prague and the following year visited Poland. Footage of some of these games was fleetingly shown on national television. There are now around 40 players in the country, with half local and half expats. Chudachik aspires to lead Slovakia into ICC membership but more clubs will need to be established to meet the required criteria.

Slovenia

Slovenia provide another example of a young man visiting England, falling in love with the game and introducing it when returning to his homeland. Borut Cegovnik learnt cricket in Kent as a boy in the mid-1970s, and convinced enough of his friends back home to play to form a cricket club in the town of Mezica. However, this remained an isolated outpost until the late 1990s when cricket was established in the capital Ljubljana. Soon after the Ljubljana club was established in 1997 a national team was formed that competed in the European Representative tournament in 2000. In a pleasing twist of fate the former team from Mezica saw footage of the national team on television and reformed their club. Two more clubs were formed in 2005 and the Slovenian Cricket Association was founded. Over the next five years new clubs were formed in Maribor and in Majsperk and Ptuj in the north-east of the country.

Slovenia has competed in international tournaments in Austria, Croatia, Cyprus, Belgium and Estonia and hosted ICC Europe division 3 in 2011. They gained affiliate membership in 2005 after being a prospective member since 2000, receiving some support from ICC Europe to meet membership criteria. Domestic cricket consists of a six-team league, a nine-team T20 cup and a championship for primary schools. The strongest club, Ljubljana, competes in the Austrian league.

Slovenia has a much more mature development programme than many other countries in the region. Over 5,000 schoolchildren have been introduced to the game through a programme begun in 2003 and this interest has been sustained with regular inter-school matches. This is a major focus of the Slovenian Cricket Association made possible by volunteers making regular school visits. They are also looking to help schools develop facilities, including outdoor nets, in their grounds. In higher education the association have worked with the University of Sport in Ljubljana to introduce a three-month cricket module as an option for students.

Spain

As with France, Spain has great potential as an emerging cricket nation. It has a large, relatively affluent population with a great sporting heritage, an ideal climate for the game and an increasingly multicultural population including many from cricket-playing cultures. Spanish sun and siestas has always been a considerable draw for English expats and there has been a sustained interest from these communities in playing the game. It was Brits who formed the first Spanish cricket club, in Madrid in 1975. They also recruited players from Indian and West Indian residents in the city. The game spread to Barcelona by the early 1980s and a club fixture between the two city clubs was played in 1982 to mark the football World Cup. By 1986 there were eight clubs in the country and the formation of the Malaga Cricket Association, that provided organisation for the game in the country and eventually became the national cricket association. By 1990 the game was fully unified in Spain and in 1992 Spain became an affiliate member of the ICC. By this time there were clubs in several major cities as well as Mallorca, Marbella and the Costa Blanca.

By the mid-1990s the country boasted a purpose-built cricket ground in Mallorca and a multi-year sponsorship deal with an insurance company to establish a national league. International fixtures were played against Italy and Portugal. Grounds at Cartema and the Sporting Alfas Club became popular as touring destinations for English clubs and an MCC tour helped the associations' efforts to increase umpiring and coaching capacity. More cricket was being played across the country and momentum was building. Recognition by the Spanish government sport's body helped raise cricket's profile and enabled it to bid for funding and get support for development. In Javea the town administration agreed to and helped deliver training sessions for schools. Spain played an active role in the European Cricket Federation and extended their relationship with the MCC, benefitting from specialist coaching. These organisations helped provide Kwik Cricket kits to support a schools programme and increase participation levels.

Spain was an active participant in regional tournaments at senior and youth level in the first decade of the new millennium, though never threatening the leading teams in the region or coming close to qualifying for global competitions. There are over 30 clubs in the country and domestic cricket is split into regional leagues. At the end of the season the leading clubs in each region compete to be national champions. There is also a national T20 cup held on an annual basis.

Cricket Spain has been active in developing cricket in schools, with support from Derbyshire County Cricket Club who helped set up and implement their schools programme. This is comprised of a training programme for PE teachers and the provision of training materials and equipment, including Kwik Cricket sets and Spanish language training manuals. Supporting the schools programme Cricket Spain have adopted the Street20 format, holding participation events in visible destinations such as city centres and parks. This has helped raise the profile of the sport in the country, especially outside the regions dominated by expats. They have also sought to piggyback on the popularity of beach festivals, ensuring beach cricket is featured and thereby marketing the game as a fun, accessible recreation. These initiatives have helped boost participation numbers but the lack of funding to provide regional development officers has meant that the interest has not been sustained or led to incorporation of new players into clubs.

Although there is quite a lot of cricket played in Spain there have undoubtedly been some missed opportunities to grow the game. An example of this is the Sporting Alfas club located at the Costa Blanca seaside town of L'Alfas del Pi. Enterprising cricketer Andrew Bond approached the local town mayor in the 1990s with a pitch for a pitch, if you'll excuse the pun. The mayor, Tony Fuseli, had a dream to create a Sports City of Olympic standard that could generate income and attract thousands of visitors to the town. Bond saw an opportunity to make cricket part of this project and promised that if he provided land for a cricket ground he would be repaid with 2,000 visitors a year to the town through cricket tourism.

He was clearly a persuasive salesman as the mayor provided a plot of land that had been a pitch and putt golf course but was soon, well after the bunkers had been flattened, transformed into the Columbus Oval in 1996. A festival of cricket was organised to celebrate the completion of the ground and the sports minister for the Valencia province attended. With these connections made Bond hoped that with the support of municipal leaders a strong of cricket clubs could be formed along the Costa Blanca coast.

Over the next few years the club became one of the most popular destinations for touring clubs from England. It did draw significant numbers to the town, albeit not quite the 2,000 promised, which provided a boost to local hotels and restaurants. More encouraging still, the profile of cricket in the area increased which brought young local players into the game. There were two ingredients for success so seldom found on the continent: the support of civic authorities and engagement of the local population. If the club had had support from the ICC to develop facilities, perhaps an academy, then this momentum may have spread to other towns throughout the region establishing cricket as an increasingly popular local sport, not just the preserve of expats. Sadly Andrew Bond died and without his vision, commitment and connections his dream died with him. Perhaps, if investment had been forthcoming, southern Spain could have become a cricketing destination to rival the UAE.

But many of the factors that have led to the Alfas being such a popular club to tour remain a huge opportunity for cricket in Spain. The weather in the south allows for cricket to be played outdoors almost all year round and it is a short, cheap flight from the UK. This appeal is not just limited to club cricketers looking for a slog and sangria either, it has attracted county teams wanting an all-year training base.

The La Manga sports club caters for a wide range of sports and the cricket facilities are arguably the best on the continent. ICC Europe has used La Manga as the base for their academies, elite training camps and a regular host for regional tournaments. Cricket Spain has also made it their base, running summer camps and evening courses. La Manga have broadened their reach, further attracting English counties looking for a pre- and post-season training base at a fraction of the cost of traditional locations such as the West Indies or South Africa. Cricket Spain used this draw to establish a partnership with Essex County Cricket Club in 2012. They can access the facilities in return for helping develop cricket in Spain through specialised coaching, development visits and bringing over talented young Spanish players into the Essex academy and league set-up. Development officers from the county have visited Madrid, Barcelona and the Costa Blanca to train local children and introduce Cricket Spain to coaching aids and philosophies developed by the ECB. This partnership has also led to twinning programmes between schools. There were similar problems faced in poor urban neighbourhoods in both Essex and Barcelona, where cricket was being played but without support or direction. The county and Cricket Spain shared experiences of meeting this challenge and developed an integrated programme of school support and street cricket initiatives to address it. Earlier this year Norlington School visited Alicante and Murcia on a four-day tour, accompanied by Essex Cricket Board coaches, visiting schools and competing in a tournament.

Cricket in the country is largely focused on the Catalunya region where there are 37 clubs, but there are also clubs in Murcia, Andalucia, Madrid, Valencia, the Canary Islands, Balearic Islands and one in Galicia. This often means clubs travelling 400km to play a league game. Cricket development is led by a director of junior cricket who works with regional development officers to run introductory courses and a schools programme. All schools are sent a cricket kit, containing information and promotional materials about the game, details on the support available from Cricket Spain to run cricket sessions and Kwik Cricket equipment. Regional development officers follow up with specific schools that show an interest. The objective is to train PE teachers to run and promote the game in their schools. In parallel Cricket Spain are looking to increase the number of junior coaches in each region, to support both clubs and schools. Regional development programmes feed in to a national development structure, that includes a national academy drawing the best players from all regions for specialist training and the selection of national teams at under-17 and under-19 level. The idea is to have a development pathway that enables a young cricketer to progress from being introduced to the game in a school, to joining a club, progressing to a regional development programme and joining the national academy and being selected for international age group cricket.

Unfortunately for Cricket Spain just as their development plan was starting to bear fruit the level of support from ICC Europe was reduced, making it difficult to fully implement and achieve the objectives set out. In particular the scrapping of ICC-run regional age group tournaments below under-19 has removed the final step in the development pathway, making it more challenging to enthuse young Spanish cricketers to commit to cricket over other sports. They have had more success than most in attracting sponsors in the past and this source of income will be critical now that ICC grants have been reduced.

On the field success has been modest to date, although one Spanish player, Tariq Ali Awan, made headlines by making two international centuries in a day at the Messonghi Beach ground in Corfu. The 38-year-old smashed 150 off 66 balls against Estonia in the morning and then after a restorative lunch returned to make a 55-ball 148, including 16 sixes, against Portugal in the afternoon.

Sweden

A Swede returning from a spell in London where he had learnt the game founded a club in Gothenburg in 1883, but he clearly didn't win his countrymen over as it only lasted a few years. Then in the 1920s there was a similarly foreshortened attempt to introduce cricket into a boarding school in Lundsberg. But this did not have the success of Zuoz in Switzerland and failed to lay the foundations of cricket in the country. Then in 1948 embassy staff from cricketing nations formed the Stockholm Cricket Club as far back as 1948 and organised games between embassy teams and visiting ships throughout the post-war years. When a club formed in Helsinki in the 1970s they became regular opposition. By the mid-1970s there were clubs in Lund, Gothenburg, Marietad, Jonkoping, Varnamo and Trollhatten. In 1978 Danish cricket enthusiast turned Nordic cricketing missionary Kogs Ready set up a team for Swedish girls and boys in Bjarred and attempted to set up a national association, but his ambitions were frustrated as failure to secure a ground saw the project die before it could flourish.

Cricket in Guttsa began in 1984 when a regular English visitor persuaded local football players to play a village match. After the match they'd have a drink at the local brewery. Five years later, in the brewery, where else, they decided to form a cricket club. Guttsa were then influential in the founding of the Swedish Cricket Federation in 1990 and they became an ICC member the following year. As in Norway the country saw a significant increase in levels of immigration in the 1990s bringing more cricketers, or those from cricket-playing cultures, to the country. But cricket in Sweden stalled when they failed to meet player eligibility guidelines introduced by the ICC. The context for this was a philosophical difference of opinions between those who were content for Sweden to host expat cricket and those, led by Guttsa, who wanted a reformed national body with the primary purpose of encouraging native Swedes to play. Guttsa boycotted the league when their pleas were not heard and a proposal for all league teams to include at least four Swedish citizens, two of them Swedes, was blocked. As a result of this infighting Sweden did not compete in international tournaments from the mid-2000s as player eligibility was an issue. This was a factor in some of the strongest clubs in the east, such as Malmo CC, joining the Danish league.

The situation has improved in recent years with a more settled cricket population and greater levels of consensus in domestic cricket. Sweden resumed playing in regional tournaments in 2010. In 2011 they won European division 3 in Slovenia and then came second in division 2 held in Corfu the following year, seeing them promoted to division 1. They were outclassed at that level, but participated in ICC Europe division 2 in 2016.

Though slightly behind neighbours Norway in developing the game Sweden has made significant progress in the last five years, seeing them overtake countries with a much longer cricket heritage on the field and off it. As immigration policies have relaxed so more people from the subcontinent have sought employment and found cricket in the country. The level of formal cricket has increased significantly, with over 40 clubs in the country. Although the greatest concentration remains in Stockholm there are now cricketing communities in Malmo in the south, Gothenburg in the west and Umea in the north. This has meant an expansion of domestic cricket where there are now three senior divisions and youth leagues at under-15 and under-20 level. Reflecting the tastes of many of the players the most popular format is T20 although games are also played over 40 overs. In addition to officially registered players competing in organised leagues there is also an increasing number of people playing informal, recreational cricket, typically with a tape ball in public areas. If these are incorporated into formalised cricket Sweden will have one of the largest playing communities in the region.

The federation has introduced some youth initiatives, including training courses in schools and indoor and outdoor tournaments for boys and girls in different cities. They also promote the game at sports events that are held in different regions to promote physical exercise and the health benefits of sport. They also run coaching courses and training days for PE teachers. As in Norway the federation get a considerable boost in funding from the government for cultural integration. This funding is considerably more than they receive through the ICC and enables them to support development initiatives that are beyond the reach of many countries in the region.

In 2015 cricket became an officially recognised sport in Sweden and this has provided additional government support and funding. This enabled a new dual pitch ground to be built in the southern Stockholm suburb of Skarpnick.This significantly improved cricket access and facilities in the city and ICC Europe were sufficiently impressed to grant Sweden hosting rights for World Cricket League Europe Qualifier division 2, in which they came runners up and were promoted to division 1. They have an influential champion too in the British embassy who hosted the teams during the recent tournament. A documentary is being produced that looks at the role cricket is playing in promoting ethnic inclusion in the country, a topical issue in the national press. The number of teams is growing rapidly across the country and the board are attempting to place a greater emphasis on youth development. Former Sussex seamer Paul Hutchison is currently combines the roles of national coach and kit supplier.

Switzerland

Thanks to the inspiring example of the Zuoz college, along with the multinational make-up of the United Nations city of Zurich, cricket has a long history in Switzerland. But today it is best known for its ice cricket tournament in glamorous St Moritz. This event, established in 1988, attracts teams from as far afield as Hong Kong and India. The games and more importantly the Alpine backdrop make it one of the most photographed and therefore recognisable cricket venues on the continent.

The Swiss Cricket Association was founded in 1980 with six member clubs. They became an affiliate member of the ICC in 1985 and by 1993 membership had increased to 16 clubs and there were 350 players in the country. They played an important role in supporting development of emerging cricket nations in the region by hosting the European Nations Cup in 1997 and were then regular participants in the European Cricket Council Trophy. In 2009 in the expanded regional structure they were promoted from the bottom rung, division 5, and were on an upward trajectory, due to play in European division 2 in 2011. However, this progress was halted when they were suspended from the tournament for having two rival governing bodies, neither of whom were recognised by the Swiss Olympic Committee. This breached ICC requirements and led to a 12-month suspension that was followed by Switzerland losing their affiliate member status. At this time the country were ranked 72nd in the world. It meant that Swiss cricket lost its membership grant, the opportunity for targeted assistance and the opportunity to play in officially sanctioned events.

Since its exclusion Switzerland has continued to play in international tournaments, albeit those not officially sanctioned by the ICC. They are part of a loose agglomeration of affiliates, or former affiliates in their case, who organise and participate in tournaments such as the Tri Nations Cup and Central European Development League. Swiss youth teams regularly tour within Europe, often to club sides in Denmark and the Netherlands, and are also regular visitors to the UK. They are one of the countries that have been supported by Surrey-based cricket coaching company T20 International, who have run coach-training sessions and youth camps in the country.

There are currently 23 clubs in the country with the greatest concentration around Zurich and Geneva, but also in Berne, Basel and St Gallen. The domestic league is played in 40- and 20-over formats and there is an annual youth tournament held at Zuoz. Switzerland are also one of a number of countries including Hungary and Poland that have established 'native' teams to develop indigenous talent. Cricket has been introduced to some schools with assistance of local government associations. In addition to the historic ground in Zuoz there is now a dedicated cricket ground in Cossonay, near Lausanne. Other grounds are shared with other sports and use artificial matting pitches. The main sponsor is Mr Pickwick Pubs, who are the title sponsor of the domestic T20 tournament.

Ukraine

Other than the odd dusty reference to games played by British residents in Odessa in the 1880s cricket was not played regularly in Ukraine until the mid-1990s when immigrants from the subcontinent and the Middle East organised matches in Vinnitsa. This community grew to sustain nine teams and a local league by 2002. The Ukrainian Cricket Board, established in 2000, runs a national league, established in 2006, and a Kiev league, with 15 participating teams in total. The winners of each league contest an annual champions trophy. Most games are played at the Voskhod Stadium, a football venue converted for cricket use. In 2014 cricket enthusiast Wayne Zschech converted a carrot field into a cricket field in the town of Kagarlyk, 50 kilometres from Kiev. Ukraine have submitted an application for ICC membership which is still pending. There are plans to introduce the game into schools. In 2016 Ukraine won the much-hyped Mediterranean Cricket League, held in Split, Croatia.

The Future

An Uncertain Future

THE brutal slashing of ICC funding and the withdrawal of direct support from ICC Europe has left the future of cricket on the continent uncertain. The whole region bristled with anger and frustration, cricket administrators scratched their heads and weighed up future career possibilities in insurance or sales and club cricketers the length and breadth of the continent would have been forgiven for wondering whether alternative sports offered them better prospects. But from this uncertainty sprang a resolve to succeed despite the odds. To fill the vacuum national boards began working more closely together, arranging regional tournaments as a focal point for their players.

Organisations like T20 International looked to play their role, coaching children and mentoring local coaches in countries the ICC had abandoned. While some were still leaving online streams of vitriol others were looking to find sponsors and establish new clubs. Austerity had hit European cricket just as it had hit European economies. The strategic plans boards had drawn up with ICC development officers were put on the shelf. Just as they had developed plans to progress cricket in their countries the funding to implement them was withdrawn. It was a cruel, cruel tease.

There was hope. Hope that with the end of Srinivasan and Clarke's reign of terror the ICC may be a smidgen kinder to the region. But the noises from the corridor of power suggested that even if funding and opportunities below Test level increased they would go to the ICC's 'priority markets' and it wasn't likely any continental countries would be on that list, though Germany's remarkable rise in participation may see them make the cut. Like a government department or local authority downscaling after an austerity budget the boards had to identify what they had to stop doing. Many had to stop paying staff, pull school projects, cancel plans for new grounds, tell excited young cricketers that there was no money for development camps. It didn't augur well for the future. Their only option was to target an increase in scorecard funding and secure income from other sources. What does the future hold for countries that aren't able to?

There is sufficient enthusiasm and commitment to ensure that cricket will always be played. For players of a South Asian background the game is so integral to their culture they would continue to play even if they had to use a fence panel for a bat. Cricket may not have seized the imagination of many native people in the region but it is a sport that quickly burrows into the very core of the soul and its enthusiasts will continue to play come hell, high water or the abandonment of the ICC. Without funding and direction, however, there is a risk the game could become disjointed and unstructured. Running cricket in a country of a million or more people with a single paid administrator and a budget of $15,000 doesn't sound easy, and it isn't. Running leagues, maintaining discipline and order and keeping a disparate membership happy and voting for you is nigh on impossible without adequate resources and the backing of the regional office.

The likely outcome in such circumstances is that many players will leave authorised leagues for alternative forms of the game free of match fees or regulations. Other than the pride of becoming national champions there isn't that much of an incentive if development pathways are removed and the national team doesn't have official fixtures. In long-established clubs the desire to continue a proud history and stay true to the visions of founding fathers may be strong. In this context leaving an official league would be considered by many members to be foolish, maybe even a betrayal. But appealing to this sense of heritage and unity is a harder sell to newly founded clubs who may have a more insular, pragmatic view.

In such a scenario people would still play cricket but not within a unified community supporting each other in attaining a long-term vision. There are already signs that the region is at risk of such fragmentation. National boards often spend as much time persuading members not to join breakaway leagues as they do trying to effectively run their own. Such breakaway leagues often have a rich backer, an appealing franchise-based model and a promise of glory, glamour and sparkling pedestal for the winners. What they invariably lack is any provision to stimulate youth development. They may well entertain players and spectators but they don't seek to address the fundamental challenges of cricket in the country.

This fragmentation of the game could lead to most countries slipping out of official tournaments and remaining permanently under the ICC's radar. In such a scenario it is hard to see how many countries could meet the criteria necessary to retain ICC membership which could result in them losing government funding too. Cricket would revert to a recreational sport played predominantly by certain ethnic groups. The recruitment drive around the turn of the millennium would be a distant memory and the ICC membership reduce considerably. In short a minority game would become even less relevant and ever more marginalised.

This is only a potential scenario but the fact that it is even possible is testimony to the scale of the risk taken by the ICC in all but withdrawing funding and support. Continental Europe may not contain the markets they are targeting for growth but nevertheless they have invested a considerable amount in the region and have jeopardised a return on this investment. They hope that others will pick up the bill and finish what they started, helping member boards deliver the strategic plans they helped draft. But the lack of faith they have shown is hardly a ringing endorsement of the project and national boards will struggle to get the funding they need. Recent rhetoric from the ICC indicates that they have chosen Ireland as the European country on which to focus funding. A line appears to have been drawn, and continental Europe sits nervously beneath it. The argument that the scorecard grant ensures fair and merit-based funding looks defensible enough on paper but in reality meeting the targets needed to significantly increase their rankings requires pump-priming grants. And guess what, ICC Europe's budget for targeted grants has been removed. In one sense scorecard funding is fair, but seen another way it appears something of a stitch-up.

There is, however, a brighter alternative future that may yet materialise. If the vast number of tape-ball cricketers on the continent are successfully assimilated into cricket communities the participation levels will rise and, in time, national teams in the region will become more competitive. This could increase funding both through ICC grants and government reward for cricket's role in social inclusion which in turn could see continental teams rise through the World Cricket League, increasing their performance grant and inspiring more to commit to the game. If luck and results go their way the Netherlands could qualify for both the World T20 and World Cup and play Test cricket into the bargain. This would surely secure a major sponsor, raise the profile of cricket, help professionalise the sport and attract young people to the game. Denmark's investment in youth could see a golden generation claim ODI status and a place in global showcase events. In the post big three era the ICC may even decide that the affluent, sports-mad countries of continental Europe are attractive future markets afterall and boost funding. With such support Germany could boast 150 clubs and 15,000 players by 2020.

Both scenarios could happen as the future hasn't been written yet. The optimists will continue to dream and the cynics will adopt the doom-mongering they so passionately espouse.

For many followers and champions of the game in the region a bright future can only be secured by breaking away from the ICC.

They cite the rejection of Woolf's recommendations as evidence that the full members will never allow the ICC to reform from a private members' club to a global governing body for the sport. The greed and short-termism that has seen the World Cup revert to ten teams is so repugnant to many that they have lost all hope. Instead they want to see a new organisation developed on truly equitable and meritocratic principles that focuses on long-term development of the game. They foresee a utopian future that the ICC is powerless to ruin. I have a lot of sympathy for this view and there is no doubt that if you were designing a global governing body for cricket it would be refreshingly free from the ICC's historic baggage and feudal governance model. But I'm not convinced it is realistic and for a region with some of the oldest cricket boards in the world to divorce from the global cricket community seems a shame, however shabbily they have been treated.

One of the arguments, one supposes, for such discussions never make it in to the press releases that follow ICC meetings, for the ICC largely withdrawing support for the region is that they don't feel they have had or are likely to get a return on investment. Or put in more stark terms they feel that if the limit of potential in the region is to facilitate cricket amongst immigrant communities then they would rather invest elsewhere. Somewhere like Nepal or Afghanistan, for instance, where cricket has penetrated into the national sporting consciousness.

But if this is indeed the reasoning it contains several assumptions that should be challenged. Firstly, that increasing the number of people playing cricket in a region, whatever their ethnic background, is not worthwhile in itself. Secondly, that a country like Germany doubling its number of clubs within a decade on a meagre grant does not constitute return on investment. And thirdly that affluent, sports-mad European countries with high populations do not make the cut as exciting future markets worth investing in.

* * * * *

As it stands the ICC's development in the region looks to be a failed experiment. At least that appears to be their self-assessment. But I think it has been judged prematurely and through blinkered eyes. If everyone with an interest in cricket on the continent thriving works together towards a shared vision the region can yet emerge as an exciting growth area for the game.

This at least is my vision. And below are my thoughts on how this can be achieved.

Securing Recognition and Funding

Cricket in much of the continent is vulnerable, its future built on unstable foundations. For several decades the ICC sought to bring stability, continuity and the building blocks for long-term success through the funding and support of ICC Europe. But recently they have begun to question their return on the investment and on reflection have decided to largely withdraw from the region. They wish it all the best of course, but they want others to fund and deliver their objectives for them. For this to happen cricket needs to become an Olympic sport and any further delay risks unravelling all of the progress made since the development programme was launched.

In recent decades the ICC has been very successful in generating revenue through its global events. It is the richest sport in the world bar football. But it is also by far the greediest. The most powerful full members have a guaranteed slice of a cake that gets bigger in every rights cycle. This makes their fickle financiers very happy indeed. They have control and a long-term, increasingly lucrative stake in the game. This is the reason why they have traditionally resisted making cricket an Olympic sport despite the fact that it would make cricket a global sport, be a game-changer for global development. However, in the post big three era the chances of Olympic inclusion have improved.

The ICC is thought to favour the direct entry route, that would see the organisation themselves receive a significant funding boost above and beyond competing nations. It is more likely however that hosting cities will have to proactively include cricket, using their rights as a host to select additional sports alongside the core events. This means that national boards will have to negotiate with their Olympic committees to get cricket on the schedule. If Rome is successful in its bid for 2024 cricket will be played in Bologna.

The increase in government funding alone would be sufficient to address many of the challenges continental cricket nations face. It would help provide more grounds, improve facilities and fund development projects. While it would differ country by country some estimate that if cricket was included in the Olympics national boards could receive 100 times the level of funding from their governments that they currently receive from the ICC. This would, of course, be quite literally a game-changer. It is the indirect, less immediately quantifiable benefits, however, that would have the most profound impacts. Olympic recognition will bring government endorsement. In turn government endorsement will increase the recognition of cricket in regional administrations and local municipalities. This will make it easier to get local support to secure grounds, introduce the game to schools and break down notions that cricket is somehow a foreign sport for foreign people. With this achieved cricket will get more media attention, helping increase participation, and be more attractive to sponsors bringing more money into the game and perpetuating a virtuous cycle for cricket in the region.

All this could happen within a matter of years with just one decision. Inclusion in the Olympics will actually help the ICC achieve its strategy to grow cricket's global economy. It wants lucrative markets, not just countries where people play cricket. In France, Spain, Germany, Italy and Russia to name just a few, continental Europe has these markets. But the ICC need to be brave. The example of rugby, which returned to the Olympics in Rio after 96 years, has shown that Olympic participation can stimulate growth in new markets. So why isn't cricket following suit? Well, in short, because including the Olympics in the cricketing calendar would prevent full members from scheduling lucrative tours.

There are encouraging signs that there may finally be the appetite within the ICC to take control of the sport they run from the self-interest of leading full members. In other words they need the recommendations of a root and branch review they themselves commissioned.

Being an Olympic sport will enable the game on the continent to flourish. The national boards will have a sustainable source of funding to build the game in their countries. But the ICC and the ECB still have a key role to play.

* * * * *

The ICC should increase the proportion of the game's wealth that is allocated to global development and its associate and affiliate members. This should not be only targeted at its teams of choice, like Ireland, Afghanistan, Nepal and the USA, but based on need and opportunity. ICC Europe should undertake a comprehensive review of constraints and opportunities across the continent, taking into account what has worked well and what has proved difficult to implement in strategic plans over the last 15 years. This will be different for different countries, depending on national circumstances and what stage they are at in their development as cricket nations. Following this analysis the ICC can work with national boards to devise a targeted investment plan. The return on investment should be considered over a long time frame, but with phased targets to be reviewed every two years.

To support development the ICC should overhaul its approach to status. Currently this is only serving to protect the inherent privileges and earning potential of full members and is depriving the vast majority of its membership of recognition, statistical relevance and the opportunity to promote the game and attract sponsors. Test status should be awarded to all teams that qualify for the Intercontinental Cup, which should be rebranded as a second division of Tests and include the two lowest ranked full members and the top eight ranked associates, with promotion and relegation between the two divisions. To support this, funding should be allocated to improve grounds and facilities in these countries to enable Test cricket to be played.

ODI and T20I status should be combined and extended to all teams competing in World Cricket League 3 and above and all teams that qualify for the global T20 qualifier. Teams should not lose this status if relegated or failing to reach the tournaments in future cycles. The World Cricket League should be extended to six divisions, with regional qualification pathways for the lowest ranked teams based on both performance and development criteria. The standard of play is of secondary importance to the value of international competition to the development strategy. Sub-regional tournaments, such as are already being established in the Balkans, Scandinavia and central Europe, should be given official endorsement and be part of the structure that feeds in to the World Cricket League. These are relatively cheap to run, thereby enabling more funding to be diverted to youth development. These tournaments should feature development events where regional members discuss challenges and opportunities and share best practice. Countries must have certainty about the criteria they need to meet to qualify for tournaments so they can embed into development planning. Investment in and commitment to youth development should be a necessary prerequisite.

The ICC should compel all full members touring England to play at least two fixtures against teams in the region with ODI/T20I status. With the future growth of the sport as its paramount focus the ICC should make their global showcase events more inclusive, with a 16-team World Cup and a 24-team World T20. This would mirror the inclusive approach of other sports and ensure cricket could celebrate a similar success to Japan defeating the Springboks in the last Rugby World Cup.

At youth level ICC Europe should run two divisional age-group tournaments at under-13, under-15, under-17 and under-19 level for both boys and girls. This will help address the dramatic loss of players across the continent from 11 to 19 and provide a focus for domestic youth development programmes.

The ICC should also make it a requirement of full member status that they play a development role within the region. Having been given this role the ECB should establish a forum for European boards where they share best practice, help shape strategic objectives and facilitate twinning relationships between continental countries and English counties. Once twinned counties can create a small team responsible for supporting development in that country. This could include facilitating club twinning programmes to schedule tours and promote player and coach exchange, planning coach, umpire and scorer training programmes to build capability in the continental country and providing leading players to participate in local leagues and county academies.

These proposals would build on the progress made under the development programme at its peak in 2011 before it was slowly dismantled. The more inclusive approach to status does not go as far as many people would wish but is intended to be a phased approach that can be accommodated within the current structure of global cricket and be broadly acceptable to full members. Full members must accept that they can be relegated in all formats and that merit-based qualification applies to them just as much as associate nations. Their enhanced regional role will benefit them in the longer term by creating more competitive teams to play regionally and a significant increase in the fan base that can make domestic cricket tournaments more commercially lucrative in the longer term. For instance it would pave the way for a lucrative T20 city franchise across Europe.

Teams below Test, ODI or T20I status should have the opportunity of playing bilateral internationals in these formats in officially sanctioned games, afforded internal status categorisation.

Finally, the ICC should make broadcasting rights available to free to air television providers across emerging markets. This may not be a lucrative source of revenue in the short term but will result in an increase in the global fan base and therefore ensure greater profitability for the sport in the future.

Making Cricket a Universal Sport

The only way for cricket on the continent to progress from a marginalised sport predominantly played by particular ethnic groups is for it to be fully integrated into schools. All countries on the continent to a greater or lesser extent have initiated school programmes but they have lacked the resources to implement a sustainable, national programme. Olympic status would provide boards with a much stronger case when approaching and working with schools. Greater recognition and backing from the government will ensure that cricket gets a more sympathetic ear and the prospect of pupils potentially representing their country in the Olympics will provide a strong incentive for schools to adopt the sport.

Introduction through schools will ensure cricket has a universal appeal and children will become more familiar with it and accept it as a natural choice of sports, rather than an activity only played by certain communities. Parents will also see this universal appeal and be more likely to support a child who shows an interest. Inter-school competitions within towns and cities and inter-regional tournaments will help embed the game into national culture and normalise the game.

National boards have a key role to play. Additional government and ICC funding can enable boards to employ full-time school development officers in each city or region. They can provide training to teachers, run training sessions and help facilitate tournaments. They can also serve as the link between schools and clubs, helping boost junior ranks in clubs and oversee a development pathway to regional and national representative sides. The ECB and the country's county partner can help by scheduling school visits to high profile events in England, helping enthuse young people with the game.

National boards can also work with schools and clubs to develop cricket apps enabling children to compare their performances and statistics with friends and peers, generating enthusiasm and creating virtual communities using new media.

To ensure schools have the capacity to adopt cricket as one of their major sports and host tournaments there needs to be investment in grounds and facilities. Collaboration between schools, clubs and local municipalities can identify available venues and build capacity. If possible this can be within school grounds but if this is not possible then in local cricket centres or extended facilities at club grounds.

These initiatives should lead to a natural increase in interest and profile that will result in more media interest and coverage. But to ensure this, school development officers should form promotion committees with teachers and local education authorities to develop and implement coordinated promotion plans.

A focus on schools will over time make cricket a more multicultural sport on the continent and therefore go a long way to addressing the issue of limited participation of native players. It will alter the widely held perception that cricket is a game played by particular ethnic groups. To support this integration of native players national boards should set targets to ensure that over a period of a decade the composition of the national team more closely reflects demographic trends in the country as a whole. This should include a gradual phasing out of aging expat players who have not learnt their cricket in the country and the inclusion of a greater number of players who have graduated through youth development programmes, including native players. This will help alter perceptions of European cricket as just a game for immigrants and also provide role models in the national team that young local and native cricketers can emulate.

The contraction of the WCL was partly due to a fear in the ICC that they were merely paying for groups of friends to play cricket abroad wearing national team jerseys. In other words that they were footing the bill for a jolly. A selection strategy based on long-term integration and cultural diversification of the game would be a robust challenge to any such fear. The composition of national teams should not just be about getting results but rather the elite squad should be the top of a development pyramid, energising and motivating all young players coming through the system.

Club Culture

Clubs should act as the local delivery agency for national development plans. This doesn't mean though that they have to surrender their own autonomy or ambitions. After all, if a club successfully boosts participation in its area it will not only deliver goals for the national board but also improve its own chances of winning leagues and trophies. Clubs need to have a soul and an independent voice and too much regulation risks stifling the development of a unique spirit and culture that will attract new members and give the club an identity in its community. However, they must acknowledge responsibility for growing the game and this is best achieved through membership criteria set by the board and development of a club charter to incentivise a development role.

As has already happened in many countries it should be a requirement at least amongst clubs in the top divisions to have youth sections and field youth teams. This culture can be promoted further through a reward system with clubs getting funding increases if their players are selected for national representative sides.

A further requirement should be that clubs have an open membership, not discriminating by ethnicity, age or gender. This does not stop clubs identifying themselves with a particular ethnic group and in the short and medium term it is likely that there will continue to be clubs dominated by certain communities. But it is important that children introduced to the game in schools can join a local club and feel welcomed.

The involvement of clubs in local events is important in ensuring cricket is an accepted and constructive presence in the community. There are many great examples of this across the continent already and it can only be hoped that members elect club chairmen that are civic minded and inclusive in approach.

National Boards

National boards play the pivotal role in developing the game in their country and it is vital that they serve the whole cricketing community rather than particular vested interests. For this reason elected officers have to either be independent of clubs or subject to a governance structure that ensures decisions are taken objectively.

There have been examples across the region of self-serving individuals furthering their own or their club's interests rather than the community overall. Examples of this include favouritism in selection and committing funding without an objective cost/benefit analysis. Abuse of positions of power is an inevitable consequence of human frailty and ego. But there has to be a process in place to make individuals accountable. This doesn't just apply to severe breaches of trust, such as fraudulent activity. After all, this is illegal in any organisation, whether in sport or beyond. But it also means being answerable for all funding that is spent. If funding is spent on sending a board member to a tournament, for instance, they must have a stated role and/or objective. Watching the cricket and enjoying a nice lunch doesn't necessarily constitute a role.

One way of building capability might be to facilitate secondments of cricket staff to national boards of larger sports, such as football. This would help develop skills and build an understanding of how a larger, more established sport operates. The ICC should approach national sport ministries to help establish these links to other sports.

There is a danger that a parochially run administration in a minority sport can get by on the odd handshake and well written speech. Such amateurism has to be held to account by members, government sponsors and the ICC. If any of these constituents are not satisfied that transparency, due process and financial probity have been upheld there needs to be an independent review and appropriate sanctions. In short, standards of governance and behaviour expected in public bodies should apply in cricket administrations.

ICC Europe should oversee governance and provide training to administrators to build capability in each country.

National Cricket Centres

It is critical for the survival and progress of cricket in the region that cricket has a permanent base in each country. It is simply not acceptable that investment in development and the tireless work of staff and volunteers could be jeopardised because a lease expires on the only cricket ground available. Cricket administrators need certainty, confidence and continuity in order to deliver development objectives. If they don't the return on investment by the ICC, governments and sponsors is not assured.

To provide this certainty and continuity the ICC should top slice their development budget to make a fund available to build national cricket centres. To ensure costs are manageable they could offer a 60%

grant, with boards working with governments and municipalities to raise the remaining 40%. These centres should include a good quality ground and an indoor training facility. They can then be used not only as a home ground for international matches and key fixtures in the domestic calendar, but also as the base for elite development and youth academies. This would represent a considerable capital outlay by the ICC, but still minimal as a percentage of the profits of the game. Looked at from a different perspective, however, it represents value for money over the long term. It will ensure that development funding is much better targeted, rather than allocated piecemeal on initiatives with a peripheral benefit, and strengthen national boards' ability to attract sponsors and backers.

The indoor training facility will help establish cricket as an all-year sport and therefore help address the leaching of young talent from the game to rival sports. Experience has shown that continuity of access is essential to player retention between 11 and 18.

Regional Hubs

One of the problems of cricket administration in the region, especially in the larger countries with populations in the tens of millions, is that their available resource has been spread too thinly. In some cases this has led to piecemeal activities across a wide area having negligible impact. An example of this has been schools projects. Arranging an event in a school can generate interest and enthusiasm but unless the initial contact is followed up it can soon become a distant memory for the children, leaving no legacy.

The same can apply to clubs. It is great when a new club is established, either where cricket has never been played before or perhaps reviving a cricketing outpost of old. But if left isolated such clubs are overly dependent on just a few players and if they leave the club can soon disappear. The common problems in these examples are lack of awareness, profile and community support. Adding dots on a cricketing map is one thing, but establishing cricket centres than can help spread cricket through a region is quite another.

One solution is the development of a hub project. This is a coordinated, multi-agency plan to establish, promote and grow cricket in a regional city or town. Working with an existing club, or a group of players seeking to establish a club, the board can meet with the municipal authority, schools, local radio/television stations and newspapers to develop a plan to establish cricket in the area, raising awareness of the game and articulating the benefits to local people. For example it could help the municipality achieve health and fitness targets, support social inclusion schemes and add to the town's tourism appeal. Once this project team has been formed a launch event can be planned, ensuring maximum exposure in the media and coordinated promotional activity through all available channels, from schools to civic speeches. The partners can then collaborate to help finance a ground and facilities, ensuring as many people in the community as possible have access and can benefit. With the media and schools on board the team is assured of publicity and hopefully a steady stream of players.

Once the club is launched and publicised a second phase of the hub project can be to establish links between the club and schools, running training sessions and perhaps also integrating cricket into the teaching of English and Geography. The partnership approach makes organising and promoting school cricket festivals or club open days much easier. In the third phase the hub can look to establish more clubs in the region to take advantage or the raised awareness and interest the publicity has generated. All being well, this can lead to establishment of a regional league and self-perpetuating cycle of growth. If this process can be repeated in four or five regional centres it could transform cricket across the whole country taking it from a minority sport few have heard of to a fast-growing sport gradually establishing a place in national sporting consciousness.

Promoting the Game

There are some excellent examples across the continent of using social media to build awareness, create a cohesive cricketing community and promote opportunities for people to play cricket. Twitter is less popular over the Channel than it is in Britain but Facebook has transformed the way cricket boards and clubs can communicate with cricketers and potential cricketers. In Germany the DCB are inundated with messages left on Facebook by players looking to join a club in their area. Elsewhere Facebook is used to promote tournaments, set up training sessions and attract new members.

There is no doubt that Facebook and other social media channels have helped galvanise cricketing communities. Recently CricHQ, a statistical database and online cricket community, has helped energise cricket leagues by recording and sharing scorecards and statistics, giving recognition for heroics on the field and a sense of importance and pride to cricket communities. All of these tools help cricketers feel less isolated and marginalised in countries where football is utterly dominant. They have helped cricket communities survive, but they have had less success in reaching beyond existing cricketers to those who may never have heard of the sport.

Access to cricket on television can be a very influential factor in growing the game. This was seen in the Netherlands in the 1980s when people could watch cricket on the BBC. Many Dutch players cite finding cricket when flicking through the channels as what got them into the game. In Norway access to cricket on Asian subscription channels has also played a key role. But occasional games on a Eurosport subscription channel and a handful of international fixtures livestreamed on YouTube have a frustratingly limited reach. One of two players may find the game through this route, but gains will only ever be marginal. Some countries have established YouTube channels, showing interviews and highlights of domestic and international games.

Newspaper coverage is also conspicuous by its absence across most of the continent. When the Netherlands played South Africa in Amsterdam in 2013 I was staggered to see that there wasn't even a reference in any of the newspapers I saw. And that was with arguably the best team in the world in town and a historical-ethnic link between the two countries. Little chance then for an Intercontinental Cup game or a league derby to be covered.

When cricket has been covered it has generally only been through a quirky, not always constructive, angle. To paraphrase many a headline I have seen 'Strange, incomprehensible game played by foreigners sees locals scratching heads.' Yes it is column inches, but it isn't useful ones. Even in England coverage of European cricket is condescending, with people discovering cricket being played somewhere they didn't expect and expressing their surprise to readers: 'Wow, what a surprise. I can't believe it. Really? I thought they were into (insert unEnglish pastime like bullfighting, dogsledding).' All jolly enough but hardly conducive to growing the game.

What is needed on the continent is for the boards and clubs to build relationships with journalists, editors and broadcasters to educate them about the game and demonstrate why cricket can be an interesting story for their readers. Take Germany as an example. If the DCB were to host a press evening at the beginning of the year and lure some journalists and editors along with a free meal, which is generally enough, they could explain the game and set out their ambitions for the game. As part of this they could show how cricket can be the hook for fascinating articles on social cohesion, development of the national team and human interest stories. Once the relationship was established a press liaison officer could manage the relationship, suggesting angles and providing photos, statistics and quotes. Journalists like nothing better than having stories written for them and over time exposure of cricket in the paper would increase, with stories helping rather than hindering the sport's development.

Partnering with Other Sports

To some extent of course cricket is in competition with other minority sports on the continent, such as baseball and rugby (except France and Italy), to raise its profile and crucially to attract youth to the game. However, minority sports face many common constraints and challenges, such as access to funding and facilities. In working together there is the potential to make funding go further, increase player pools and create a more stable and sustainable base. This has been seen in Holland with cricket often being a component of a club also playing hockey and/or football, one of the reasons why cricket facilities in the country are much better and more numerous than elsewhere in the region.

A sport that shares a similar set of skills to cricket is baseball, an American import that has proved popular in continental Europe. There are 38 members of the Confederation of European Baseball and the sport boasts double the number of players of cricket, although while cricket playing numbers are rising steeply baseball's have plateaued in recent years. Meetings between national boards could be beneficial in sharing grounds and training facilities and increasing awareness and player participation levels. Links between clubs either at regional or town level could help leverage promotional efforts by both sports, especially with support from civic authorities.

Another useful link to explore would be between rugby and cricket as they are played in alternate seasons. It would provide cricketers with a winter sport and flankers and props with a summer game, with clubs developing joint training facilities and maximising revenue streams.

Cricket Tourism

The ICC has quite rightly challenged the culture of dependency many countries have on their grant. However, rather than simply cut the level of funding to force boards to frantically scrabble for alternative revenue sources, a more constructive, collaborative approach would have been to work with national boards to identify and maximise other revenue. This was a small part of the old development officer role but was perhaps not given enough prominence, leading to the sudden slashing of funding.

With sponsorship being very difficult to secure for a sport with such a low profile, with even the Netherlands struggling at times to get shirt sponsor deals for World Cups with a billion viewers worldwide, cricket tourism is an area countries should focus on. The ice of the north and the sun of the south have proved a very attractive draw for travelling visitors, especially from the UK. In some instances, such as Ice Cricket in Estonia, revenue from such visitors has made a significant contribution to cricket development. There have also been some very encouraging examples of cricket boards working with tourism departments to demonstrate the value of cricket to boosting visitor numbers, such as Corfu and Schiedam. There are other successful precedents in the wider region too, with Jersey increasingly marketed as a cricket destination, for both club tours and international tournaments.

The twinning programmes with English counties can help facilitate cricket tours to countries, bringing revenue into clubs and the wider economy. This can help cricket by generating goodwill amongst local beneficiaries who are then more likely to support the game and help it become part of local culture. The establishment of national cricket centres can help the cricket tourism offer too. Traditionally cricket tourists have gone to the region for a cheap, cultural experience and a quirky cricketing anecdote. They have put up with the poor facilities, perhaps even seeing this as part of the charm. However, with the professional training facilities national cricket centres would offer they could attract higher calibre teams looking for cheaper alternatives to the West Indies or South Africa. This could include schools, colleges, universities, minor counties, counties and even ECB national age group squads. Revenue from such tours or partnerships could then be re-invested into domestic development programmes and increase non-ICC income on the scorecard ranking.

Professionalisation and European Franchise Cricket

As the only continental country to qualify for the ICC's High Performance Programme the Netherlands is the only country in the region to be supported in the professionalisation of their cricket. This saw the adoption of corporate management structures, including a chief operating officer, an increase in the number of paid professionals in the KNCB and the introduction of a structured youth development programme. Other continental nations, such as Denmark, have also professionalised in at least some of these areas.

A natural evolution of the High Performance Programme and TAPP scheme was to establish professional leagues and a career path for leading cricketers. A first step towards this was taken in the North Sea Pro Series, where Dutch regional teams played against each other and Scottish counterparts. It was hoped that once the series was established these games could be given List A and first-class status. This process was advanced further in Ireland and there was an eyebrow-raising precedent set when fast bowler Craig Young decided to move back to Ireland to become a professional cricketer rather than progress his county career.

In the Netherlands the series has principally served as an 'A' team structure to help those on the fringes of the national team bridge the gap from club to international cricket. But could it one day evolve into a commercially viable professional league enabling Dutch cricketers to make a career from the game in their homeland? That is, in truth, a long way off and there would need to be a groundswell of interest in the game to make it even a vague possibility. But borrowing a phrase from the Remain campaign, continental cricketers could be 'better together'. For while paying to watch Dutch regional teams seems a remote prospect a franchise-based tournament played in European capitals may not be so far-fetched. Currently only Amsterdam and Copenhagen have the facilities, but with increased funding and the establishment of National Cricket Centres this concept could just be viable by 2020. It would need to be very well marketed and be planned in conjunction with a broadcaster and media partners, but it could just create the surge in interest and profile the game in the region needs. Similar dreams in the USA have fallen on their face, so expectations would need to be managed in case it led to funding being wasted that could have been better spent on more tangible, sustainable outcomes. Nevertheless, it is a vision perhaps to aspire to.

In parallel to city franchises the extension of ODI and T20I status would make it far easier to market regional internationals. For example you could envisage a T20I tri-series featuring the Netherlands, Denmark and Germany proving popular given a concerted promotion drive and support from the media. The ECB, in the extended regional role I have advocated, also have a crucial role to play. They should commit to fixtures against leading countries in the region, as they have done with Ireland. Cricket has more to be gained by England playing internationals against Ireland, Scotland, the Netherlands, Denmark and Germany than an instantly forgettable five-match series against Bangladesh.

Ultimately, though, the career prospects for continental cricketers will be determined by whether the sport can break into the mainstream. If it can then it will attract money and the region's cricketers can get their share.

* * * * *

There are a lot of ifs and buts in the proposals I've set out. There are never any guarantees and factors and events as yet unknown could yet determine an altogether different future for cricket on the continent. But isn't it more invigorating to hope and strive than throw in the towel and sulk? If you are inspired, if you feel you've read a rallying call rather than a eulogy, then there is hope indeed.

Participation and Grounds

TO enable comparison these statistics show senior and junior player numbers for 11-a-side hard ball cricket. Also included is the new ICC player category for 'modified games' that are any competitive forms of cricket held either indoor or outdoor. This is where considerable growth has been seen.

	Players 2004	**Players 2014**	**% Increase**	**Modified Games**	**Grounds 2004**	**Grounds 2014**
Austria	240	615	156%	113	4	3
Belgium	405	780	93%	1275	8	15
Bulgaria	-	555		118	4	6
Croatia	90	240	167%	42	2	4
Cyprus	165	300	82%	380	2	7
Czech Republic	15	90	500%	410	0	2
Denmark	1810	1875	4%	1801	36	35
Estonia	-	45		367	2	2
Finland	385	315	Minus 18%	100	0	6
France	825	1140	38%	4940		
Germany	750	2970	296%	3217	10	26
Gibraltar	320	435	36%	390	3	1
Greece	450	615	37%	200	2	3
Hungary	-	225		3400	-	1
Italy	720	2250	213%	2255	5	21
Luxembourg	105	120	14%	0	1	2
Malta	45	210	367%	0	1	2
Netherlands	4230	4020	Minus 5%	1730	96	80
Norway	270	1215	350%	2269	4	5
Portugal	105	255	143%	91	2	3
Romania	-	180		501	-	2
Russia	-	435		1450	-	3
Slovenia	-	240	-	392		2
Spain	460	1515	229%	1470	5	12
Sweden	165	510	209%	797	7	19
Switzerland	255	-		-	2	-
Totals	11,810	21,150	79%	27,708	196	262

Break down of participation by region in 2014 Pie Chart of Current Player Numbers Total = 381,344

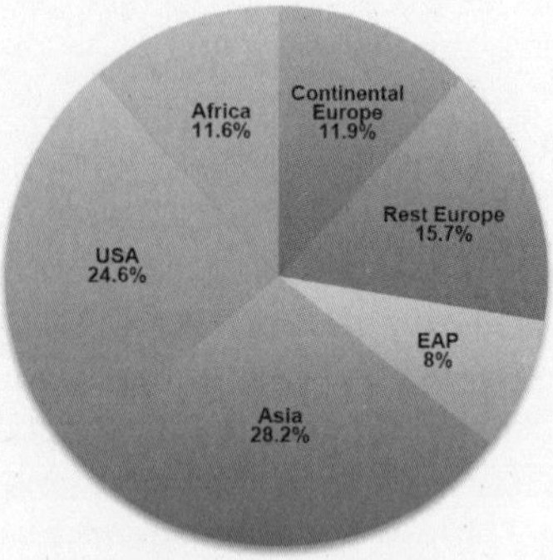

Break down of participation by region in 2004: Total = 103,345

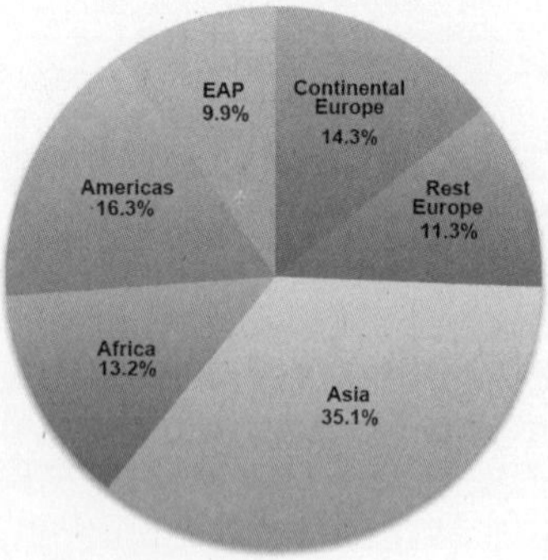

Cricketer Participants in Continental Europe

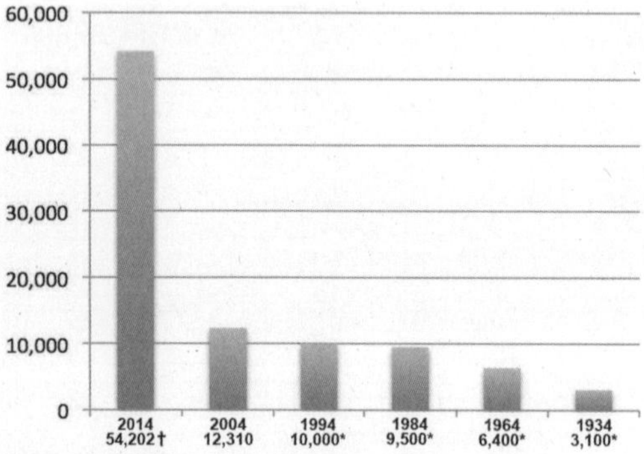

*Estimates. The 2014 and 2004 figures are ICC statistics.

†This figure is comprised of approximately 22,000 players with the remainder anyone who has taken part in an introduction to cricket event or coaching clinic.

% growth by region in last decade

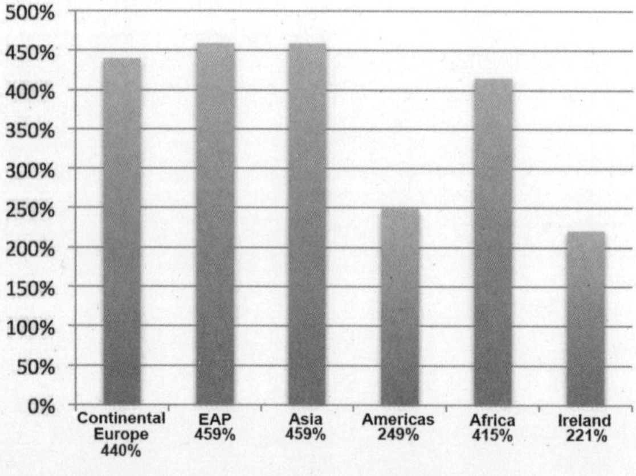

One-Day Internationals
Leading Batsmen

Player	Country	Runs	Matches	Average	100/50
Ten Doeschate	NL	1541	33	67.00	5 / 9
Szwarczynski	NL	1102	41	29.78	0 / 10
Zuiderent	NL	1097	58	23.84	0 / 8
Borren	NL	1004	58	22.31	0 / 5
T Cooper	NL	976	23	48.80	1 / 8

Leading Bowlers

Player	Country	Wickets	Matches	Average	Economy
Bukhari	NL	57	46	28.08	4.71
Ten Doeschate	NL	55	33	24.12	5.03
Borren	NL	46	58	35.21	4.91
Seelaar	NL	42	37	31.64	4.73
Schiferli	NL	33	30	30.54	4.67

T20 Internationals
Batting

Player	Country	Runs	Matches	Average	Strike Rate
Myburgh	NL	636	27	26.50	123
Swart	NL	621	26	27.00	116
Borren	NL	618	40	20.60	122
Barresi	NL	596	32	22.07	121
T Cooper	NL	404	18	28.85	132

Bowling

Player	Country	Wickets	Matches	Average	Economy
Ahsan Malik	NL	43	28	14.81	7.33
Bukhari	NL	43	38	18.13	6.64
Seelaar	NL	26	36	20.73	6.49
Van der Gugten	NL	23	22	19.39	6.77
Borren	NL	18	40	33.50	6.87

ICC Trophy Records

Leading Batsmen

Player	Country	Runs	Matches	Average	100/50
N Clarke	NL	1040	18	74.28	5 / 3
Zuiderent	NL	897	24	69.00	3 / 5
T de Leede	NL	832	42	26.83	0 / 5
R Gomes	NL	772	18	59.38	3 / 2
Lefebvre	NL	745	43	25.68	1 / 1

Leading Bowlers

Player	Country	Wickets	Matches	Average	Economy
Lefebvre	NL	71	43	11.64	2.47
O Mortensen	DEN	63	26	10.41	2.45
Schiferli	NL	41	17	16.24	4.16
S Vestergaard	DEN	37	27	14.83	3.45
T Hansen	DEN	37	22	15.72	3.86

World Cricket League

Leading Batsmen

Player	Country	Runs	Matches	Average	100/50
Barresi	NL	1064	37	36.69	1 / 9
Borren	NL	1007	44	34.72	1 / 5
Klokker	DEN	965	27	38.60	1 / 6
A Northcote	IT	928	34	29.00	1 / 5
T Cooper	NL	744	16	53.14	1 / 5

Top Runscorers for Other Continental Nations

Country	Player	Runs	Matches	Average
Belgium	J Farmiloe	122	5	30.50
Germany	M Fernando	589	19	31.00
Gibraltar	Ferrary	353	12	32.09
Norway	Shabbaz Butt	408	18	27.00

Bowling

Player	Country	Wickets	Matches	Average	Economy
Bukhari	NL	71	46	22.32	4.25
Ahsan Malik	NL	47	29	18.26	4.34
Munasinghe	IT	46	30	21.98	4.31
R J Iqbal	GER	43	23	15.88	3.88
Bashir Shah	DEN	36	27	24.58	4.67

Top wicket-takers for other continental countries

Country	Player	Wickets	Matches	Best Bowling
Belgium	Khaliq Abdul Rehman	11 11	4 5	5-20 3-22
Gibraltar	Mirpuri	16	12	6-61
Norway	Waheed	20	17	6-56

First-Class Records (those born or learnt their cricket in a continental country)

Batting

Player	Country	Runs	Matches	Average	100/50	Teams
Kervezee	NL	4621	97	29.81	6 / 27	Netherlands Worcestershire
Lefebvre	NL	1494	77	20.46	1 / 3	Somerset Glamorgan Canterbury
Amjad Khan	DEN	1466	108	16.85	0 / 6	Kent Sussex
Zuiderent	NL	1328	31	28.86	2 / 9	Netherlands Sussex
T de Grooth	NL	892	20	26.23	1 / 5	Netherlands

Bowling

Player	Country	Wickets	Matches	Average	Teams
O Mortensen	DEN	434	157	23.88	Derbyshire
Amjad Khan	DEN	347	108	31.62	Kent Sussex
Bakker	NL	193	69	28.01	Hampshire
Lefebvre	NL	149	77	36.23	Somerset Glamorgan Canterbury
A van Troost	NL	146	71	38.45	Somerset Griqualand West

Bibliography

Bowen, R. *Cricket: a History of its Growth and Development Throughout the World.* 1970

Coldham, J.D. *German Cricket: a brief history.* 1983

Connelly, C (ed.) *Elk Stopped Play.* 2014

Frith, D. *The Golden Age of Cricket 1890 – 1914.* 1978

Haigh, G. *Sphere of Influence.* 2010

Haigh, G. *Uncertain Corridors.* 2013

Labourchere, P.G.G. Provis, T.A.J., and Hargreaves, P.S. *The Story of Continental Cricket.* 1969

Malcolm, D., Gemmell, J. and Mehta, N (eds.). *The Changing Face of Cricket: from imperial to global game*

Morgan, R. *Encyclopedia of World Cricket.* 2007

Morgan, R. *Real International Cricket: A history in a hundred scorecards.* 2016

Swanton, E.W. (ed.). *Barclays World of Cricket.* 1986

Waddell, D. *Field of Shadows.* 2014

Wigmore, T and Miller, P. *Second XI: Cricket in its Outposts.* 2014

Tim Brooks is a cricket writer and commentator specialising in global development of the game. He has extensive experience of writing on European cricket and has worked with ICC Europe, Norway and Germany on developing strategies to raise the profile of cricket in the region. Tim is Head of Cricket for QTV Sports and contributed a chapter to the acclaimed *Second XI: Cricket in its outposts.*